MAKING AND DRESSING

Dolls House Dolls

MAKING AND DRESSING

Dolls House Dolls

In $^1/_{12}$ Scale

SUE ATKINSON

(of Sunday Dolls)

David & Charles

A DAVID & CHARLES BOOK

Typeset by ABM Typographics Ltd, Hull
and printed in Italy by Milanostampa SpA
for David & Charles
Brunel House Newton Abbot Devon

Foreword

WHEN DAVID & CHARLES *asked me to recommend an author to write a book on making and dressing dolls-house dolls, I thought immediately of Sue Atkinson of Sunday Dolls who has an international reputation among collectors for exquisite miniature dolls which are beautifully dressed in authentic period clothes. Sue consulted her team of needlewomen who gave her their wholehearted support – and this delightful book is the result.*

Many dolls' dressmakers are reluctant to work in $^1/_{12}$ scale as these tiny garments seem so fiddly to make by conventional methods, but Sue has been generous with her knowledge and experience, and the book includes all the innovative techniques for miniature dressmaking which the Sunday Dolls team has developed over the years.

This book will be of value to both dollmakers and miniaturists who will find inspiration in the gorgeous colour photographs and practical help in the full-size patterns and instructions. Using these methods, even the beginner can make and dress residents for any dolls' house from country cottage to stately home in costumes of any period from the eighteenth century to the present day.

Venus A. Dodge
1992

Contents

Introduction

I AM ASKED FREQUENTLY how I began to make dolls professionally and why I called my business 'Sunday Dolls'. It started with a childhood passion for dressing dolls, using handkerchiefs and scraps of ribbon. Years later, my daughter's dolls needed replacements for the rather shoddy clothes they arrived in, and I found that even the smallest garment had to be properly cut and sewn if it was to look good and withstand play and laundering. This led to miniaturising my daughter's entire dolls' wardrobe from swim-suit to smocked party dress. Then I tried to make the dolls as well and discovered the fascination of transforming two-dimensional fabric into three-dimensional dolls. I thoroughly enjoyed making hundreds of these rag dolls, adding moulded felt faces to some of them. In the days before reproduction porcelain dolls were available in Britain, I wanted to make a modern version of the lovely Victorian dolls for today's children. Experiments with a form of fibreglass were quite successful, but it was an unsuitable material to use at home. These resin dolls were similar to those made for Victorian children, which were brought out for supervised play on Sunday – hence 'Sunday Dolls'.

I heard that reproduction porcelain dolls were being made in the United States, and, after replying to an advertisement, I started to correspond with Joy and Wayne Parker in Canada. I bought a number of their lovely Swallowhill dolls and eventually spent a blissful week in their workshop learning the craft of dollmaking. When production switched to dolls-house scale, they invited me to be their British and European agent. Over the years we have been able to co-operate in developing their doll range and to share the search for the specialist haberdashery that is required to dress them. The demand for fine fabric, narrow ribbons, lace and braid, hair, patterns and helpful gadgets has led to an exciting worldwide treasure-hunt. This enterprise grew so large that it threatened to over-shadow the dollmaking, so the haberdashery part of the business has now been transferred to The Dollshouse Draper.

In order to sell kits, made-up examples were needed for display. Requests for dressed dolls soon became a steady international demand and I have been lucky to have the help and support of a team of talented needlewomen who have achieved tremendously high standards in miniature doll dressing. They have evolved fine needlework techniques to create realistic period costumes which complement the lovely houses and furniture that are available to the serious dolls' house collector. Our aim has been to make each 'person' as realistic and as authentic as possible.

This book has been written to help and inspire others to achieve similar high standards, but also as a permanent acknowledgement of the skill and dedication of the Sunday Dolls team, and of the craftsmanship of Swallowhill dolls.

Dolls' houses have enormous charm for many people and for many reasons. It may be the attraction of anything miniature, or nostalgia for the dolls' house that was once owned or always longed for. Admiration for the skill of the miniature craftsman or the need to create might lead to this absorbing hobby, but for most people it is the magic of a small world of sheer escapism. The imagination can take you wherever you wish from palace to garden shed, whether it is historically accurate or wildly fanciful. Collectors can acquire a Tudor cottage or Palladian mansion, a copy of their own home, a shop, school, church or pub. A display cabinet, bookcase, aquarium or an upturned drawer can be turned into a satisfactory room-setting in which to display small treasures. In this miniature world there is no consideration of rent, rates or heating bills. There can be kitchens full of unpaid servants and delectable food without cooking smells – even the flickering flames in the open hearth can be controlled by the touch of a switch. No one actually carries buckets of coal upstairs for those endlessly polished grates, scrubs the floors or blackleads the stove.

Although some purists will not allow inhabitants to intrude on the perfection of their rooms, most modern collectors aim to show activity – the family eat, play and sleep, they have visitors, scatter their possessions and pursue their hobbies. Servants are seen cooking, washing and cleaning, and off-duty they might warm their feet by the fire or ease them in a mustard bath. Life and humour can be breathed into these small figures with a little thought – you can have guests for tea or dinner, nursery squabbles, messy kitchen accidents and amorous intrigues above and below stairs. Delicious scenarios can be carried out, but realistic poseable 'people' are essential. Given these, specific families, famous people, and a huge range of recognisable characters are possible – the parson, schoolteacher, doctor, solicitor, farmer, pedlar, businessman, shopkeeper, publican, and many more.

Before you start to dress the dolls, an approximate date should be decided for your house. If its architecture is Tudor or Georgian, it could be furnished and inhabited entirely in its own period. The earlier it is, the fewer pieces of furniture will be required, but suitable items will be more difficult to find and may have to be custom-made. The house could also be shown occupied at a later date, perhaps with Victorian furniture, and anything of an earlier style as 'antiques'. The fashion worn by the lady of the house will set the deadline, and there should be absolutely nothing in the house of a later period, however tempting. This includes furniture, kitchen and domestic appliances, fabric and wallpapers, carpets, lighting, pictures, ornaments, books and even the toys in the nursery.

When you have decided the period when time was 'frozen' in your dolls' house, you will find patterns and instructions in this book to make a family, their servants and friends and to dress them in the latest fashions. The beginner will discover that many of the methods and patterns are simple – provided that he or she has a knowledge of basic needlework – but I hope that the more experienced dollmaker will find a stimulating challenge in some of the more elaborate styles.

1

ℳaking the dolls

As you plan the residents of your dolls' house, there are several factors to consider, the first of which is the scale of the dolls. To determine this, establish the scale of the dolls' house and apply it to human proportions.

Most modern collectors' houses are in $^1/_{12}$ scale where 1in (2.54cm) represents 1ft (30.48cm) in real life. A few are half that size in $^1/_{24}$ scale and children's dolls' houses from about 1910 to the present day are likely to be in $^1/_{16}$ scale – ($^3/_4$in to the foot). Old houses (Victorian and earlier) are usually larger, possibly $^1/_{10}$ or even $^1/_8$ scale. If you are in doubt, measure the height of the door or ceiling and compare it with a real house, but bear in mind that old cottages have low ceilings, mansions have high ceilings and a dolls' house may have disproportionately high ceilings for ease of access. Modern dolls' houses are usually true to scale, but there are considerable variations in earlier houses which might make the choice of doll size a compromise.

Another way to judge the size of your dolls is by trial and error. Make a simplified doll from a roll of paper or piece of card and adjust until it looks the right size for the room and furniture.

Whatever scale is used, the proportions must look right when the doll is dressed and wigged. Measurements and patterns are given for $^1/_{12}$ scale and other scales can be calculated from these. As a general guide, a man in this scale will be 6in (15cm) tall, a lady 5$^1/_4$-5$^1/_2$in (13-14cm), and children 3$^1/_2$-4in (9-10cm). But not all adults are the same size (or weight), so there should be slight variations in height. Older people tend to shrink a little, so the grandparents could be a little shorter, and maybe a little stouter. A good mixture of tall and short, stout and thin will add realism and character to the family. The relative ages of the children should also be considered so that they can be carefully planned and graded in height. Make sure that the mother is a suitable age in relation to the number and ages of her children. Unless a caricature is required, be careful that the lady and her hat are not taller than her husband – it may sometimes be true in life, but it looks odd in dolls.

Arm length is often a problem, because arms must not look too short or too long. A good general guide is that when the arms are outstretched at shoulder level, the distance from fingertip to fingertip should be equal to the

fig 1
ℱigure proportions

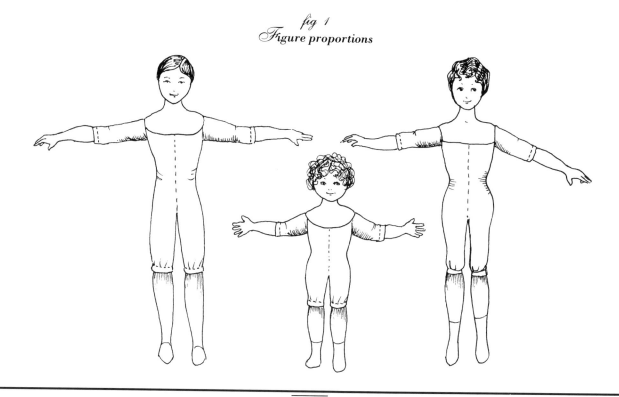

height. Each joint will take up a little of this length, so it is better to allow a fraction extra for shoulders and elbows. A 6ft (1.8m) man will be 6in (15.25cm) tall, but his overall arm measurement should be 6¼in (15.9cm). If the doll is to hold anything large, such as a basket or tray, then one or both arms should be made extra long. On a figure holding a baby, the arm that crosses the body should be made long enough to look as if the child is held securely. If the figure is to be sitting or kneeling, then extra length must be allowed for hip and knee joints. Consider the finished height of the doll before you model a head and limbs and use Fig 1 as a guide for the doll's proportions.

Although it is possible to make your own porcelain dolls, the initial outlay on equipment is considerable; you will need a kiln, moulds, slip and paints, all available commercially, but it is advisable to learn how to use them from a good teacher before you make the investment. There are dollmaking courses in Britain and the United States, run by firms which supply dollmaking materials – for example, Recollect – and who advertise in specialist publications. However, most people prefer to use a porcelain-doll kit or model their own dolls in hobby clay.

CHOOSING A KIT

Many dollmakers offer a wide range of porcelain-doll kits which are made from commercial moulds, from their own sculpting, or from a mixture of sources. In choosing which to buy, there are a number of criteria, apart from price. Look for the following points:

■ A comprehensive range of realistic heads with well-defined features – including men who look like men – all in a consistent scale and covering all ages.
■ Good flesh-coloured bisque with a smooth finish.
■ Delicately painted eyes with a good expression, gently blushed cheeks and soft mouths.
■ Arms and legs which are properly proportioned, and well-defined hands with fingers shaped to hold accessories.
■ Proper arrangements for attaching the limbs and clear making-up instructions.
■ Long, slim necks, preferably with separate shoulder-plates to allow for movement.
■ Ladies with deep shoulder-plates and full-length arms to wear low-necked gowns.
■ Heads with or without moulded hair as required. Usually, moulded hair can be wigged over.
■ A choice of special requirements – for example, bare feet with moulded toes, pointed ballet legs, heavy boots for workmen or Santa Claus, bent knees for sitting.
■ A choice of ethnic types.

Some dollmakers will undertake commissions, sculpting portrait dolls from photographs, but this can be expensive. A remarkable likeness can be achieved by careful choice from a comprehensive range of heads and by using the right hairstyle and clothes – for example, everyone will recognise Queen Elizabeth the Queen Mother if the doll has a soft round elderly face with grey hair and is dressed in an off-the-face hat and a flowing coat in pastel colours.

A making-up service is offered by some dollmakers so that the body comes ready to dress. Send for catalogues, look around at the shops and fairs, then buy the best you can afford as it is very disheartening to put a lot of work into making beautiful clothes for an inferior doll. Porcelain dolls are breakable, but if the colours are properly fired they have the great virtue of being washable. This means that if you are not satisfied with the finished doll, you can remove the head and limbs from the body, soak off any traces of glue and begin again.

MODELLING DOLLS

MATERIALS
Ideally, each member of a dolls-house family should be sculpted individually. This can be done in traditional potters' clay, which is grey in colour but dries off-white. The disadvantage with clay is that it has to be kept damp while it is modelled and then kiln fired. There are also hobby clays, such as Das, which harden in air but are rather fragile. Both potters' clay and hobby clays will need to be painted flesh colour.

Much easier to use are the self-coloured hobby modelling compounds which are pleasant to work with, do not dry out, and are hardened by cooking at low temperature for a short time in a domestic oven. Fimo, Sculpy and Cernit (available from craft shops) are the best known of these compounds and they come in a wide range of blendable colours. As they will not harden until they are baked, a number of pieces can be made and cooked together. If the flesh colour is rather bright, it can be improved by mixing with white or translucent in a ratio of two parts flesh to one part white, with the addition of a pin-head quantity of blue and brown. This will just 'dirty' the colours to a convincing flesh tone and be very close to the colour of fired porcelain bisque. (The blue and brown colours can be paint or any other suitable colorant as the quantity is so small.) Work on a piece of clean plastic laminate, greaseproof paper or aluminium foil, with clean hands. Knead and roll until the colours are completely blended – using a rolling-pin makes this easier – and work the material until it is soft and malleable.

METHOD
Work with a doll or picture in front of you to use as a

guide. To make the head, roll an egg-shape of Fimo (or similar material) approximately ¾in (2cm) long and push a pipecleaner into the lower end. A man's head should be slightly larger than a lady's, and a child's head should be smaller and rounder. Wrap Fimo around the pipecleaner and blend upwards to make a slim neck and jawline for lady dolls, fuller and stronger for men, or slim and short for children. Roll out and cut a thin square of Fimo to make the shoulder-plate and push the pipecleaner through the centre. Blend the lower end of the neck into the shoulder-plate, and curve the shoulder-plate over a pencil or a piece of dowelling. (Check that the shoulder-plate is deep enough for a lady doll wearing a low neckline.) Gently slope the shoulders and smooth any angles. The distance between the front and the back of the shoulder-plate should be approximately ½in (1.3cm) to allow it to fit neatly onto the body.

Using your fingertips and a toothpick, gently shape and round the features. Indent the eye-sockets about halfway down the head. Add a tiny piece of Fimo for the nose (slightly larger for men) and mark in the mouth, halfway between the nose and the chin.

Unless you are very experienced, do not attempt to model eyelids and lips, as these are best painted in this scale. Ears should project slightly between eye and mouth level, but they could be omitted for women and children. Keep rotating the head so that you look at it from all angles. Check that the eyes are level and the same size, that the nose is straight and the mouth does not droop.

Model the arms and legs onto pipecleaners. To allow movement at the elbow or knee, the Fimo should finish just below the joint. For arms, start with a slender roll of Fimo, insert the pipecleaner and gently roll and shape,

curving the fingers inwards and separating the thumb, so that the hands look relaxed. Fingers can be defined with indentations, and the ends just separated and moulded into the fingertips. Legs are made in the same way, and the end of the roll should be bent and shaped to form the foot. Boots or shoes can be modelled, marking toe- and heel-caps, buttons and lacings. The shoe parts can be made in coloured Fimo, with contrasting soles and buttons, so that painting is unnecessary.

When the head and limbs are finished, lay the parts on a piece of cooking foil over a baking sheet and cook in the oven, following the manufacturer's instructions. The oven must be at a steady temperature before the parts are put in, so if you are not confident that the temperature control on your oven is absolutely accurate, try a sample at a lower setting to reduce the risk of overcooking or burning.

PAINTING

Heads and limbs modelled in potters' clay or Das should be lightly sanded with very fine-grade sandpaper before painting, but Fimo pieces should not be sanded as they are self-coloured and harden to a smooth surface.

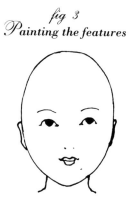

fig 3
Painting the features

Use acrylic paints, which work well on all modelling compounds and can be blended to make subtle mixed shades, and fine, good-quality brushes. Test colours on the back of the head. Paint clay and Das pieces matt flesh-colour and allow to dry thoroughly before painting the features (see Fig 3).

To paint the eyes, draw a fine arc in brown to represent the upper lashes, and a flat-topped circle in colour to represent the iris – it is not necessary to paint in the white of the eye. Paint black pupils into the centre of the irises, ensuring that both face the same direction, and add sparkle to the eyes with a touch of varnish or clear nail-polish when the paint is dry. Eyebrows should be painted as a fine line in light brown for women and children, but as a darker and thicker line for men.

Paint mouths in a soft peachy colour rather than pink, and keep them fairly small. Do not mark in nostrils as this can look very ugly and is unnecessary on a modelled nose. Cheeks are blushed by rubbing in a little of the

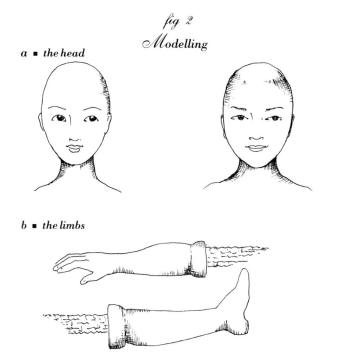

fig 2
Modelling

a ▪ the head

b ▪ the limbs

peachy mouth colour with a cotton bud or fingertip.

Allow the paint to dry thoroughly before putting the head onto the body and wrap it in tissue paper and a small polythene bag to protect it as you make up and dress the doll. Acrylic colours are not fired in like china paints and although they are quite stable, constant handling might remove them. The head can be sprayed with a matt acrylic varnish to seal the paint.

MAKING MOULDS

PLASTER MOULDS

A two-part mould can be made in plaster of Paris using your own modelled head or an old porcelain head. This mould can then be used to reproduce the head in a modelling material such as Fimo. (It is important that the head that is used to make the mould has no undercuts, such as the angle of the chin or nose, which would prevent it from being withdrawn from the mould.) It is not practicable to use commercial doll moulds for making Fimo heads, because they are overlarge (to allow for the shrinkage of porcelain during firing) and because the oils in Fimo would spoil the surface of the mould for future use with porcelain.

You will need a small waterproof box which is large enough to take the head – that is, approximately 3in (7.6cm) each way. This might be a plastic icecream or margarine container, a cardboard box lined with aluminium cooking foil or one built from interlocking plastic bricks such as Lego. You will also need:

- Modelling clay or Plasticine
- Plaster of Paris (potters' or dental grade)
- Soft soap or washing-up liquid
- 2 soft sponges – for example, cosmetic sponges
- Small plastic bowl or container for mixing
- 1 small and 1 large bowl for soaping
- 4 marbles or ball-bearings for 'keys'

The head from which you are taking the mould must be made waterproof. Any openings, such as a hole at the top of the head, should be closed with Plasticine. A porous head – for example, one made of Das or potters' clay must be given a thin but complete coat of varnish and allowed to dry. (The spray varnishes used by artists are excellent for this purpose.)

Soften the clay or Plasticine and form a bed by pressing a layer about ½in (1.3cm) deep into the bottom of the box. Hold the head horizontally in profile at eye level and determine how it should be tilted to make sure that there are no undercuts at the nose or chin – usually the chin will need to be higher than the forehead. Keeping this angle in mind, set the head into the box using more clay or Plasticine to build up the bed to the correct angle.

fig 4
The head mould

a ▪ *the head in the mould box*

b ▪ *half-mould showing 'keys'*

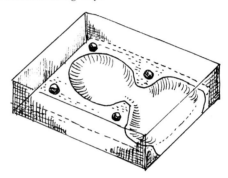

The dividing line where both sides of the mould will release the head must now be determined and marked with chalk, grease pencil, crayon or lead pencil – whatever will work on the head you are moulding. Keep the marker absolutely vertical, with the point touching the clay bed, and carefully trace around the head – the resulting mark is the dividing line. Build up the clay or Plasticine to the dividing line and smooth the surface. Press three or four small marbles or ball-bearings half into the clay for 'keys', spacing them evenly around the head. These 'keys' will form depressions in one half of the mould which correspond to bumps in the other half, thus 'locking' the mould and ensuring that both halves fit properly together and will not slip (see Fig 4).

Using a small bowl and hot water, mix about two parts water to one part soap. Squeeze a sponge in the soapy mixture to make very thick suds. Squeeze the sponge out until it is just slightly wet, then carefully pat the soap onto the head. Leave the sponge in the soap mix. Using a large bowl and cool water, squeeze the second sponge until it is just damp and dab off the soapy film. Repeat this process at least eight times until a film appears on the head. This film will last about fifteen minutes, so the next part must be done immediately. (If an interruption occurs between the soaping and pouring the plaster, resoap four or five times to replace the film.)

Half-fill a small bowl with cool water and sprinkle on the plaster of Paris until dry islands rise above the surface of the water. Leave this to slake for one minute, then stir very slowly and gently, trying not to make air bubbles which would spoil the mould. Mix for about a minute. Pour the plaster into the mould box at one corner, until the head is covered by at least ½in (1.3cm). If the box is on a table, tap the underside of the table sharply several times to encourage any bubbles to rise to the top of the plaster. When the plaster begins to cure it will become quite hot. Wait at least an hour after it has cooled before working on the second side of the mould.

Carefully remove the contents of the box without separating the clay and plaster. (If Lego has been used, the walls can be removed and rebuilt.) Invert the mould and gently lift off the clay or Plasticine without unseating the head. Put the plaster half-mould with the head in it back into the base of the box. Remove the marbles or ball-bearings – the depressions they have made are the first half of the 'keys'. The second half 'bumps' will form in these depressions when you pour the second half of the mould.

Repeat the soaping procedure, but this time both the plaster and the head must be thoroughly soaped. (Stinting on the number of soapings can prove disastrous as it might be impossible to separate the finished mould.) Soap at least ten times and make sure the plaster has a good shine. Mix the plaster of Paris and pour it on as before. Leave to harden for at least an hour after the plaster cools. Remove the mould from the box and smooth off the sharp edges with a knife or file. Lift the upper part of the mould straight upwards so that it is not damaged – a sharp pull is usually necessary. Ease out the head slowly and carefully. Making moulds requires considerable patience.

You will now have a two-part mould with locking 'keys'. Write the name of the head on the outside of both halves using a grease pencil or crayon. Close the mould, secure it tightly with two or three strong elastic bands, and leave it to dry at normal room temperature. Do not use direct heat to hasten the drying as this will cause the plaster to deteriorate. Store the mould with the separating line horizontal so that it will not warp. After the mould is quite dry – usually two or three days – it can be used for making dolls.

Before use with Fimo (or similar modelling compounds), the inside of both halves of the mould must be thoroughly coated with soft soap or a commercial release agent. Knead the Fimo so that it is soft, smooth and malleable, then, working with the front (face) half of the mould, press small pieces of Fimo firmly into the features. When the cavities for the nose, chin, etc are filled, press in more Fimo to fill the rest of the face. Fill the back half of the mould in the same way.

A pipecleaner, folded back at the end so that it will not pull out, should be inserted into the neck before the two halves of the head are pressed together. (The pipecleaner will be used to attach the head to the body.) For a shoulder-head, gently scrape out a little of the Fimo under the shoulders so that it will fit over the body. Carefully remove the head from the mould and smooth the join between the two halves. Check for any imperfections and with a toothpick make any alterations to the features – for example, open the mouth or add wrinkles. Cook on foil in the oven as described. If the halves have not joined properly, they can be cemented with a little Fimo and rebaked.

The methods described above can be used for making moulds of arms and legs, but great care must be taken to plan where the dividing line will be on the arm to avoid an undercut which would make it impossible to release the limb from the mould.

RUBBER MOULDS

Two-part moulds can also be made from RTV (room temperature vulcanising) rubber. Initially, this is more expensive than plaster, but the definition in the mould is excellent. Being flexible, rubber moulds are easier to use and with care will last a long time; using Lego to make a box exactly the right size will minimise the quantity of rubber needed. The chemicals involved are toxic and can irritate the skin, so care should be taken to work in a well-ventilated room, preferably with an extractor fan, and to wear plastic or rubber gloves. A coloured catalyst is added to the white liquid rubber to make it set. The two liquids should be mixed very slowly to avoid air bubbles, until the uniformity of the pigment indicates that mixing is complete. It is most important to follow the manufacturer's instructions exactly, and to use their release agent instead of soap. With a fine brush, paint a thin layer of mixed RTV rubber onto the modelled head, ensuring that there are no air bubbles, particularly in the eyes and mouth. When this layer begins to set, slowly pour rubber into one corner of the mould box until the head is covered. The rubber will take about twenty-four hours to 'cure', when the mould will be ready for use. Coat the inside of the mould with release agent and press in the Fimo as described above. The parts are removed from the mould by easing the rubber carefully away from the Fimo which will be soft and should be handled gently.

Simple one-piece babies or dolls' dolls can be reproduced in Fimo using a one-piece mould. Seal any porous material with varnish and treat with release agent. Secure the doll face-up to the base of the mould box with a small lump of clay, Plasticine or Blu-Tack, and make the mould as before. Remove the mould from the box, slit the thin film of rubber at the doll's back and, by easing the mould, extract the doll.

When using a one-piece mould, care must be taken to push minute scraps of Fimo right into the ends of the limbs and features, then fill the body firmly and round off

The Manikin-Makers
The body construction method using padded pipecleaner limbs strung with elastic to a porcelain shoulder-head

the back. Remove the soft Fimo doll carefully by easing back the mould. The limbs may be a little elongated as they are removed, but they can be pushed back into shape and the body reshaped. However, any imperfections will be concealed by clothing. Bake the Fimo doll as described above. Blushed cheeks and only very basic features will be needed. Hair could be painted, but the tiniest mohair curl peeping out from a gathered lace bonnet is prettier.

MAKING BODIES

MAKING UP OLD DOLLS

Victorian dolls-house dolls were usually 'shoulder-heads' – that is, the head and neck were moulded in one piece with a curved shoulder-plate. The earlier china heads were glazed white ceramic with moulded hair usually painted black, sometimes pale yellow. Contemporary hairstyles were used, those with a centre parting being the most common. Heads were mass-produced in several sizes and sold very cheaply. The arms of these dolls were unglazed, often with barely marked fingers, and there was very little to distinguish left from right. The legs, also unglazed, had fashionable but improbably small feet. The dolls were sold as kits and on stuffed cotton bodies. Much rarer were superior-quality heads with more delicate features and ornate hairstyles, some of which had their own headgear and were known as 'Bonnet dolls' – even if the bonnet was actually a top-hat. These dolls had glazed arms and legs, often mounted on jointed wooden bodies, and are now valuable. Similar but larger half-dolls made of ceramic to the waist were frequently mounted on skirt-shaped pin-cushions or tea-

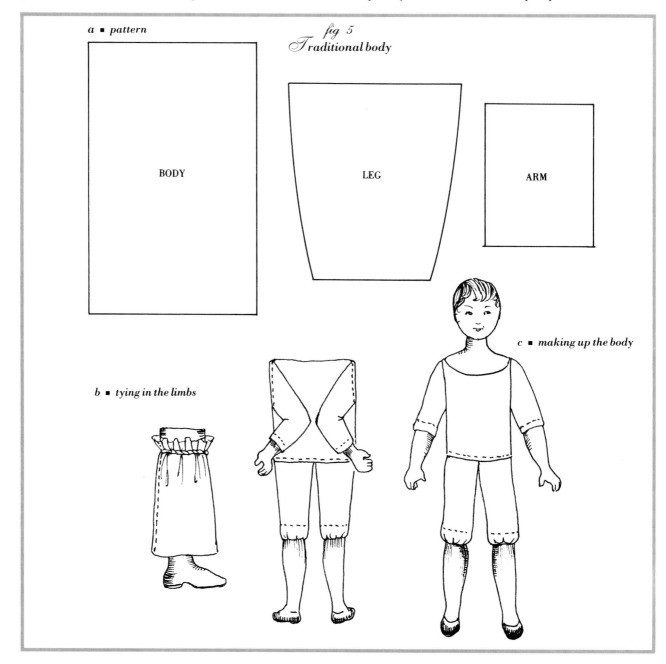

a ▪ pattern

fig 5
Traditional body

BODY

LEG

ARM

b ▪ tying in the limbs

c ▪ making up the body

cosies and these are still in production.

Reproductions of old heads are available, complete with the appropriate limbs. It is also possible to buy old heads, but beware of new heads which have been artificially aged. Genuine old heads are usually made of cheap pottery and show considerable signs of wear, as many have been retrieved after being buried for years in rubbish tips. It is most unwise to repaint rubbed features as modern paint looks wrong and this will devalue the doll. Dressed sympathetically in old faded fabrics, they look delightful and at home in an old house. Unfortunately, old heads are usually found without limbs, but it is possible to buy new white limbs specially made for use with antique heads. If one old limb is available, then a second can be modelled to match, but the shape, texture and colour are important. If the head is white china, then the limbs should be white and have a bisque (matt) finish. Any imperfections in the modelling can be disguised with long sleeves, gloves, mittens, muffs, fans, bouquets, or with a tiny scrap of lace handkerchief. As some of the originals were made with simple leather arms, often coloured, new arms could be made from fine old gloves. Soft leather boots, decorated with braid, ribbon bows, buckles and buttons can be made onto covered pipecleaner legs. Legs are not quite as important for ladies and a voluminous dress could conceal a paper cone or stuffed base.

Traditional Victorian-doll bodies were usually made from squares of cotton (see Fig 5). Cut two squares with sides wide enough to go around the top of the arms and provide the seam allowance, and two to fit around the legs. Slight shaping is needed to allow room for turning right side out. Fold the fabric in half and seam down the long side, shaping in at one end so that it will fit closely over the top of the limb. Insert the limb from the wide end so that the seams will be at the underarm or at the centre back of the leg. Secure by winding strong thread several times around the limb just below the ridge, finishing with a tight knot and a dab of glue. Gently pull the tube back over the limb and stuff with a little dry sawdust. Stitch across to make elbow or knee joints, then add more sawdust to the upper legs, but leave the upper arms almost empty. Cut two squares for the body. Tack the arms onto the top of each side of the square, and the legs to the bottom edge, checking that they are the right length and that the hands and feet will be facing the right way. With right sides together, stitch the front to the back body, leaving the bottom edges open. Turn right side out, stuff firmly with sawdust and stitch the bottom edge closed. Glue the shoulder-head onto the body.

Even if you keep the stuffing in the legs to a minimum, these dolls do not sit properly, which explains why the inhabitants of so many antique dolls' houses are either lounging inelegantly, standing stiffly to attention or have taken to their beds!

MAKING UP DOLL KITS

The modern porcelain-doll kit is made from flesh-coloured bisque. This is porcelain formed by a 'biscuit' firing without the subsequent glazing which is applied to table or ornamental porcelain. Bisque is very hard and cannot be filed or drilled once it has been fired. It is brittle and will shatter if dropped or knocked, so hands and feet are very vulnerable and should be protected as much as possible during making up by wrapping in bubble or tissue paper.

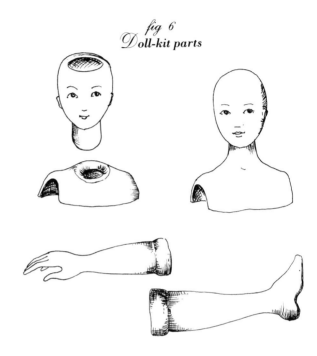

fig 6
Doll-kit parts

The doll parts are hollow, and a kit will have either a swivel-head, which fits into a shoulder-plate with matching central holes, or a shoulder-head in one piece. Arms will usually finish somewhere between the wrist and the elbow, and legs at mid-calf. If the body is also provided, this is known as an 'all-bisque' doll, meaning that no cloth or stuffing will be needed and the head will fit into a hole at the top of the body, or be joined to it (see page 23). Complete arms and legs will be included so that there is jointed movement at neck, shoulder and hip. There are also a few, very expensive, miniature dolls made with fully articulated bodies, jointed at shoulder, elbow, waist, hip, knee and ankle.

There is no right or wrong way to make up a doll kit. Whatever method is used, the requirements are that the head and limbs should be firmly attached to a poseable body to give the right overall proportions. The legs should be sufficiently strong to support the body, the arms strong enough to hold suitable accessories and the figure should be flexible to allow for sitting or kneeling. As it is always a problem to find fabrics which are fine enough for clothes, the body should be very slim, especially at the waistline, to allow for this. Extra padding may be needed at bust and hips to give a fashionable outline, support fitted garments, or to thicken the waistline for stout people. This is best done after the body is made, when the padding can be shaped by stitching. For a lady, insert tiny balls of cotton-wool or polyester wadding to form the bosom (before closing the bodice), arranging the padding to achieve the correct figure shape. Drawers can also be lightly stuffed to give more realism to the hips and bottom, which will help to support a bustle. For really stout gentlemen, study pictures to see where on the body the padding should go, and thicken the legs so that the figure is realistic. Arms should always be kept slim, otherwise they will not bend, but tiny tufts of padding can be slipped inside the gathering at the top of the sleeves to ensure that they stand out.

BOUND PIPECLEANER BODIES

One simple and satisfactory body-making method which requires no sewing, uses strips of wadding wound around pipecleaners (see Fig 7). For each doll you will need:

Head and limbs
- 5 pipecleaners, 6in (15cm) long

- 6ft (2m) strip of polyester wadding, ½in (1.3cm) wide
- Thick white PVA glue
- Plastic foam draught-excluder, ¼in (6mm) wide (optional)
- Wire-cutters or old scissors
- Ruler

Make a scale drawing of the doll and keep it in front of you to check measurements. Make sure that you have pairs of limbs and use enough pipecleaners in each limb to fill the space snugly, and enough glue to be sure they are secure. For adults, glue one or two pipecleaners into each leg. When dry, twist the pipecleaners together so that, with both feet facing the same way, the length from sole to sole is 9½in (24cm) for a man and 8½in (21.6cm) for a woman. For children, glue one or two pipecleaners into one leg, and cut them so that when the other leg is fitted the feet are 5¾in (14.6cm) apart, or for a toddler, 5¼in (13.5cm).

Glue pipecleaners into one arm, then measure and cut so that when the second arm is put on, the length from

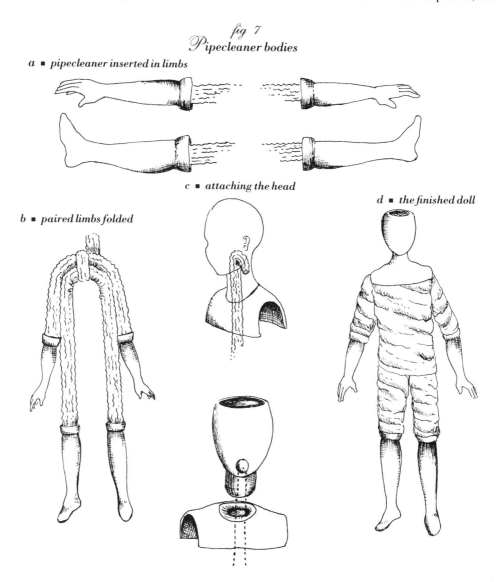

fig 7
Pipecleaner bodies

a ▪ *pipecleaner inserted in limbs*

c ▪ *attaching the head*

d ▪ *the finished doll*

b ▪ *paired limbs folded*

Afternoon Duties
The butler and parlourmaid demonstrate the relative proportions
of man and lady dolls

fingertip to fingertip is slightly more than the final body height. Allow about 6¼in (15.9cm) for men, 5½in (14cm) for women and 4-4¼in (10-10.8cm) for children. Put aside until the glue has dried.

Extra strength and thickness can be added to the legs by sticking self-adhesive foam strip (sold for draught-proofing windows) along the length of the pipecleaners before binding. Bind each pair of limbs with strips of wadding, securing the loose end with a dab of glue. Use only one layer for the arms, but the legs should be thicker. Fold arm and leg lengths in half (unless uneven arms are required for a special pose), making sure that the legs are the right way round and that the hands are facing forwards on their correct sides. (A good way to check is to hold the doll facing away from you, to see that they match your own hands and feet.)

If you are using a shoulder-head, hold together the mid-points of the two pairs of limbs and bind them with a pipecleaner, cutting the ends to fit into the head. Check again that the limbs are matched properly and that the shoulder-plate is in contact with the 'shoulders'. Bind the body from the hips upwards with a strip of wadding, working in a figure-of-eight around the neck until there is sufficient thickness to support the shoulder-plate. Apply glue liberally to the inside of the shoulder-plate and to the pipecleaners which fit into the head. Seat the head on the body, tipping it slightly forward so that the eyes are not staring straight ahead.

If you are using a swivel-head, attach it to the shoulder-plate with strong, thin cord elastic. Starting from under the shoulder-plate, thread the elastic up through the central hole and into the head. If the head has two holes at the top, go up through one, down through the other, and back through the neck and shoulder-plate. If the head is open at the top, secure the elastic by threading it through a small bead, or by knotting it around a short length of bent pipecleaner. Tie the ends of elastic tightly around the fold point of the prepared limbs. The head will then be attached firmly and able to swivel freely. Bind the body with wadding strip, starting from just below the waist, winding round and under the shoulder-plate until it is the right shape. (Children will require very little padding, and extra bulk at the waist should be avoided for fashion ladies.) Using strong thread, bind and stitch the wadding to hold it in place, adding extra pieces to build the required shape.

For a smoother finish, add a top layer of binding cut from thin white jersey, or cover the body with felt as described in the next method.

FELT-COVERED BODIES
This method for making bodies uses a sewn felt 'skin'. To make each doll you will need:

Head and limbs

- Good-quality white felt, 6in (15cm) square
- 5 pipecleaners, 6in (15cm) long
- Polyester wadding or cotton-wool
- Thick white PVA glue
- Needle and thread

The felt should be of top quality with no faults, otherwise it will split when stitched. Choose heavy commercial, rather than 'art' felt, and white rather than flesh colour (even for black dolls) as a colour may show through thin clothes.

Check that the limbs are paired. For men, glue one or two pipecleaners into each leg. For ladies, glue the legs onto each end of one or two pipecleaners. For children, glue the legs onto the ends of one or two three-quarter-length pipecleaners. Make up a pair of arms as in the previous method and set aside for the glue to dry. Fold ladies' or children's limbs in half, leave men's legs separate.

Trace the body pattern (Fig 8a) onto thin card. With the greater stretch of the felt going across the body, and using a soft pencil, trace around the pattern and cut two body pieces. Check that the end of the felt leg fits exactly around the top of the porcelain leg, trimming to fit if necessary. For a lady, draw around inside the dart, fold the dart from point to point, stitch exactly on the curved line and clip. Repeat on the reverse of the second body piece so that both darts will be on the inside.

With right sides together, stitch the centre-front seam on the same side as the darts and clip the curve. Run a line of glue along the end of the felt legs and wrap them around the top of the porcelain legs so that the join is at the inside, as in trousers. Check that the feet are facing the front and are correctly paired. Oversew neatly up the leg to the crotch and down the second leg, fastening off securely. For men, twist the pipecleaners together to form the 'spine', folding over at the top if they are too long.

Stuff the legs firmly with wisps of stuffing, working around evenly using a small blunt wooden stick, such as the end of a fine paintbrush, as anything sharp might pierce the felt. Add only a small quantity of stuffing at a time so that it does not become lumpy, and roll the limb between finger and thumb to give a smooth finish. Rejoining the thread at the crotch, continue oversewing and stuffing up the centre back, keeping the body slim.

A variation of this method is to stitch the darts and the centre-front seam as described, then oversew the back seam by hand or machine zigzag stitch on the outside. When smoothed out, this will make a flat butt join at the back and avoids turning the felt body inside out, which might stretch it out of shape. The prepared legs on pipecleaners are then inserted into the body, glued, sewn and stuffed as before.

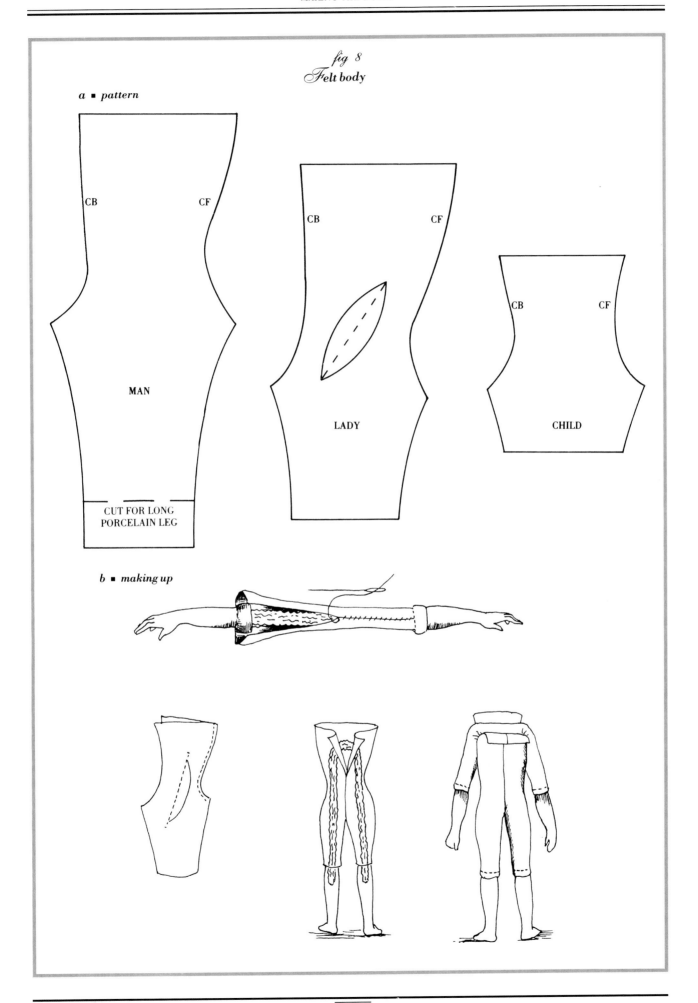

fig 8
Felt body

a ■ pattern

CB   CF

MAN

CUT FOR LONG
PORCELAIN LEG

CB   CF

LADY

CB   CF

CHILD

b ■ making up

Cut a strip of felt to fit around the top of the porcelain arms, and long enough to cover the pipecleaner and lap over each arm. Apply glue to both ends of the felt and wrap it around the porcelain arms. Oversew the arm seam closed, but do not stuff as the felt provides sufficient padding.

Attach a swivel-head to its shoulder-plate as previously described, but knot the elastic around a short length of toothpick (or pipecleaner). Lay the prepared arms across the top of the stuffed body and try the assembled head to check the overall height of the doll. Adjust the stuffing in the body until it is right and trim any surplus felt. Lay the prepared arms on top of the body, checking that the hands face the right way and are on the correct sides. Fold the body felt over the arms and stitch securely in position. Check once more that the height will be right, then glue on the head, tilting it very slightly forward. This method gives a very neat finish, but it may still be necessary to reduce the waist by binding with thread, and to add small scraps of stuffing or felt to give a better bustline.

PIPECLEANER DOLL'S DOLLY

A simple dolly can be made from Fimo and pipecleaners or a small wooden bead can be used for the head; these can be bought with the features already painted. To make the doll you will need:

- Small piece of flesh-coloured Fimo
- One ½in (1cm) bead (optional)
- 1 pipecleaner, 6in (15cm) long
- Coloured Fimo or paints for shoes and hair
- Scraps of ribbon and lace for clothes
- Viscose hair or embroidery silk for wig

Cut a 2¾in (7cm) length of pipecleaner. Fold it in half for the body and legs, and bend up the two ends a little to form feet. Cut a 2in (5cm) length of pipecleaner for the arms and slip it through the body about a quarter of the

fig 9
Pipecleaner doll's dolly

way down. Fold over the right arm to the left, and the left arm to the right, so that they are firmly wrapped around the body (see Fig 9).

Roll a ½in (1cm) ball of Fimo (or glue the bead) and push it onto the end of the folded pipecleaner to form the head, leaving a short neck above the arms. Bend the arms forward into the chosen position and cover the ends with a little Fimo, shaping it into rudimentary hands. Cover the legs and feet in the same way (using coloured Fimo for socks and shoes if required). Moulded hair should be added now, but hair, socks and shoes can all be painted later. Make sure that the limbs are in the right position, then bake in accordance with the manufacturer's instructions. Paint the features and blush the cheeks very simply. Dress the doll in gathered ribbon or lace and wig with a hair curl or embroidery thread.

This method can be scaled up to make a whole family, and would be particularly suitable for a child's dolls' house, or a family project. Making the dolls in a larger size would give more scope for detailed hands and feet, and more ambitious faces, but they look best if the clothing is simple.

STRINGING AN ALL-BISQUE DOLL

Most babies, toddlers, ¹⁄₂₄-scale dolls and some adults are made entirely of porcelain bisque. These usually present no problems and it is easy to see how to put them together. The smallest will probably have the head and torso in one piece, with holes pierced at the top of each limb to correspond with holes at shoulders and hips. To assemble the doll you will need wire-cutters, a small pair of needle-nosed pliers and copper wire, either natural or tinned to look like silver. If this is not provided with the kit, use heavy 13amp fuse-wire, 22 or 24swg (standard wire gauge) or about 0.6mm diameter, from a hardware shop. The wire should pass through the drilled holes easily and be pliable enough to bend into a small loop (Fig 10a).

Nylon fishing-line may be used instead of wire – this is fastened with small knots, which can be fused using a small soldering iron – and is neater than it sounds, as the fishing-line is almost invisible.

For dolls with separate heads, these should first be joined to the body with elastic. If there are two holes in the top of the head, the elastic will loop around them, but if the top of the head is open, the elastic should be brought up and passed through a bead or round a scrap of pipecleaner. Usually the loose end of the elastic will exit at a hole provided between the legs, where it can be knotted. If there are two holes between the legs, the knot can be concealed within the head or the body to give a neat finish. If no body holes are provided, the elastic should be looped around a short length of toothpick wedged under the shoulders and if no holes are provided in the top of the head, elastic can be looped over a short length

fig 10
Stringing all-bisque dolls

a ▪ *wiring the limbs*   b ▪ *stringing with elastic*

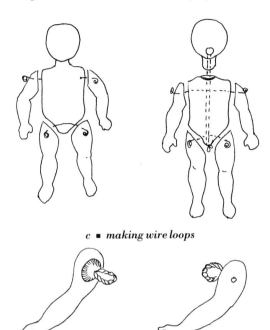

c ▪ *making wire loops*

of toothpick pushed up into the head and wedged above the neck (Fig 10b). (A folded length of fine copper wire will make a threader for pulling elastic through the body.)

To wire the limbs, start from the outside, thread the wire through one arm, through the body and out through the other arm. Use pliers to twist one end of wire into a tiny loop (twice round for very fine wire), then cut the other end long enough to make another loop. Wire the legs in the same way and press in any sharp points so that they will not catch on clothing.

Another traditional method is often seen on old dolls, but requires considerable patience. The limbs are held on with thin cord elastic which is threaded in the same way as wire. With the elastic stretched (and therefore thinner), push a sliver of matchwood into the hole in the limb and glue it in place. While the glue is setting, the elastic must be held taut, using locking forceps or a similar device. When the glue is absolutely dry, use a craft knife or scalpel to pare both elastic and wood level with the porcelain. The resulting neat finish is well worth the trouble, especially if the join is to be left exposed.

Sometimes the limbs are not pierced, but have a small loop or pierced bump which fits into a hole in the body. Attach these limbs with elastic which should be pulled tight before knotting.

PROBLEMS

Occasionally, a porcelain-doll kit poses problems, but with a little ingenuity, solutions can be found. If there is no passageway through the body, the limbs should be glued on in the required position and reinforced with a glued gauze bandage, or an undergarment.

If the body holes are crooked or rather large, the legs will not hang evenly. In this case, wire the left arm diagonally down across the body to the right leg, and vice versa. If the body is not hollow, then a small cardboard or plastic patch can be glued on top of the oversized hole and a new hole pierced in it. If all else fails, the fault may be concealed by gluing the limbs into the knickers or sleeves.

If the hole in a bump is too small to take elastic, make a wire loop through it, twisting the ends together several times to secure. The elastic can then be threaded through the loop and joined either side to side or diagonally across the body. If these bumps are broken, or the holes are clogged or are not there at all, then a replacement loop must be made. Take a short length of wire, fold it over and twist the ends together, leaving a small loop. Insert the ends into the limb and fix them in place with household cement or a mixture of glue and paper-tissue. Leave until completely dry before attempting to string (Fig 10c).

It is important that the limbs are properly attached, hanging well and moving freely before you begin to dress the doll.

2

Dressmaking – equipment and materials

EQUIPMENT

THE EQUIPMENT NEEDED FOR dressing miniature dolls is very simple and can be obtained from most haberdashery (notions) departments. Sewing needles, which should be kept clean, should be fine, short and sharp – 'sharps' or 'betweens' are best, as longer needles tend to bend when making small stitches. Size 12 is the finest sewing needle, although an even finer size 15 is obtainable in long beading needles; however, these bend easily and are only suitable for stab stitching up and down straight through the fabric.

Many people assume that everything made for small dolls must be hand-sewn, but quite a lot can be sewn by machine, especially underwear and long seams. Ensure that the machine is running smoothly with the tension perfectly adjusted, and fit the smallest sized needle. Sewing and machine needles blunt quite quickly and it is remarkable how much difference a new one can make. Use very fine thread – 180 polyester is excellent.

A pair of very sharp scissors which are kept only for cutting fabric and thread are essential; another pair should be kept for cutting paper. A few sharp pins, a ruler, eyebrow tweezers, and a syringe with a blunt nozzle to dispense small quantities of glue will all be useful. Always use a sharp pencil for pattern marking as ink is easily transferred to fabric, and mark fabric with tailor's chalk to avoid soiling. The blunt end of an artist's paintbrush will be invaluable for turning garments and a long latched hook called a rouleau/loop turner, or small locking artery forceps (haemostats), are helpful for pulling through sleeves.

Lidded food containers – even the most fragile acetate ones from the supermarket – are invaluable for storage, but remember to label the contents. To avoid eye-strain, it is advisable to work in good natural light, but if this is not possible, use an adjustable hobby lamp – the type with an illuminated magnifying lens is useful for fine work.

Two major difficulties in miniature sewing are to prevent the fabric from fraying and to eliminate bulk, particularly in hems. A great help with both problems is 'Fray Check', which can be painted onto fabric and forms a thin invisible film; however, it should be tested first on a small scrap. If Fray Check is used when making a hem, only one turn of fabric will be required; when it is painted just outside the stitching line, it will prevent a seam from pulling away. It can also be used to make non-fray ribbon and as a stiffener for fans, hats and parasols.

For top-class work which is expected to last a long time, it is inadvisable to use glue on fabric because although modern glues are effective, no one yet knows what they will look like in a few years' time. Some glues turn yellow and some will hold only for a year or two, so it is better to rely on sewing and use glue only for a temporary hold or where it is absolutely necessary – for example, on hair and shoes. The best glue to use is a non-toxic, thick white PVA (polyvinyl-alcohol) which will dry clear, matt and slightly flexible; Aleene's Tacky Glue is recommended.

If fabric must be glued, paint a thin line on each piece, wait until it is tacky, then press the pieces together very gently. This will prevent the glue from oozing through the cloth and staining it. A line of glue is often necessary to tack a ribbon or trim in place, but it should be reinforced with an occasional stitch in matching or invisible thread.

For convenience and economy, dispense the glue from a curved nozzle syringe (available from craft suppliers). To fill the syringe, remove the plunger, pour or squeeze the glue into the barrel until it is about half-full and replace the plunger. Turn the syringe so that the tip is upright and wait to allow the bubble of air to escape. The plunger can then be pushed down fully and the syringe will be ready for use.

To prevent the glue from drying up, always leave the syringe partly full and keep a cap on the end when it is not in use. If the syringe has been unused for some time, a pin pushed down the nozzle will generally clear any dried glue blocking it.

QUICK REFERENCE LIST OF EQUIPMENT

- Sewing needles (sizes 10-12 sharps or betweens)
- Machine needles (size 10)
- Polyester sewing thread (180)
- Small sharp scissors
- Small sharp pins
- Eyebrow tweezers
- Glue syringe and PVA glue
- Tailor's chalk pencil
- Sharp HB pencil and ruler
- Small paintbrush (or similar) for turning
- Rouleau/loop turner or locking forceps (optional)
- Fray Check

All fabric and trimming should be carefully pressed before cutting out, as the slightest wrinkle will show later and could distort the shape of tiny pieces. A miniature ironing-pad can be made from an offcut of hardboard or particle board, which has been padded and covered in cotton (preferably removable for laundering). A better

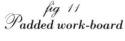

fig 11
Padded work-board

version can be made from laminated plastic board by padding the rougher side and making a cotton cover with a draw-string hem which fits comfortably around the edge, but leaves plenty of clear working space on the back (Fig 11). This makes a small portable working surface for drawing and cutting, which reverses to become an ironing-board. A slim firmly stuffed roll, for use when pressing awkward places, can be made from fabric scraps. For a crisp professional finish, constant pressing is required, so keep a steam iron handy – a small travelling iron is ideal – and check the sole plate regularly to make sure that it is clean. Take care when ironing fabrics not to mark or overheat them, so always test a small sample first and use a pressing cloth.

FABRICS

Thin, closely woven cottons and silks are the easiest fabrics to handle and give the most satisfactory results. Plain China silk, known as 'Habotai', is available in a wide range of colours, and will gather, pleat and drape well, but the heavier slubbed-weave silks fray easily and the knubs can be difficult to stitch. Avoid anything which frays or is loosely woven as it may pull away at the seams. Cottons with a stiff finish can sometimes be softened by washing. Modern synthetic fabrics like nylon and polyester were designed specifically to hold their shape and not to crease in normal use and consequently are too stiff and springy for miniature work. Old silk may be lovely, but it must be examined carefully; anything stained or faulty must be discarded. It is heartbreaking if the fabric disintegrates while it is being sewn or fitted. Sometimes part of an old garment is still strong enough to use, or can be reinforced with gauze or the thinnest iron-on backing. Gathering or draping may not be possible, but it can be used flat or pleated for a skirt. Fine white cotton lawn or silk will be needed for underwear and shirts.

Traditionally, suits for dolls-house men were made of felt, but this looks clumsy, especially as the surface tends to fluff. Men's clothes look far more elegant and convincing when they are made in silk or cotton bonded to an interlining. Small checks and stripes for modern suits are most likely to be found in men's shirting fabrics. Market stalls and the darker recesses of fabric shops often produce the less-favoured drab colours which will resemble tweed in this scale – for example, dress-weight denim, known as chambray, which will look like Irish tweed.

Charity shops are a marvellous and inexpensive source of fabric, and often have small-patterned silk ties which make lovely cravats and waistcoats. Fine silk or cotton jersey, which will be needed for stockings, can be cut from underwear or T-shirts – a man's white jersey evening-dress scarf is just right for making silk stockings for Georgian men or liveried servants in breeches. Thin kid-leather gloves make excellent belts, shoes and handbags.

In the search for the right fabric, everything should be considered for its possibilities in small scale. Sometimes a border around a scarf or a print in a fairly large scale can be used if the design and colouring are delicate, so that the overall pattern is not obvious, particularly when the fabric is pleated. Conversely, some very small patterns are unsuitable because the colour contrast is strong and the design will stand out too sharply.

The most elaborate Victorian ladies' costumes were often made from two or three different fabrics, with a wealth of trimmings, fringeing, ribbons and embroidery. With planning, it is possible to reproduce these costumes in miniature. Different fabrics can be used as an overlay on the bodice, sleeves and skirt and edged with braid or lace; or a draped apron front and gathered train could introduce a second fabric, repeated on cuffs or hat trim. Provided that the work it kept neat, there is almost no limit to the amount of detail which can be added in this way.

Helping Hands
**The children play with the simple equipment needed for making
dolls' clothes**

Scarlet Ribbons
The pedlar sells laces and ribbons to a lady wearing the Day Dress
(1850–60) watched by her husband in the Frock Coat and son in the
Early Victorian Suit

3

*D*ressmaking methods

DRESSING DOLLS IN ¹⁄₁₂ SCALE is not just a matter of making very small clothes. The miniature dressmaker has many problems to overcome and must be prepared to abandon some conventional techniques to obtain the right effect. It is not practical to make tiny garments which can be taken on and off. The difficulty is that there are no fabrics to scale – even the finest available needles and thread are hopelessly coarse, fingers seem giant-sized and the tiny garments infuriatingly small. However, by making the best of what is available, together with a little ingenuity, it is possible to re-create the most elaborate and detailed fashions.

HOW TO USE THE PATTERNS

The patterns are designed for slim flexible dolls of approximately 6in (15cm) for men, 5¹⁄₂in (14cm) for women and 4in (10cm) for children. A seam allowance of ¹⁄₄in (6mm) is included on the patterns, but to avoid confusion seam and gathering lines are not shown.

Great accuracy is needed in cutting out both patterns and fabric, as even the slightest variation will make a big difference in this scale. If only half the pattern piece is shown, trace it as a full piece – do not cut the folded fabric. Trace the pattern in pencil onto thick paper or card, transferring all the markings. Draw around the pattern onto the fabric or interlining and cut out just inside the pencil line, then check your pattern again with the book.

Pattern pieces are very small and easily lost, so they should be identified and kept together in a labelled plastic bag or envelope. Add a note of any alterations which have been made, together with a scrap of the fabric as a further reminder.

Before cutting the fabric, cut a toile for the main pattern pieces in paper kitchen-towel or strong paper-tissue, cutting the toile on the bias where it is shown on the pattern. Pin or tack the toile on the body and make any necessary adjustments – this is particularly important for the bodice, for which a good fit is essential. Check the bodice, sleeve, skirt and trouser lengths, as even small dolls vary considerably in size, so it is impossible to give a pattern which will fit them all.

BONDING

Most of the patterns in the book are designed to be cut in fabric that has been bonded to fusible interlining. Trace the pattern onto the interlining using a sharp pencil, then dry iron to the wrong side of the fabric and cut out, or bond a sufficient area of fabric and cut the pattern from this. To avoid constant repetition, this will be referred to in the patterns which follow as 'bonding' or 'bonded fabric'.

Where extra stiffness is needed, patterns are cut in two layers of fabric with Bondaweb sandwiched between them (see Chapter 2). This will be referred to as 'double-bonding' or 'double-bonded fabric'. Double-bonded fabric, cut on the bias grain, retains some 'give', and cutting with sharp scissors will give a neat non-fraying edge.

CUTTING

Press all fabrics before cutting. Cut the lining exactly the same size as the fabric piece and on the same grain. Check whether the pattern recommends bonded or double-bonded fabric and, if you are using iron-on muslin, be sure that it is bonded with the weave of both fabrics in the same direction. Keep seam allowances even and check whether you need to trim the seam allowance for a hem or lining which will not be sewn. Cutting the fabric on the bias may seem extravagant, but very small amounts are involved, and it really does make a big difference to the fit and hang of tiny garments. For shaping the bodice, bias cutting is better than darts, which are difficult to stitch accurately and tend to form sharp points. With striped and checked fabrics it will also give an interesting effect although care must be taken to reverse the stripe for each sleeve or side of the bodice; fortunately, most striped silks are woven through the fabric.

SEWING TECHNIQUES

Use the smallest, sharpest needles and the finest available matching thread. Invisible thread has advantages, but be careful not to melt it when pressing. To avoid knotting and splitting, thread the needle with the loose end of thread as it comes from the reel and start and finish sew-

The Dressmakers

*The ladies, wearing Edwardian Blouses and Skirts, show the
pattern-cutting method and tools for making trimmings*

ing by securing with several stitches rather than a knot. If you are using a sewing-machine, leave long thread ends so that they can be secured. The machine zigzag stitch is excellent for attaching lace, but apart from top stitching around a tailored jacket, try not to let any machine stitching show. Use small running stitches or back stitch for seams, and avoid stretching seams cut on the bias, especially around hems. On edges which may be stretched out of shape, it is advisable to run a line of hand or machine stay stitching just outside the sewing line, especially around the neckline on jackets.

Seams should be neatly trimmed and the slightest curves clipped and pressed at each stage, as it will be impossible to do it later. Corners must be cut across and the seams pared right down before turning. Run a blunt tool along the inside of the seam to turn a facing back crisply and use a toothpick rather than anything metal to ease out the point of a collar.

Where fabric is to be gathered, two rows of gathering thread sewn close together will give a neater finish and make it easier to distribute the fullness evenly; it is essential to do this when gathering a lot of fabric into the waist.

■ SETTING SLEEVES

In miniature scale it is very difficult to set gathered sleeves into the armhole from inside, so they are attached by the following method. Run a gathering thread around the top edge of the sleeve, then stitch the underarm seam. Fit the sleeve onto the doll over the bodice, pull up the gathering thread and arrange most gathers to the top.

fig 12
Stitching the sleeves

a ■ to the armhole

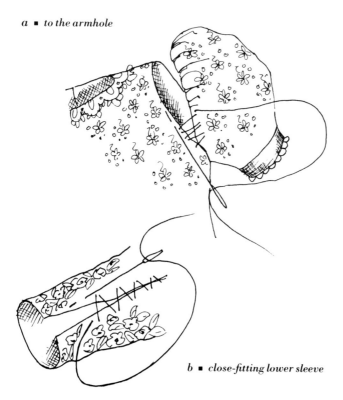

b ■ close-fitting lower sleeve

With the underarm seams matching, slip stitch or ladder stitch the sleeve onto the bodice at the natural armhole and tuck in the raw edges with the point of the needle (see Fig 12). With a very full sleeve it may be necessary to stitch around twice. For sleeves which are to fit smoothly to the shoulder, as on a man's coat, the gathering thread is still needed for easing, but there should be no actual gathers.

When the sleeve is attached to a low-necked dress, it should be stitched as far as possible around the underarm, and the gathers pulled up tightly so that the sleeve sits on the shoulder-plate. If necessary, a tiny dab of glue will help to hold it in place. Tight-fitting sleeves which cannot be seamed and turned should be fitted at the armhole, then slip stitched on the arm.

■ CUFFS

Cuffs give a nice finish to sleeves, but should be really neat. If the sleeve is not wide enough for the hand to go through, leave the end of the sleeve seam open, and slip stitch after the garment is fitted. It is usually sufficient to fold under (and press) the end of a tight-fitting sleeve. Cuffs can be made from narrow lace or broderie anglaise, or from a folded strip of fabric. Fancy shaped cuffs, collars, yokes, panels and pockets can be cut from bonded fabric and the raw edges covered with braid.

■ FASTENINGS

Avoid making any actual fastenings. Although minute hooks and eyes can be made with wire wound on pins, they will not withstand use. Fastenings on a lady's dress can be indicated by beads sewn where possible from the inside before fitting or, for early fashions, by lacing with a pair of threads stitched through the fabric. For a man's coat that is worn unbuttoned, stitch beads on the right-hand side and represent the buttonholes on the left-hand side with single stitches.

■ HEMS

Usually the hem is the last thing to be sewn on a full-size garment, but in miniature dressmaking, hems should be avoided as much as possible by lining with silk, fine lawn or organdie, and should always be finished before the skirt has been sewn onto the doll. If a hem is unavoidable, use a loose catch stitch to pick up one thread from the garment and a tiny stitch from inside the hem.

Bonded interlining is also used to turn up straight or curved hems without stitching. Turn up the hem once, snipping any curves, and iron the interlining to lap over the raw edge. This is particularly recommended for trouser legs and sleeve ends and is described in the patterns as 'bonded to hold the hem in place'. Most of the patterns in the book begin with the hem and work up to the waistline where the bodice is slip stitched over the skirt and covered with a belt, sash or trimming.

■ PLEATING

Pleating evenly is difficult on full-size garments, but in $1/12$ scale it has to be absolutely perfect. This can be done by using a special grooved heat-resistant rubber pleater made by d'Anne Ruff Miniatures (see Stockists). The edge of the fabric should be finished first with a hem or lace edging, or sealed with Fray Check.

fig 13
Using the pleater

To use the pleater (see Fig 13), lay the fabric across the board and press it into each slot with the aid of the two plastic cards provided; one card holds down the first pleat as the second card is inserted. The fabric must be kept perfectly straight and pressed in firmly. When the required length of fabric has been inserted, press it with a steam iron or over a damp cloth. Secure the pleats at both the top and bottom edges with narrow strips of iron-on backing, and leave in a warm place until it is bone dry. Gently lift out the fabric, which is now corrugated and can be sewn through the top strip, then pull away the two strips. This gives excellent controlled fullness instead of bulging gathers. If knife pleating is required, the corrugated fabric can be pressed flat between the two holding strips by pushing the pleats in one direction with the iron. The strips can then be removed. Pleaters are available in a choice of three widths of pleat in various depths and can be used to make narrow trims, bonnet lining, panels of tucks or complete skirts. Use only natural fabrics – for example, silk or cotton – as man-made fibres like polyester cannot be pleated crisply by this method.

■ TUCKS
Victorian drawers and petticoats were often decorated with rows of tucks. Care is needed in marking and pressing the creases evenly before stitching, but the results are worth it. To make tiny tucks, fold the fabric with wrong sides together, measuring carefully so that the crease is perfectly level, or the tucks will not meet exactly at the seam. Press, then stitch on the outside with small running (or machine) stitches. The next crease is made so that there will be a small gap between tucks. On a straight gathered petticoat, it is easier to stitch the back seam first, then make the creases and stitch the tucks all round. This is not possible on the legs of drawers, which are best sewn flat.

MAKING TRIMMINGS

■ RIBBON ROSES
Fabric flowers small enough for $1/12$ scale are almost impossible to obtain and dried flowers are brittle. However, delightful roses can be made from narrow pure silk ribbon, using a rosemaker tool, which is a forked needle mounted in a handle. A small dot of glue is needed at each turn and this can be applied with a pin, but it is much easier to use a glue syringe filled with white PVA glue. Holding the rosemaker in the right hand, insert the ribbon into the fork from the left (see Fig 14). Rotate the tool twice and apply a dot of glue to the base of the ribbon to form the centre of the rose. Fold the ribbon forwards and downwards once, rotate the rosemaker half a turn, and glue again. Holding the rose with the right index finger, fold the ribbon backward, glue again and rotate half a turn, fanning out the ribbon slightly at the top to form the petal, but pulling it tight at the stem where it is

fig 14
Making ribbon roses

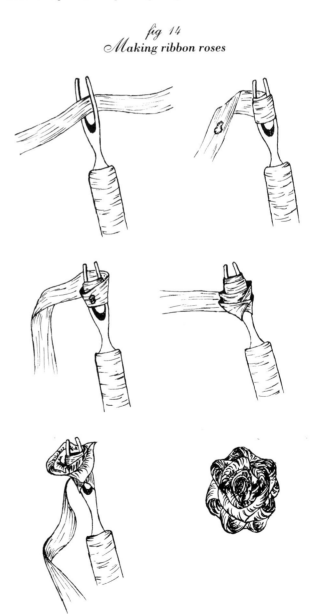

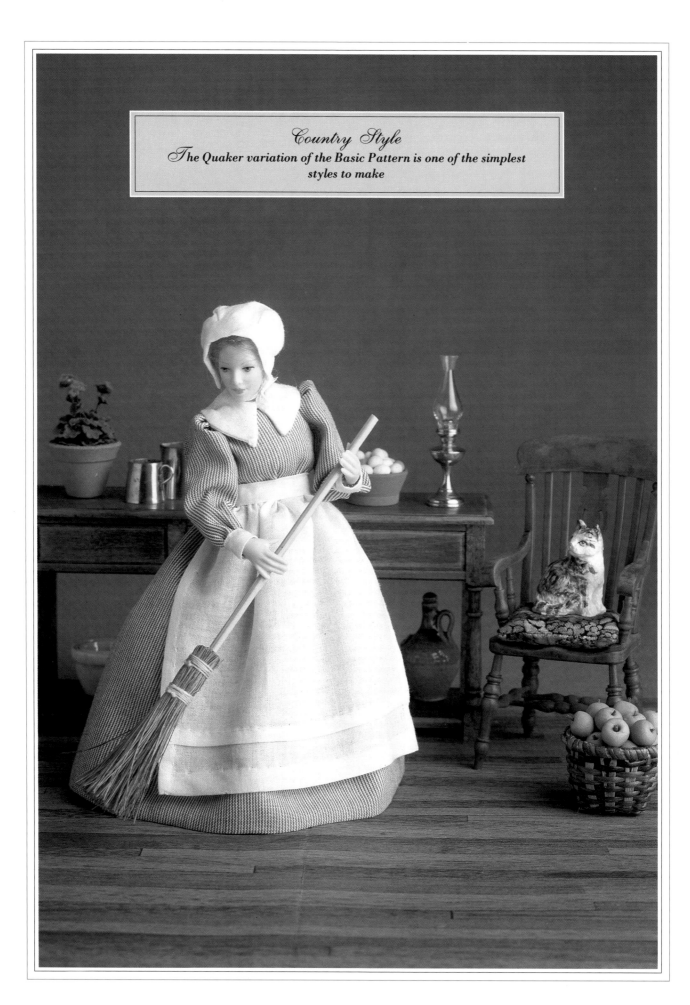

Country Style
The Quaker variation of the Basic Pattern is one of the simplest styles to make

Paying Calls With Mama
The Edwardian mother and daughter wear their most Elaborate Dresses to visit friends

glued. Repeat, arranging the folds of ribbon so that the petals are well spaced. Once you have the knack of leaving the ribbon loose at the top and tightening it where it is glued, a lovely rose emerges. Continue until the rose is the required size, then cut the ribbon and glue the end tightly around the base. Crease the bottom of the rose with a thumb-nail and ease it off, gently pushing it into shape before the glue hardens. A little practice is required, but the results are very worthwhile.

Rosebuds can be made simply by rolling and gluing the ribbon. Two close shades of ribbon look very pretty, or try ombré shaded ribbon. A felt pen can be used to add extra colour shading. Roses made in several slightly different shades look more effective than those all in one colour. Add tiny loops of green ribbon for leaves. The roses can be used on dresses, in hair, on a ribbon around the neck or wrist, on bonnets, parasols or shoes, or can be glued to green wire to make a bouquet.

■ ROSETTES

Pom-poms or rosettes of narrow ribbon make lovely trims for baby bonnets and dresses. They can be made with a rosette maker, which is a block of wood with ten smooth pins set evenly in a circle (see Fig 15). To keep the wood clean it is advisable to impale a small piece of grease-proof paper on the pins before you start. Onto this, glue or wax a tiny square of paper as the base for the rosette. A drop of glue is needed at each stage, for which a glue syringe filled with white PVA glue should be used.

Use 2mm silk ribbon or good quality gift-tie torn into narrower strips – six to eight strips from the normal width works well.

The rosette is made by repeatedly winding the ribbon across the pins in a figure-of-eight, gluing each loop as it crosses the centre. Start by gluing the end of the ribbon at the centre. Wind it around one pin, apply a dot of glue to the centre and press down the ribbon. Wind it around the pin diagonally opposite to the first one, then back to the second pin and so on, gluing at the centre each time and keeping the ribbon uncreased and untwisted as it is wound around the pins. Work at least three times around the circle (four times if the ribbon is very narrow). Cut the ribbon and glue the end to the centre. With a strong needle, ease the rosette gently off the pins, taking care not to crease the ribbon. Fluff up the loops so that it is a complete pom-pom. Do not leave the rosette on the pins while the glue dries or it may be difficult to remove. Clean off any surplus glue before reusing the rosette maker.

■ BOWS

Tiny bows are very effective in miniature work, but are fiddly to make by hand. However, perfect bows can be made using a bowmaker, which is an arrangement of pins around which the ribbon is looped and tied. Different sized bows can be repeated identically and will not come undone. A bowmaker can be made from polished pins nailed into a block of wood (Fig 16a) or very quickly by slipping a pair of fine knitting-needles into a piece of corrugated cardboard cut from a packing carton (Fig 16b).

Measuring along the length of the corrugations, cut the cardboard about 3in (7.5cm) shorter than the knitting-needles. Insert two knitting-needles between the ridges spaced to make the width of bow required. The block-of-wood bowmaker can be held firmly on the table with Blu-Tack, but the card variety is best held between the knees. Wind the ribbon around the pins and knot halfway

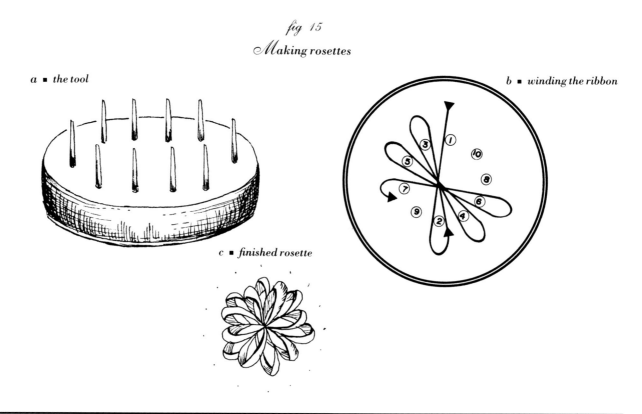

fig 15

Making rosettes

a ■ the tool

b ■ winding the ribbon

c ■ finished rosette

Making bows

a ▪ *with a bowmaker*

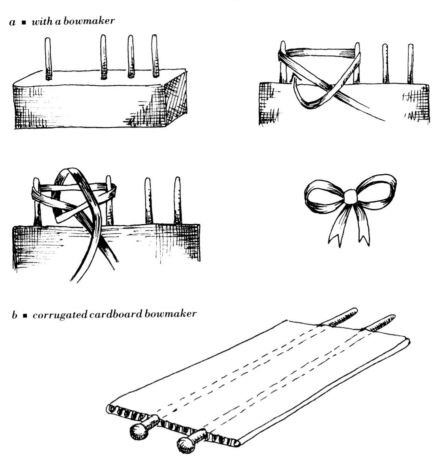

b ▪ *corrugated cardboard bowmaker*

between them, as shown in Fig 16a. Pull the two ends together, trim at an angle and slip the bow off the needles. Nylon or polyester satin ribbon is too stiff for very small bows, but this method works extremely well with pure silk ribbon.

▪ EMBROIDERY

Embroidery can add a delightful finishing touch to garments for girls and ladies, especially on underwear. Simple flower embroidery worked in lazy-daisy stitch and French knots or feather stitching on a petticoat hem look particularly attractive. Use a fine needle and one strand of embroidery silk.

▪ INSERTION

A small zigzag stitch can be used to insert a band of lace which has two straight edges between two pieces of fabric. The lace can also be stitched on top of the fabric, but it looks much better if the fabric is cut away behind it. Fake insertion can be made by machining two rows of small zigzag stitching, leaving space between for a line of running stitches using two or three strands of embroidery thread. Narrow ribbon can be threaded through most insertion lace, even if there are no special holes, and finished with neat bows.

4

A brief history of fashion

'FASHION' BEGAN AS AN EXPRESSION of the power and wealth of the ruling class who guarded their privilege to such an extent that some fashions were permitted only to the monarch. It would have been a brave and audacious courtier who tried to outshine Queen Elizabeth I!

Gradually, styles spread down the social scale, from town to country and from Europe to the new colonies. As the centuries progressed, fashions changed more rapidly and became available to more people.

In the dolls-house world, interest in fashion usually begins with the elegant eighteenth century, although for earlier periods, styles can be researched in books on fashion, history and contemporary portraits. Historians will appreciate that in the following notes many years and

small changes of fashion have been condensed to give a general impression of the period.

GEORGIAN (1740–1800)
(Fig 17)

In the middle of the eighteenth century, world trade was flourishing and imported fabrics were rich and varied – silk, satin, brocade, velvet, lace and fine muslin were fashionable and an English silk manufacturing trade was based in Spitalfields. Fabrics were expensive, so the hand-sewn clothes were lined to help preserve them as they might be unpicked and restyled several times.

■ LADIES

Ladies wore tight-fitting bodices over stiff, decorative

fig 17
Georgian styles, 1740–1800

stomachers, with wide skirts open at the front to show elaborate often quilted, petticoats. Necklines were low and square, framed in lace and sometimes covered by a fine neckerchief. Sleeves were tight to the elbow with flared frills cut shorter at the front to reveal a froth of lace. Colours were light and bright; yellow, pink and blue were very popular. Hair was worn drawn off the face and styled in a bun or flat plait. Caps with gathered crowns and face-framing frills gave way to outsize lace-trimmed mob-caps and flat straw-hats. Delicate muslin aprons were worn by fashionable members of society.

By 1770 gowns had become more elaborate, often with front lacing and heavily decorated with ruching. Hair was drawn upwards over pads and decorated, with ringlets on the shoulder, in a style made famous by Marie Antoinette. Ladies often wore ribbon around their necks, trimmed with a bow or flower. White stockings with high-heeled shoes decorated with buckles or bows were fashionable for many years with both men and women.

During the 1780s, the 'shepherdess' style became popular with ankle-length skirts drawn up and draped into 'panniers'. Muslin fichus became fashionable again, as were the outsize hats immortalised in the paintings of Thomas Gainsborough and Sir Joshua Reynolds. Sprigged and striped fabrics were popular and hairstyles were soft with curls around the face.

■ CHILDREN

Babies at this time and until the end of the eighteenth century were tightly swaddled. Very young girls and boys wore low-necked short-sleeved muslin dresses until they were about five or six years old, when they were dressed like miniature adults. Girls wore small versions of their mothers' dresses, complete with long boned corsets, and boys wore formal suits. Around 1780 there was a reformation in children's clothes and older girls continued to wear their simple muslin dresses with large mob-caps or straw-hats (a style which was later adopted by their mothers); boys wore linen shirts and trousers, a garment previously worn only by sailors or countrymen.

■ MEN

For most of the eighteenth century men wore long flared coats that were cut away to display gorgeously embroidered long waistcoats, and knee breeches with silk stockings and buckled shoes. Cravats, lace cuffs and tricorn hats were fashionable. By 1700 wigs were generally worn — initially styles were long and curly, but by 1740 they were shorter at the sides and tied back with a large black bow; from 1750 they were usually drawn off the face into formal rows of curls. As the century passed coats became less voluminous and waistcoats shorter. Breeches became tighter and were worn with boots. Subdued shades of blue, green, dark red, brown, grey and black became popular for these more restrained styles.

■ SERVANTS

Clothing was expensive and most servants wore second-hand or third-hand garments from which the valuable lace and buttons had been removed. Women servants wore simple print dresses with large mob-caps and fichus and long straight aprons. A man servant would wear breeches with the typical long waistcoat over a shirt with full sleeves. In the wealthiest households, the footmen and coachmen wore the braided livery which is still seen occasionally today.

REGENCY (1800–30)
(Fig 18)

By the end of the eighteenth century the fashion was for classical pseudo-Greek simplicity in architecture, furniture and clothes.

■ LADIES

Ladies wore slimmer and softer dresses which were often made in muslin. They were usually white, high-waisted, and low-necked, with short puffed sleeves, and were worn over ankle-length pantaloons. Shoes were dainty flat slippers with ribbon ties. Hair was worn in Grecian style, drawn up into an elaborate bun or cut very short, with tiny curls and tendrils on the forehead, temples and nape of the neck. Large mob-caps were worn indoors, and straw-hats, tall face-framing poke-bonnets, or turbans were worn outdoors.

After 1805 skirts became shorter and were accentuated by rows of elaborate trimming at the hem; short 'Spencer' jackets with tight sleeves covered by short puffed oversleeves were worn for warmth. Very large shawls were fashionable, the most prized being from Kashmir, although cheaper copies were manufactured at Paisley in Scotland.

■ CHILDREN

Little girls looked enchanting in low-necked, high-waisted muslin dresses. The waistline on boys' trousers was also cut high and sometimes buttoned to a shirt trimmed with frills at collar and cuffs. Both boys and girls wore sashes. These styles were later revived and popularised in the 1890s by the Victorian illustrator Kate Greenaway.

■ MEN

The elegant young men of the day did not adopt the classical Greek look, but the outline of their clothes changed. Waistcoats were shortened to the natural waistline and coats were cut higher at the front to display the bottom of the waistcoat, although they remained at knee length at the back. Breeches and boots gave way to long tight-fitting trousers, which at first were drop-fronted but later had a fly-front opening. Shoulders were broad and accentuated by slightly gathered sleeve heads. Woollen broadcloth in subdued colours was used for coats, but waistcoats were still made of gorgeous silks and brocades. The wig was abandoned in favour of short natural hair, and high-crowned hats, sometimes decorated with a buckle, were the fashionable headgear.

fig 18
Regency styles, 1800–30

EARLY VICTORIAN (1830–60)
(Fig 19)

■ LADIES

By 1830 the waistline was back in its natural place, skirts became stiffer and fuller, and were balanced by outsize 'gigot' sleeves and huge shawl collars. Necklines were low and shoulders bare for evening, presenting a curious mixture of modesty and exposure. Pastel colours were fashionable again for sprigged cottons and chintzes in floral patterns. Darker colours like sage green, plum, deep rose, amber and tobacco browns gradually became popular. Hair was worn elaborately curled and trimmed with ribbons and flowers.

The fuller, often three-tiered gathered skirts of the 1840s–50s required numbers of stiffened and padded petticoats to support them, until the crinoline cage was introduced in about 1855. This was made of calico reinforced with hoops of whalebone or steel. Sloping shoulders were fashionable, dress bodices neat and waists drawn in with tight corseting. Sleeves were tight at the armhole, flaring into three-quarter-length 'pagoda' sleeves over gathered undersleeves of soft fine material. The customary pale colours for summer, with more sombre tones for winter, changed dramatically with the introduction of aniline dyes in the 1860s, which made purple, cerise, viridian and royal blue immediately

fashionable. Queen Victoria's passion for tartan made it popular for everything. The conventions of mourning kept whole families dressed in black for long periods, although black lace and braid trimming were popular at other times. The fashionable hairstyle was centre-parted, looped back into a neat bun with ringlets, or coiled around the ears in braids. Indoor caps, worn by married women, were delightful confections of lace, ribbon and flowers. Wonderfully decorated bonnets, which framed the face and had a frill to cover the nape of the neck were worn by all women until richly trimmed small hats replaced them.

■ CHILDREN

Babies were still restricted in their movements as the old-fashioned swaddling clothes were replaced by binders, wrappers and a number of long petticoats. Baby gowns were long and full, and gave plenty of scope for beautiful decorative needlework. Delicate lace was used on hems and as insertion, often alternating with rows of tucks, whitework embroidery and hemstitching. Out-of-doors, Victorian babies wore long carrying capes and bonnets in fine wool or quilted silk, often trimmed with swansdown.

Once again children were seen as small adults and were required to be fashionable. Girls' dresses echoed the full-skirted line of their mothers' but were shorter and worn with long decorative pantaloons. Small boys also

fig 19
Early-Victorian styles, 1830–60

wore dresses, sometimes over trousers, and outsize caps with tassels were very popular. Older boys wore similar clothes to their fathers.

■ **MEN**

As the first hint of the crinoline skirt appeared, a short full-skirted frock-coat was introduced for men. This became narrower and shorter through the 1840s and began to resemble the suit jacket as we know it today. Men's clothes became less restrictive and the frock-coat was worn only for formal occasions, with a matching waistcoat (vest) and trousers, and a top-hat. Side- or centre-parted hair was brushed down at the sides to join with side whiskers.

MID-VICTORIAN (1860–80)
(Fig 20)

■ **LADIES**

Gradually the skirt fullness was drawn to the back to form a bustle and train of complicated cut and elaborate decoration. For day-wear, bodices were high-necked and tight fitting, beautifully shaped and trimmed; sleeves were usually wrist length and tight with cuff interest. Evening gowns were magnificent with very low necklines and only a vestige of sleeve. Fabrics were rich, dark and sombre and two or three contrasting fabrics were often combined in one outfit, trimmed with a profusion of pleating, ruching, fringe, braid and ribbon.

Pads of false hair supported the high elaborate hairstyles that were decorated with chignons, or ringlets, and curled fringes (bangs). Small trimmed hats were worn perched on top, usually with a slight forward tilt.

■ **CHILDREN**

By the 1880s it was recognised that children required greater freedom and their clothes reflected this. Girls' dresses hung loose from high yokes and were made in warm dark fabrics for winter and washable cottons for summer. Eyelet embroidery (broderie anglaise) could now be made by machine and this was widely used for trimming underwear, dresses and the starched pinafores which were universally worn except for very best. Young boys still wore dresses, sometimes over trousers, although older boys now wore practical worsted suits with short trousers, stockings, boots and caps. This outfit (known in America as the Buster Brown suit), was

Georgian Style ►
At the betrothal of their daughter to a neighbours' son, both ladies and the little girl wear Georgian Gowns open at the front to show elaborate petticoats. The men and the boy wear Georgian Suits with embroidered waistcoats and lace ruffles at wrist and throat

fig 20
Mid-Victorian styles, 1860–80

generally popular, but the velvet suit with lace collar (immortalised by Frances Hodgson Burnett in *Little Lord Fauntleroy*) was considered suitable wear for wealthy boys in 1889.

■ MEN

Three-piece lounge suits, made in tweed checks and plaids, and the knickerbocker suits which were popular for countrywear, were worn with turned-down collars and broad ties. Double-breasted caped 'Inverness' overcoats and short fly-fronted coats in dark wool cloth were popular. The three-piece lounge suit buttoned high with small revers was worn for all but formal occasions with a tall bowler hat (Derby), although a cap or 'deerstalker' were customary for countrywear. Straw boaters were popular during the summer, and spats were frequently worn over boots or shoes in bad weather.

■ SERVANTS

The Victorians introduced uniforms for servants, except the housekeeper who usually wore plain black. Cooks, housemaids and kitchenmaids wore washable cotton dresses with white caps and aprons. Elasticated sleeve protectors to keep sleeves rolled up and top aprons of coarser unbleached fabric were worn for dirty jobs. The parlourmaid (who might double as housemaid or cook in the morning) wore black with a fancy lace or broderie-anglaise-trimmed apron and a tiny cap with streamers at

the back. Indoor male servants usually wore black suits, sometimes with horizontally striped waistcoats, donning tailcoats and white gloves for formal duties. Vertically striped waistcoats were often worn by outdoor staff, although coachmen and grooms would have livery.

LATE VICTORIAN (1880–1900)
(Fig 21)

■ LADIES

From 1887 the bustle was reduced in size and had disappeared by 1890. Women's more active lives required simpler clothing. Hip-length flared jackets were worn over tailored skirts, cut flat or slightly draped at the front, and gored or pleated to give fullness and a slight train at the back. Bodices were very dainty with high necklines and fronts which bloused slightly over elongated waists, often accentuated by wide V-shaped belts. Outsize 'leg-of-mutton' sleeves were fashionable and flat braiding and frogging were used as trimming. Evening gowns remained long and trailing with several flounces at the hem and had outsize puffed sleeves. A choker necklace of ribbon or pearls was fashionable. Vivid and garish colours were still popular and considered a sign of affluence as the dyes were expensive. Hair was worn puffed over pads and fastened with a bun on top, to which a large flat straw-hat or boater could be pinned.

fig 21
Late-Victorian styles, 1880–1900

■ CHILDREN

As a fashion set by the closely related royal families of Europe, sailor suits were popular for both winter and summer. Girls usually wore a short pleated skirt under the bloused top and boys wore trousers, cut straight or gathered below the knee. Both boys and girls wore black stockings and boots. Girls' coats were often made three-quarter length and, like their parents, children always wore hats out-of-doors – usually flat boaters or berets for girls and caps for boys. Even the poorest child in rags and bare feet would wear some sort of hat, however battered.

■ MEN

The frock-coat remained correct formal wear, but the straight front edges were rounded to give a smooth 'swallow-tail' line. Businessmen might wear black striped trousers with a short black jacket and waistcoat, and a bowler hat; otherwise, men wore worsted or tweed lounge suits with short jackets and wider trousers, sometimes with the new permanent turn-up. In the country, tweed 'Norfolk' knickerbocker suits were worn with thick stockings and boots, and for holiday-wear or sports, white flannel trousers with a striped blazer and flat straw boater were introduced. Black evening suits were still much the same shape as in 1815, with the coat cut short in front and long at the back, but were worn with wider black trousers, often with a silk stripe covering the out-side seam. Formal dress shirts were stiff with high starched collars and were worn with white bow-ties and low-cut waistcoats. (Butlers and waiters wore a similar suit, with a black waistcoat and black bow-tie.)

EDWARDIAN (1900–10)
(Fig 22)

This period, notable for the growth of the Suffragette Movement, brought greater emancipation for women and a general softening and simplifying of clothes. Most of the world was at peace and the wealthy filled their lives with the social round, each engagement requiring a different set of clothes throughout the day.

■ LADIES

The S-silhouette was accentuated by a high-necked, bloused bodice balanced by a smooth graceful skirt with fullness and padding at the back, supported by elaborate boned corsets. Silk, satin, velvet, georgette, crêpe and linen in subdued colours, or black and white, were liberally covered with lace, beading and braiding. Hats were huge and magnificently decorated. By 1910 skirts became slimmer, and for a while were so ridiculously narrow at the ankle that they were known as 'hobble skirts'. Colours and decoration were influenced for a time by the costumes for Diaghilev's ballet *Scheherazade* and black, orange, jade, cerise and violet were fashionable colours. Gradually, dresses became softer and less structured. By 1914 the hemline was above the ankle with long, slim skirts, which were often slit to give greater freedom. Shoulders were softer with much draping.

■ CHILDREN

Babies' clothes were simplified and dresses were shortened to above ankle length. The introduction of the perambulator made long gowns and carrying capes impracticable. The sailor suit was still popular for both girls and boys. Girls' dresses were often gathered from a high yoke and were sometimes drawn in with a sash at the waist or hipline. Washable pinafores were worn for school and play. Girls began to wear pleated serge tunics over white blouses for games and exercise in the gymnasium, and this outfit was soon adopted as general school uniform. Boys wore tweed knee-length trousers with knitted jumpers or tweed jackets. The Sunday suit was made in dark cloth and worn with a large white Eton collar. Striped blazers, previously worn only for sports, began to be worn as a distinctive school uniform.

■ MEN

Men's clothes changed very little and shirts with turned-down collars were worn with lounge suits and soft hats for all but the most formal occasions. Trousers were pressed to form a crease in the front and back following a fashion set by King Edward VII.

BETWEEN THE WARS

The mass-production of cheap clothes, the invention of rayon (known as artificial silk) and the emancipation of working girls with money to spend brought a great revolution in dress. The cinema, newspapers and magazines showed the latest Paris fashions and the shops vied with each other to have cheap copies within days. The flappers shortened their skirts, shingled their hair and danced and sang until the Depression of 1929 cast its blight over the industrial nations.

The 1930s saw hems down to mid-calf, and although dresses were soft and flowing, many women wore tailored skirts with blouses or knitted jumpers. Home knitting was immensely popular, particularly for children's wear and men's pullovers, especially in Fair-Isle patterns. Babies wore short dresses and lovingly knitted matinée jackets, bootees, bonnets, pram suits and shawls. Small girls wore short dresses, often knitted in fancy stitches, and small boys wore shorts and jumpers.

The basic cut and fabric of men's clothes changed little in this period – details of the tailored suit went through minor changes and generally clothing became less formal. Navy and grey suits replaced black, soft homburg and trilby hats replaced the bowler and short-jacket dinner suits (tuxedos), worn with a black bow-tie, became acceptable wear for all but the grandest evening functions.

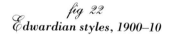

fig 22
Edwardian styles, 1900–10

5

Dressing the dolls

WHEN DRESSING LARGER DOLLS, the usual order of work begins with the underwear, progresses to the clothes, then the footwear, hat and accessories. In miniature dressmaking, this is not practicable as the dolls are so small and making the footwear after the doll is dressed would probably spoil the costume. So conventional methods must be abandoned in favour of the following sequence of working.

SEQUENCE OF WORKING

1 Make or paint the stockings and shoes.

2 Finish the hems on underwear, seam and fit to the doll just below the waistline. Add bustle or hip padding.

3 Make up the skirt or trousers, line and add trimmings. Adjust the length at the waistline and fit with the raw edges upwards.

4 Add yokes, trimmings and buttons, and stitch bodice or waistcoat. Add padding under the bodice to improve a lady's figure. Close the bodice by stitching where it will be best concealed. Turn up the lower edge of the bodice and hem over the skirt (and apron).

5 Finish the sleeve ends, stitch the underarm seams. Gather the tops of the sleeves and slip stitch to the armholes on top of the bodice.

6 Finish the neckline, waistline and the bodice trimming.

7 Protect the doll up to the neck in a plastic bag while making the wig.

8 Add jewellery, hat and accessories and put the doll onto a dollstand.

FOOTWEAR

PAINTING

The porcelain dolls supplied in kits often have moulded boots or shoes which may come ready painted or can be painted with a fine brush, using enamel paints which are available in small tins. Contrasting colour on the soles will make a realistic finish and decoration can be added by marking toe- and heel-caps, laces, bows, buckles and buttons, or they could be elegantly two-toned. Trim-

mings can also be glued on to conceal a less-than-perfect edge – picot edging looks particularly good around the top of boots. Should the kit come with footwear which is wrong for the period, the moulding can usually be disguised sufficiently by over-painting in white or flesh, and covering with the required style. To distinguish between black stockings and black boots or shoes, either paint the stockings very dark grey, or use matt black for the stockings and gloss black for the boots. Pure white paint for socks is rather stark, but it can be toned down with the merest touch of grey or yellow. With a steady hand and a fine brush, a fancy finish could be added to sock tops (see Fig 23 for examples).

MAKING FOOTWEAR

Fabric socks or stockings and silk or leather boots and shoes make a tremendous difference to the appearance of the finished doll and are not difficult to make. They will enlarge the legs and feet and are a good way of disguising feet which are badly shaped or have unsuitable moulded styles.

■ STOCKINGS AND SOCKS

Fine net, thin jersey, lace and lace edging are the most useful materials for making socks and stockings. The choice is governed by the doll's costume as both the stockings and shoes should be complementary in colour and correct for the period – for example, both men and women in the eighteenth century wore white and coloured stockings, often with 'clocks' embroidered at the side, above the ankle. These can be imitated by painting on a simple design in crayon or paint. There was a fashion in the mid-Victorian period for horizontally striped stockings which were worn by ladies and children and can be made using cotton jersey from a child's T-shirt or sock top. Fine black jersey is the best choice for Edwardian socks and stockings. Very pretty socks for children can be made from lace edging with a neat border design or insertion lace with a straight edge.

To make stockings, measure the approximate length required – the top edge will be covered by drawers or breeches and the bottom edge by the top of the boot or shoe. Cut a piece of jersey, with the stretch across the fabric, wide enough to wrap around the thickest part of the leg. With the right side of the fabric to the leg, stretch

fig 23
Examples for painted shoes and boots

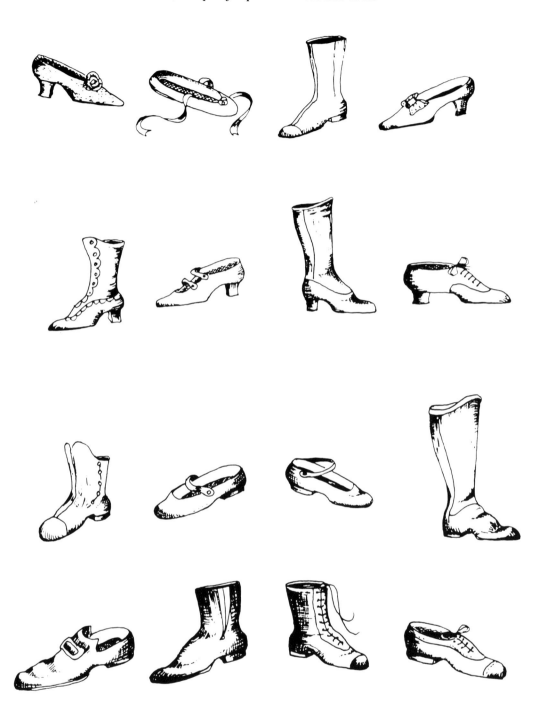

tightly, fastening the seam at the back with short pins. Keep adjusting until the jersey is taut and fits well. Ease the fabric off the leg and sew along the pin line with tiny stitches. Trim away any surplus fabric and, starting at the foot, roll the stocking back up the leg, making sure that the seam is flat and at the centre back. When satisfied with the fit, glue in position on the foot and at the top of the leg. Alternatively, working with the wrong side of the fabric to the leg, fasten with pins as before. Cut away the surplus very closely, then, removing one pin at a time, slip stitch the two edges together on the leg (Fig 24a).

A third method is to remove the pinned stocking and cut away all the surplus fabric. Run a line of glue down the back of the leg and, when it is tacky, stretch the fabric back onto the leg. Working from the top, glue the fabric so that it just overlaps. Trim the stocking away from underneath the foot where it would be too bulky.

Socks made from lace edging are glued just low enough on the foot to be covered by the boot or shoe. They can be cut from wide lace using the top edge. Decide how high the socks are to be (although this is likely to be determined by the width of the lace). If the doll is to have

fig 24
Making footwear

a ▪ stockings   *b ▪ shoes*

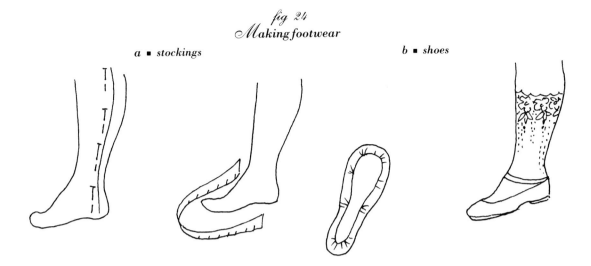

slippers or strap shoes, the lace must start near the toes. For bar and ankle-strap shoes, two widths of narrower lace could be used as the strap can be arranged to conceal the join. Cut a piece of lace more than long enough to go around the foot. Spread glue over the foot and ankle and, starting from the toes, gently press on the lace, working down each side over the ankle and up the leg. Press and ease the lace around the foot, making sure that there are no wrinkles. Trim away the surplus and finish by sewing or gluing so that the pattern at the top edge meets exactly. Jersey socks can be made in the same way as stockings with the top raw edge turned in and caught with a stitch or dab of glue.

▪ SHOES

Shoes can be made from silk ribbon or the finest gloving leather, which must be unflawed and should be prepared by stretching and working until it is soft and supple. Small offcuts may be found in craft shops or obtained from glove manufacturers (see Stockists); old kid gloves are excellent. Really sharp scissors are essential to cut a clean edge on the leather.

To make shoes, cut a strip of leather (or ribbon) (about 1½ x ¼in (3.8 x 0.6cm)) to go right around the foot. Place the centre of the strip on the toes and pull the leather firmly around the foot, trimming to make a butt-join at the back of the heel. There should be very little leather showing around the top of the foot, otherwise the shoes will look clumsy. Trim the lower edge of the strip so that it just curves comfortably under the foot, but does not quite meet at the centre, and make tiny snips all along this edge.

Apply glue under the foot and to the heel and fit the strip back on, making sure that the sides are even and that there is a perfect join at the heel. Turn the snipped edge under the foot, working it round and trimming where necessary so that it lies flat. Cut a neat sole in stiff light brown paper or matching leather slightly smaller than the foot, (curved nail-scissors will help with this) and glue in place. Paper soles often look better than

leather which shows the cut edge unless it is very fine. For a bar or ankle-strap, cut the narrowest possible strip and tuck the ends in position inside the shoe, adding a bead button on the outside (Fig 24b). The front of the shoe can be decorated with a buckle or short length of silk ribbon gathered into a rosette; eighteenth-century shoes need high tongues trimmed with metal buckles. Slippers for Regency ladies might have narrow silk-ribbon ties, glued into the shoe, and crossed around the ankles.

Stacked heels can be made with pieces of paper and moulded heels should be painted or covered with a scrap of shoe leather. The shoes can be painted or varnished with Fray Check which gives a glossy finish (see Fig 23).

▪ BOOTS

Boots can be made using a similar method, from a small square of supple leather, working and snipping it on the foot and up to the ankle until the shape is nearly right. Applying glue will further soften the leather and make the final fitting easier. Toe- and heel-caps, laces, buttons and scallops can be marked with felt pen or paint; braid around the top edge makes a nice finish. Double picot edging up the centre will give the impression of lacing, or this can be made by gluing on crossed threads (see Fig 23).

Men's heavy work-boots or boots for Santa Claus can be made by first adding a little modelling to enlarge the feet; use a self-hardening or oven-baked clay such as Das or Fimo for this job. The remodelled feet are covered with leather as before, but make thicker soles and heels. With patience, long boots can be made, but the legs might need extra padding to give the right shape. Spurs can be made from copper wire that is twisted and glued around the heel, with rowels made from star-shaped sequins. Wellington (rubber) boots are made most convincingly by over-modelling on the leg in coloured Fimo, using the appropriate contrasting colour for the sole.

Reference to costume books or contemporary illustrations will provide examples of footwear for each period.

The Southern Belle

The young lady sits in her corset and petticoats while Mary,
wearing clothes made from the Basic Pattern, brushes her hair

UNDERWEAR

LADIES

Authentic as it may be for a doll to wear a complete set of underwear and corset for the period, the constant problem of the thickness of material makes it impracticable. It is better to leave most of the unseen to the imagination and to concentrate on the garments which will show.

Making decorative underwear can be simplified with a little planning. The fabric can be prepared first with inserted lace, tucks and lace hem, and the drawers and petticoats cut from it (Fig 25). This is particularly convenient if some of the work is being done on the sewing-machine. Hems and rows of tucks are more difficult on a shaped or bias-cut garment, but rows of lace can be applied by hand or machine.

Flannel petticoats can be made from brushed cotton or wool/cotton shirting fabric in red or pale stripes and should be finished with a heavier torchon lace to represent tatting. Broderie anglaise (eyelet) is correct for Victorian or later underwear, provided the design is small enough. If it can be found wide enough with a delicate edge, then the whole garment could be made from it.

Although a corset is not recommended under clothes, a pattern is given for a lady doll who is wearing only her underwear, or to make an accessory for the dolls' house. Corsets can be made in silk, tartan, jacquard, brocade or cotton, trimmed with lace or broderie anglaise and ribbon bows.

Drawers are relatively modern and therefore incorrect on dolls of a period earlier than *c*1800. However, as most people turn female dolls upside down, it looks better if the cloth parts of dolls dressed to represent earlier periods are covered with plain fitted drawers, made just wide enough to pull on.

The shape of the petticoat should follow the line of the dress with no gathers under a slim fitted dress. For bustle styles, keep the front flat and take all fullness to the back, which should be cut longer to allow for the bustle pad, shaped to lie under the train. A bias-cut petticoat will fit and hang better than one cut on the straight grain of the fabric. If very full petticoats are needed to support a wide skirt, they can be made in tiers. A double ruffle of lace at hem level will also help and iron-on backing can be used for extra stiffening.

The patterns are shown to include the lace edging, so allow for this when cutting out.

- **BUSTLE PAD**

(Fig 28b)

This can be cut in cotton, stitched and turned, but is much easier made in white felt which can be oversewn from the outside and stuffed just before closing. Attach around the waist with fine cord, or stitch in position just below the waist.

For Georgian styles, a larger pad may be needed to act as a 'pannier' support.

- **CORSET**

(Fig 26)

Cut the shape in medium-weight iron-on interlining and press onto the wrong side of the fabric. Cut out, leaving 1/4in (6mm) of fabric all round. Using a little glue (Prittstick or similar), fold the extra fabric onto the wrong side of the corset and press. If the corset is to be lined, do this now using a bonding agent and trimming the lining to shape.

Stitch the darts, starting at the centre front and fastening off firmly with back stitching. Snip each dart at the centre and press towards the centre front – using a point presser or sleeve board will make this easier. Press the bottom half first, then the top, spreading out the curves. Turn to the right side and top stitch the corset on the lines shown in Fig 26a. If you are sewing by hand, use back stitch or prick stitch. As you sew, manipulate the corset to stretch the darts above and below the waistline. The stitching will help to make the correct shape.

Make eyelet holes on the back edges using metal eyelets or use an awl (stiletto) and paint with Fray Check.

fig 25
Fabric prepared for cutting underwear

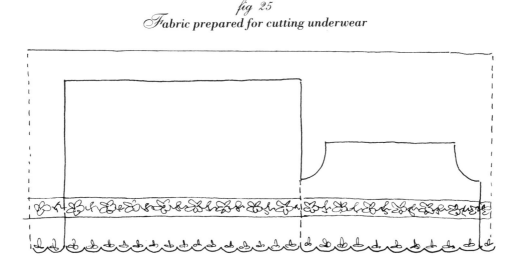

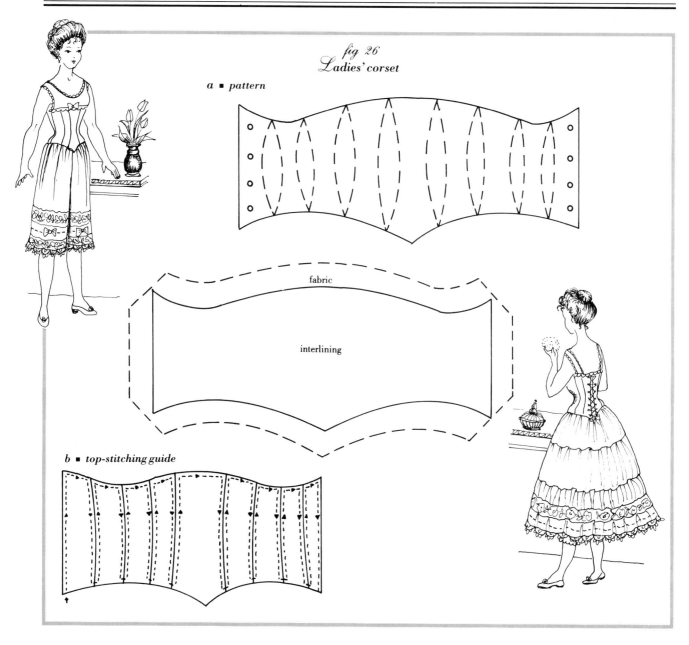

fig 26
Ladies' corset

a ▪ *pattern*

fabric

interlining

b ▪ *top-stitching guide*

Trim the top edge with broderie anglaise, lace or ribbon. Fit onto the doll and lace with thin crotchet cotton, adding extra stuffing in the bosom if necessary. The corset may be worn either under or over a petticoat.

▪ **DRAWERS**
(Fig 27)

For most periods these should come to just below the knee, but make sure that they will cover the cloth part of the leg. During the early to mid-Victorian era, long pantaloons were worn.

Cutting a toile in paper-towel is advisable so that width and length can be measured accurately, allowing for lace and tucks. Ensure that the legs are wide enough to pull over the feet and that the drawers are wide enough at hip level.

Cut two pieces and trim hems with lace, insertion or tucks. Stitch front and back seams, clip and press open. Stitch leg seams, finishing securely at the edges, and press open. Run a gathering thread at the waist edge, fit onto the doll, distribute the gathers away from the front, and stitch to the body securely just below the waist. (Before closing, a little padding can be slipped into the back to give the bottom more shape.)

For a simplified 'bloomer' effect, cut the legs a little wider, but do not hem or add lace. Stitch seams as above, but with the drawers inside out, run a gathering thread around the bottom of each leg, and insert the doll's legs into the legs of the drawers.

Pull up the gathering threads just below the knee and fasten off securely. Pull the drawers up to the waist and finish as before. This is a very quick method and is particularly suitable for dressing servants. If it looks too plain, a band of ribbon can be added or lace whipped on at the bottom of the legs.

▪ **GATHERED PETTICOATS**
(Fig 28)

These are the easiest style to make and are suitable for most costumes. Under a full skirt, two petticoats of

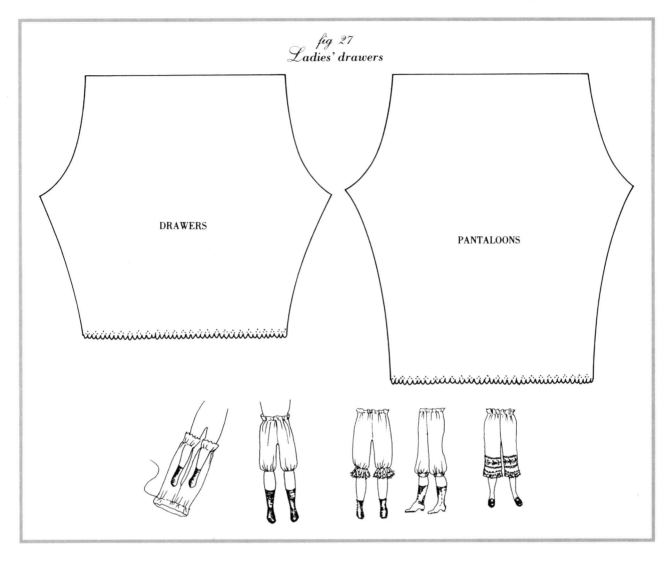

fig 27
Ladies' drawers

DRAWERS

PANTALOONS

different widths are better than one. Make the first fairly narrow and the second fuller, or make it in tiers for really good hem support. Measure the required length (usually to slightly above ankle length so that the petticoats will not show below the dress). The patterns include edge trimming, which can be as simple or as elaborate as you wish. Stitch the back seam and use a French or 'run-and-fell' seam, or trim the edges and oversew for a neat finish. Press, then run a gathering thread around the top edge and fit the petticoat onto the doll over the drawers, distributing the gathers away from the front; stitch securely to the doll just below the waist. If there are several petticoats, attach them at different levels to keep the waist slim.

Cut the tiered petticoat as shown in Fig 28 and trim the lower edge. Gather each tier evenly and stitch to the tier above, then stitch the back seam and fit as before.

- SHAPED PETTICOATS
(Fig 29)
These should be made to correspond with the shape of the dress or skirt and cut in bias fabric, with gathered lace whipped to the bottom edge and in layers above. There is one slim-shaped pattern for Regency and Edwardian skirts, a slightly fuller pattern for flared skirts, and one for late-Victorian or Edwardian skirts with a slight train. Trained petticoats might have lace or broderie anglaise frills sewn in rows down the back to give extra support to the bustle.

UNDERWEAR FOR CHILDREN
(Fig 30)
Several layers of body belts, flannel wrappers and plain and embroidered petticoats were considered essential clothing for Victorian babies, but in miniature they must be reduced to a folded nappy (diaper) and one petticoat.

Regency Style (1800–1830) ▸
As the family assemble in the drawing room before the reception, mama and her daughter wear high-waisted silk Regency Dresses and her son wears a fashionable Skeleton Suit. Both gentlemen wear Regency Suits with breeches and their little servant is dressed in exotic finery adapted from the Early-Victorian suit. The maid and governess wear simple cotton versions of the Regency Dress

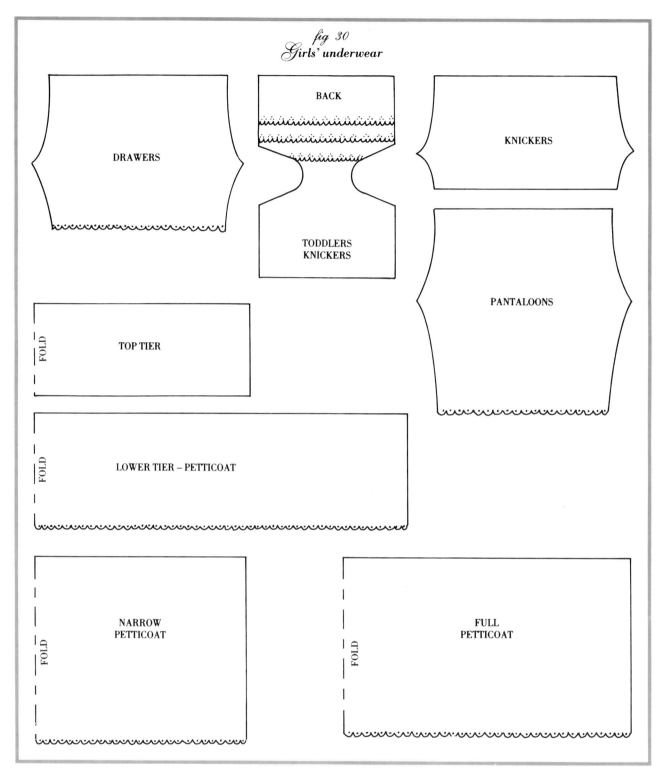

fig 30
Girls' underwear

DRAWERS

BACK

KNICKERS

TODDLERS
KNICKERS

PANTALOONS

FOLD — TOP TIER

FOLD — LOWER TIER – PETTICOAT

FOLD — NARROW
PETTICOAT

FOLD — FULL
PETTICOAT

and these can be made in the thinnest cotton jersey, preferably off-white (although Americans seem to have favoured red which washed out to pink). Neck, wrists and ankles should be treated with Fray Check, buttonhole stitched, or turned up with the narrowest possible hems. The front opening and back 'trap-door' could be fastened with small bead 'buttons'.

Washing Day
The maids, wearing clothes made from the Basic
Pattern wash and iron lace and ribbon-trimmed
drawers and petticoats

6

$\mathscr{P}$atterns for ladies

THE PATTERNS WHICH FOLLOW include styles for lady dolls from the Georgian period to the twentieth century. They are illustrated in the drawings and most are shown in colour photographs – relevant page numbers are given in the individual patterns.

The clothes are made by using the methods described in Chapter 3, which should be referred to where necessary to avoid excessive repetition. The making-up instructions given here are brief.

Specific fabric requirements are not listed as the amounts needed are so small. One-tenth of a yard or metre of fabric 36in (91cm) wide will make a simple dress and even the most elaborate crinoline or bustle style will need less than 1/4yd (0.23m). The amount of braid, lace or ribbon required will vary according to the costume and the trimming used – from approximately 1yd (1m) for simple styles to 3-4yd (3-4m) for lavishly trimmed costumes.

Suggestions are offered for footwear and underwear to complement each style and for the fabrics and colours most suitable for each costume. Appropriate wigs, hats and accessories can be found in Chapters 10 and 11.

The patterns are arranged in roughly chronological order, but begin with the basic pattern which can be used to make a wide variety of simple costumes for Victorian servants and ladies from Georgian times to the present day. This simple pattern is recommended for beginners.

THE BASIC PATTERN
(Fig 31)

The basic pattern includes a bodice in two sizes, a long sleeve, gathered skirt and aprons. See Fig 34 if you prefer to make a shaped skirt. The gathered skirt is the simplest to make, but the shaped skirt – cut on the bias and slightly gathered at the waist – gives a better line.

COOK
(Fig. 32 – shown in colour on pp62/63).
Choose small-scale check, striped or sprigged cotton print for the dress, fine white cotton lawn for underwear, dress lining, cap, apron and cuffs. Stripes and checks look better cut on the straight grain. If she is to be stout,

use extra body padding and the larger bodice pattern. The bibbed apron is late Victorian – before then aprons were usually tied at the waist, (see Fig 31).

- **FOOTWEAR**
Black boots with front lacing or side buttons.

- **UNDERWEAR**
Cotton drawers and a plain gathered petticoat, trimmed with tucks or feather stitching.

- **APRON**
Cut in cotton lawn and hem one long and two short sides. Fold the bib piece in half and seam the two sides, clip corners, turn and press. Cut a strip 8 x 1/2in (20.5 x 1.3cm), fold in 1/8in (3mm) on both long sides and press – half this length is for the waistband. Cut the remainder in half again for the shoulder straps and put the bib and straps aside.

- **DRESS**
Cut one skirt and one lining in cotton lawn or muslin. Seam the short edges together on each and press the seams open. With right sides together and centre-back seams matching, stitch the lower edge of the skirt to the lining, easing the fabric without stretching so that there are no wrinkles. Trim, turn through and press so that the lining does not show. (If the skirt is not lined, extra length must be allowed for a hem.) Check the skirt length on the doll – remembering that the waist gathers will make it slightly shorter. With the skirt seam at the back, lay the apron over the skirt and run two gathering threads through both at the waistline. Fit onto the doll, pull up and distribute the gathers evenly, making sure that the apron is central, and fasten off securely. (For a slimmer waist, cut the skirt (Fig 34) and lining on the bias grain of the fabric. Make up as before, but gather the apron separately and draw the skirt fullness to the centre back.)

Cut the dress bodice on the bias grain of the fabric, or cut striped fabric on the straight grain and make small bust darts to give shape. Stitch shoulder and underarm seams and press open. Snip around the neckline. Fit the bodice onto the doll and fold under the lower edge to fit exactly over the gathers of the skirt, trimming any surplus fabric. Slip stitch the back opening closed and, with the point of a needle, tuck in the raw edges around the neckline. Push a wisp of stuffing under the bodice for

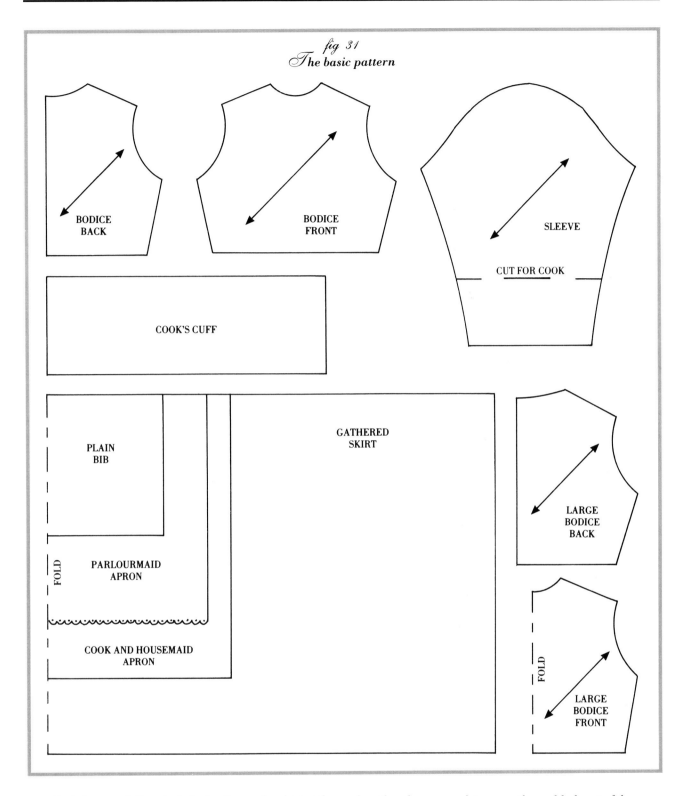

fig 31
The basic pattern

BODICE BACK

BODICE FRONT

SLEEVE

CUT FOR COOK

COOK'S CUFF

PLAIN BIB

GATHERED SKIRT

LARGE BODICE BACK

FOLD

PARLOURMAID APRON

COOK AND HOUSEMAID APRON

FOLD

LARGE BODICE FRONT

a realistic bust and slip stitch the bodice to the skirt at the waistline.

Make the collar with a short length of broderie anglaise (eyelet), or a strip of folded dress fabric or white lawn. Neaten the short edges. Snip the long raw edge and turn under around the neck. Slip stitch into position so that the ends meet neatly at the centre front.

Cut the sleeves on the bias (reversing if striped.) Run a gathering thread around the top of the sleeves and stitch the underarm seams. Fit onto the doll and adjust to elbow length *or* long enough to cover the padded part of the arm. Pull up the gathers with fullness at the top of the sleeve, matching the underarm and side seams, tuck in the raw

Below Stairs ▸
The butcher wearing Working Clothes (shopkeeper variation) calls on the cook – she and the housemaid, parlourmaid and tweeny all wear variations of the Basic Pattern

fig 32
Victorian servants

edges and stitch to the bodice at the natural armhole. A wisp of stuffing may be inserted to support the sleeve gathers.

fig 33
Making the cook's cuffs

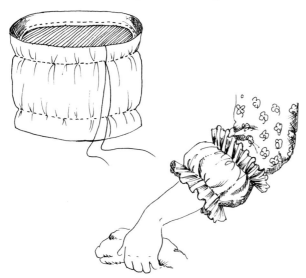

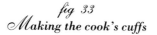

For the gathered cuffs, cut two pieces of white cotton 3 x 1in (7.6 x 2.5cm). Seam the short edges and press open, then press ¼in (6mm) turnings on both long edges. Run gathering threads ⅛in (3mm) from both edges, leaving the threads on the outside. Place the cuffs over the raw ends of the sleeves, pull up tightly and adjust the

gathers and stitch firmly in place (Fig 33).

Trim the raw edge of the bib to the required length and tack to the dress bodice at the waistline. With very neat stitches attach the shoulder straps at a slight angle to the top of the bib. Cross the straps at the back and tack them at the waistline, trimming any surplus. Fit the apron waistband around the waist, covering the raw edges of the bib and shoulder straps. Trim to fit and stitch at centre back. Add two white beads for buttons or a ribbon bow.

- HAIR

A very plain style.

- HAT

A white cotton mob-cap.

- ACCESSORIES

A mixing-bowl and wooden spoon, rolling-pin or baked pie.

HOUSEMAID

(Fig 32 – shown in colour on pp62/63)

Make the sleeves wrist length and finish with cuffs made from folded strips of white cotton. Use the pattern in Fig 31 for the apron and in Fig 34 for the U-shaped bib. Cut two bibs in white cotton, stitch together, trim and clip the neck and corners, turn and press. Adjust the length, tack to the waist and attach shoulder straps and waistband as for the cook. Make the cap shown in Chapter 11 and add a mop, broom or feather duster as accessories.

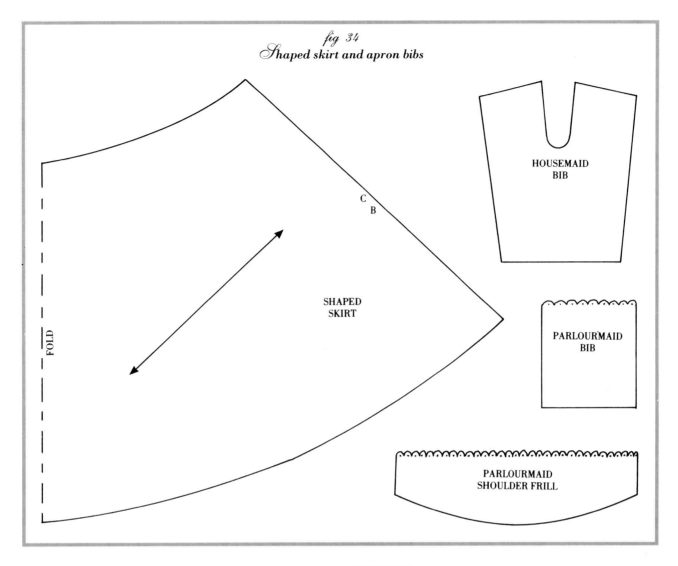

fig 34
Shaped skirt and apron bibs

HOUSEMAID BIB

SHAPED SKIRT

C
B

FOLD

PARLOURMAID BIB

PARLOURMAID SHOULDER FRILL

PARLOURMAID

(Fig 32 – shown in colour on pp62/63)

Use black bonded silk or fine cotton for the dress. Make apron, bib and shoulder frills (Fig 34) in broderie anglaise or white cotton lawn edged with slightly gathered narrow lace. Turn in and hem the sides of the apron and bib. Gather the curved edge of the shoulder frills and pull up to fit from the top of the bib to the centre back waist, tucking in the raw edges and stitch in position. Fit the waistband and finish with a ribbon bow. Make a cap with streamers; the maid could be carrying a tea-tray or a plate of cakes.

NANNY

(Fig 32 – shown in colour on p159)

She might be stout and motherly with grey hair, or a pretty young nursemaid. Her dress could be plain or striped blue cotton, with long sleeves and white cuffs, worn with a white bibbed apron. Instead of shoulder-straps, the bib could be held with two tiny safety-pins sewn on. Make a pretty little cap tied under the chin with a bow, and she could be carrying a baby, a pile of towels, or a bottle of medicine and a spoon.

TWEENY

(Fig 32 – shown in colour on pp62/63)

A pathetic little kitchenmaid eternally on her hands and knees black-leading the stove or scrubbing the floor can be very appealing. Use a child doll with a rather thin face for a twelve-year-old. Cut the dress pattern a little smaller to fit, and use a drab faded fabric with a cream apron, which could be suitably 'soiled' with watercolour or felt pen. Her mob-cap could be oversized with wisps of untidy hair escaping.

MARY

(Fig 35 – shown in colour on p50)

If you have a realistic black doll, Mary can be dressed from the basic pattern. Pad her body and make up the pattern as for the cook, using the larger bodice. Red-checked cotton or black silk for the dress and white cotton for her waist-apron, collar and cuffs are most effective. Make a little curl of black or dark brown hair to show under a white turban made from a 3in (7.6cm) square of white cotton, folded in half and tied on the top of her head. Sew on tiny gold ear-rings made from jewellery jump rings.

fig 35
Mary, balloon-seller and Granny

FLOWER- OR BALLOON-SELLER, COUNTRYWOMAN

(Fig 35 – shown in colour on p179)

These dolls could wear dark cotton print or thin wool dresses, with waist-aprons in shirting cotton in plain or muted coloured stripes or checks. Add a triangular woollen shawl with fringed edges and either a mob cap or bonnet. Fill a basket with the smallest dried flowers sprayed with hair lacquer to preserve them, modelled fruit, vegetables or eggs. For instructions for making balloons, see Chapter 11, Accessories.

GRANNY

(Fig 35 – shown in colour on pp182/183)

Use a really old-character-faced doll with grey or white hair. Make her dress in dark grey, purple or black, trimmed with lace collar and cuffs, or add a straight or V-shaped lace yoke by laying wide lace over the bodice front before sewing it to the back and covering the join with grosgrain ribbon. Add a few jet beads for buttons. Make a brooch by sewing several beads together, or join the collar with a bow. Make a small black silk waist-apron and a soft fringed shawl. If she can be seated, she could have a piece of sewing or knitting on glass-headed pins with a ball of wool, or a book or a kitten to keep her company. Spectacles or a lorgnette would be a nice finishing touch.

PEDLAR

(Fig 36 – shown in colour on p27)

This is a particularly popular doll because of the many tiny objects packed onto her basket-tray. Use an interesting older-faced doll. Choose a dark print for her dress, with a cream or striped waist-apron, plain collar and cuffs. Make her distinctive red woollen cloak in fine wool or cotton winceyette with lining to match. Stitch the small shoulder darts on the cloak and lining – cut open and press flat. With right sides together, seam down the fronts and around the bottom, trim, clip, turn and press. Run a gathering thread around the neckline through both cloak and lining and pull up to fit the neck. Trim the raw edges and bind with black ribbon to tie at the front. (The cloak can also be made in single fabric bound around the edges.) Make a bonnet of black straw or bonded fabric, trimmed with black ribbon, with a frill of white lace under the brim to represent a cap. Add a shallow basket-tray suspended from a narrow strap around the neck, loaded with ribbons, cards of buttons, bottles, books, toys or household utensils.

QUAKER STYLES

(Fig 36)

These simple costumes made in even the plainest, drabbest fabrics, have great charm. Make plain underwear with no trimming. Use the basic pattern and slightly gathered sleeves. Cut the collar in double-bonded white cotton and snip all round the neck edge to fit. (If the collar is too large, trim both centre fronts; if it is too small,

fig 36
Pedlar's cloak and Quaker collar

COLLAR

FOLD

CLOAK

trim a little from the neck edge.) Stitch trimming to the outside edge using grosgrain ribbon, bunka or picot braid – the latter looks very neat with the loops faced inwards. For a strict sect there must be no trimming at all, so cut the collar with a seam allowance in two pieces of bonded lawn, seam the outer edge, trim the seam and clip all round before turning and pressing. Tack the collar to hold it in place and stitch together at the centre front. Use the pattern for a housemaid's cap (see Chapter 11), or make a small plain fabric or straw bonnet.

PEASANT, GYPSY OR NELL GWYNNE
(Fig 37)
Use a doll with a shoulder-head because of the low

neckline and porcelain arms which come above the elbow.

Cut the blouse in Jap silk or fine white lawn. Stitch the shoulder seams from A to B, then pleat or gather from B to B to make fullness at the top of the sleeve, tucking in the raw edges. Turn in the neckline with a gathering thread, pull up a little but do not fasten off. Stitch the underarm seams and turn under the sleeve ends with gathering threads. Fit the blouse onto the doll, pull up the sleeve gathers and fasten off.

Using the basic pattern, make a slightly shorter skirt in bright fabric and trim with rows of braid. Fit the skirt over the blouse and add a short decorative apron.

Cut the waistcoat in double-bonded fabric. Stitch

fig 37
Peasant, gypsy and Nell Gwynne costume

FOLD

A

B

BLOUSE

FOLD

WAISTCOAT
BACK

WAISTCOAT
FRONT

BELT

BELT

shoulder and side seams. The neckline, armholes and front edges could be trimmed with braid. Using thick thread, lace the fronts together so that the blouse shows between – this is easier using a needle at each end of the thread. Adjust the neck gathers on the blouse and fasten off the gathering thread. The neckline and sleeves could have a narrow lace trim and ribbon ties.

Instead of a waistcoat, the wide-shaped belt could be made in thin leather or braid-trimmed double-bonded fabric. Make dark curly hair and gold ear-rings for a gypsy, or red hair and a basket of oranges for Nell Gwynne. With suitable variations in fabric, trimming and head-dress, this pattern will adapt to most European national costumes.

GEORGIAN GOWN

(Fig 38 – shown in colour on pp42/43)

Dresses of this period have tight-fitting bodices with very low necklines, so the doll should have a deep shoulder-plate, otherwise, the neckline could be filled with a fine

muslin or lace fichu. Use a stiff brocade for the under-skirt, or a plainer fabric with the front panel decorated with quilting, embroidery, rows of lace or fabric frills. The bodice and overskirt could be in pastel silk or sprig-ged or striped cotton. The stiffness and close fit of the bodice and stomacher are most important.

- **FOOTWEAR**

Silk stockings and shoes with tongues and buckles.

- **UNDERWEAR**

Although incorrect for the period, the doll will look better with knee-length drawers. Two or three full petticoats – keep fullness away from the front.

- **DRESS**

Unless the fabric is very stiff, cut the underskirt in bonded fabric and in lining. Decorate the front panel, stitch the back seams on the skirt and lining and stitch together around the hem, clip, turn through and press. Gather the waist edge and fit onto the doll, drawing the fullness away from the centre front so that the hem is ankle length. Cut the overskirt in bonded fabric and in lining. Stitch the hip darts matching A to A in both pieces and, with right sides together, seam down the fronts and

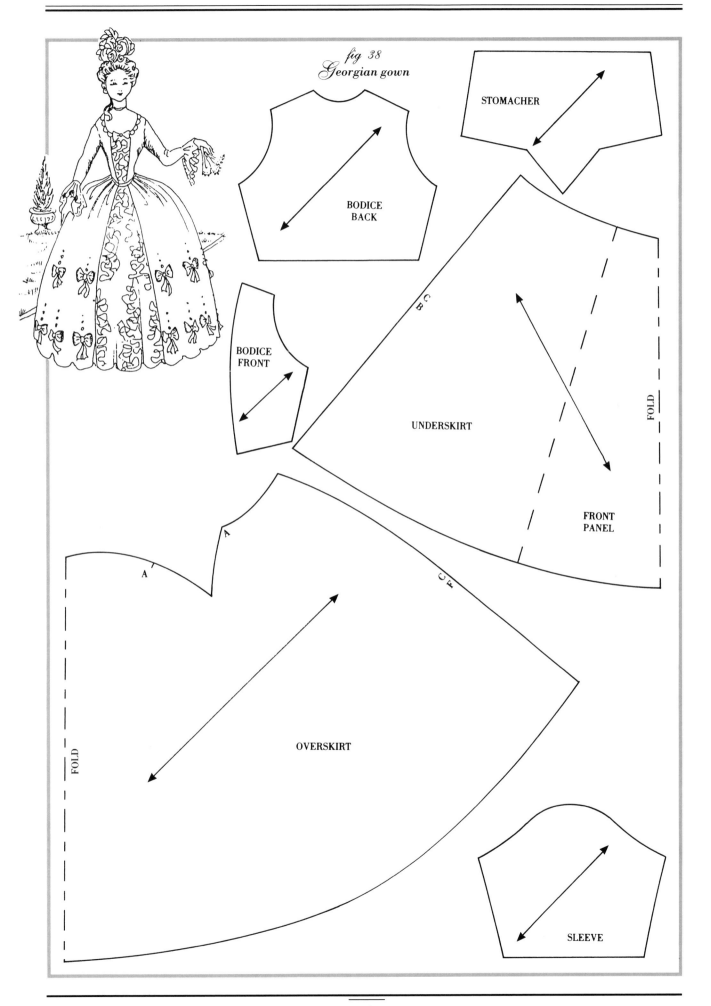

fig 38
Georgian gown

STOMACHER

BODICE
BACK

BODICE
FRONT

UNDERSKIRT

FOLD

FRONT
PANEL

OVERSKIRT

FOLD

SLEEVE

The Proposal

The elderly gentleman wearing a Georgian Suit asks the young lady in her exquisite Georgian Gown to honour him with her hand in marriage. She is reluctant

around the hem. Clip the curve, turn through and press. Fit to the doll's waist with small pleats arranged evenly so that the hem is a fraction longer than the underskirt and just clears the ground. (Decorate the front edges if required before fitting.)

Cut the stomacher in double-bonded fabric and check that it will cover the lower edge of the shoulder-plate. Decorate as required. Holding the point at the centre front, pin the sides to the doll's body and insert wisps of cotton-wool for extra shaping. With strong thread, lace the stomacher around the doll's back, pulling it tight and covering the top of the skirt.

Cut the bodice back and fronts on the bias in bonded fabric. Stitch the shoulder and underarm seams. Trim the front edges so that they do not quite meet at the waist to show the stomacher. Decorate the front edges to match the skirt and fit the bodice onto the doll; tack it in place. The front edges might be laced together with fine silk ribbon or embroidery thread. Slip stitch around the waistline and trim with braid. Cut the sleeves to fit tightly to just below the elbow. Stitch the underarm seams and make gathering threads to ease. Slip stitch the sleeves to the bodice without gathering at the armholes.

Finish the sleeve ends with delicate lace ruffles, which should be longer at the back than at the front. Use about 4in (10cm) of ¾in (1.9cm) wide lace and graduate the gathering line so that it starts and finishes at the outer edge, pull up so that the two short edges meet at the centre front of the sleeve and trim with a bow.

The dress trimming can be very elaborate – ruched ribbon from neck to hem was popular, with lots of bows and ribbon roses. Very narrow lace or gathered ribbon could be added around the neckline of the dress, and a ribbon tied around the doll's neck.

- **HAIR**

The hair should be drawn high, with softly curling ringlets and decorated with ribbons or feathers.

- **HAT**

A large frilled muslin mob-cap or a wide-brimmed hat.

MAID

Dress a maid in pale sprigged cotton. Make the dress with a slightly narrower skirt and a little lace or trimming. Make a narrow muslin apron and a fichu to cover the low neckline. Finish the sleeves with small cuffs or narrow frills in place of lace ruffles. She should wear a large mob-cap.

REGENCY DRESS

(Fig 39 – shown in colour on pp54/55)

The low-necked short-sleeved dress is made for a doll with a deep shoulder-plate and complete arms. If she has padded or cloth arms, use the long-sleeved version.

Use fine silk or muslin in white or a pastel shade for the short-sleeved dress – a tiny print or darker colour would be suitable for the long-sleeved version or for a maid. To obtain the slim high-waisted look of this period, cut the skirt in bonded fabric, on the bias, in one piece with a centre-back seam; it is essential that this should fit properly.

- **FOOTWEAR**

Dainty flat slippers in silk or kid to match the dress.

- **UNDERWEAR**

Long decorative pantaloons and a slim bias-cut petticoat.

- **DRESS**

Stitch centre-back seams on the skirt and skirt lining, then stitch them together around the hem, being careful not to stretch the seam. Clip the curve, trim and press. Decorate the hem of the skirt with a broad band of cross-cut self-ruching, rows of lace, or a pattern of braiding or embroidery, or a heavy lace motif could be used with additional bows and roses. The skirt should fit neatly under the bustline, with any easing centred at the back.

The bodice is so small that a little ingenuity is required to make it. Cut a bias strip of dress fabric (Fig 39a) and seam the short ends, on the bias, to form a loop. Press under a small turning on both long edges. Mark the loop into four equal sections which will be the bodice front, back and sleeves. Lightly mark the lowest possible square neckline on the back and front of the shoulder-plate. Run a gathering thread along the top fold of the bodice and pull up the gathers to fit this line exactly. Cover the marked line on the shoulder-plate with a thin line of glue to hold the fabric in place, and fit the bodice, with the raw edges tucked in, so that the four marked points are the four corners of the square neckline – gathers should be slightly fuller over the shoulders. Turn under the lower edge of the bodice and attach it to the skirt with a few stitches under the left arm. Gather the bottom edge of the sleeve to the next marked point, pull up the gathers tightly around the arm and fasten to the starting point, forming a little puffed sleeve. Gather across the front bodice to the next marked point and secure under the right arm. Stitch around the arm and pull up the gathers for the second sleeve, again securing under the arm, then work across the back of the bodice, gathering to fit and secure. There will now be a small gathered bodice with sleeves. Tuck in a little cotton-wool to improve the bustline and slip stitch the bodice to the skirt. Trim the neckline, cuffs and the join between skirt and bodice with narrow grosgrain ribbon or picot edging, glued to tack in place, but stitched for security. Trim the back waist of the dress with a bow and long streamers.

A gathered bodice could also be made in lace, or in self-frilled embroidered ribbon – the flat ribbon forms the neckline, mitred at the corners, concealing the join at a back corner. A thread through the edge of the frill will gather it to form sleeves and bodice. Stitch to the skirt as

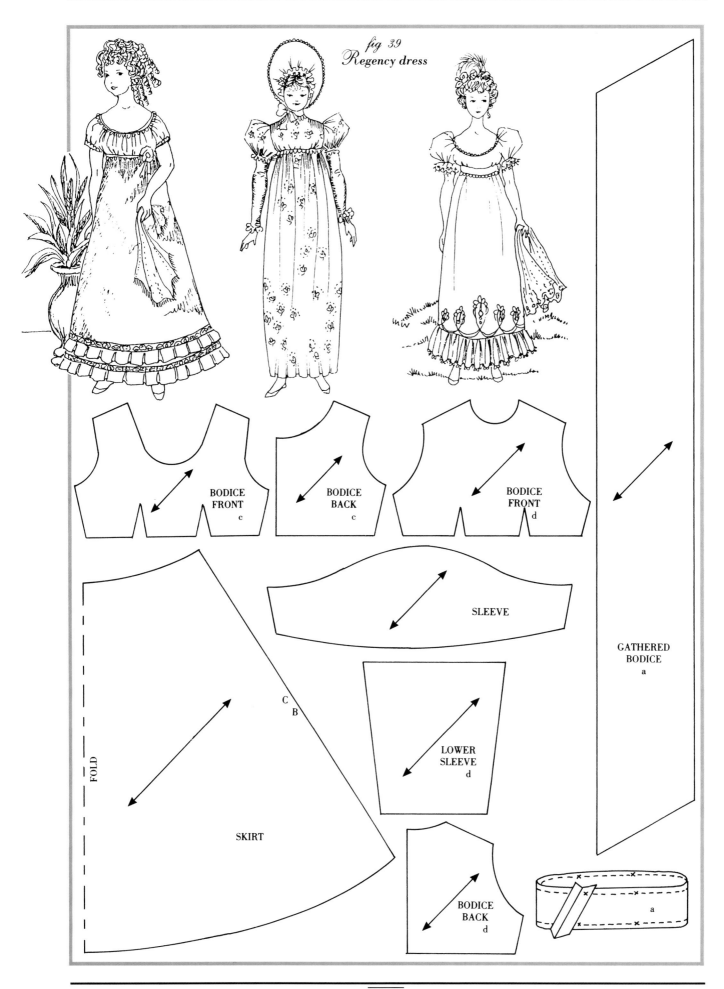

fig 3.9
Regency dress

BODICE FRONT
c

BODICE BACK
c

BODICE FRONT
d

GATHERED BODICE
a

SLEEVE

FOLD

C
B

SKIRT

LOWER SLEEVE
d

BODICE BACK
d

a

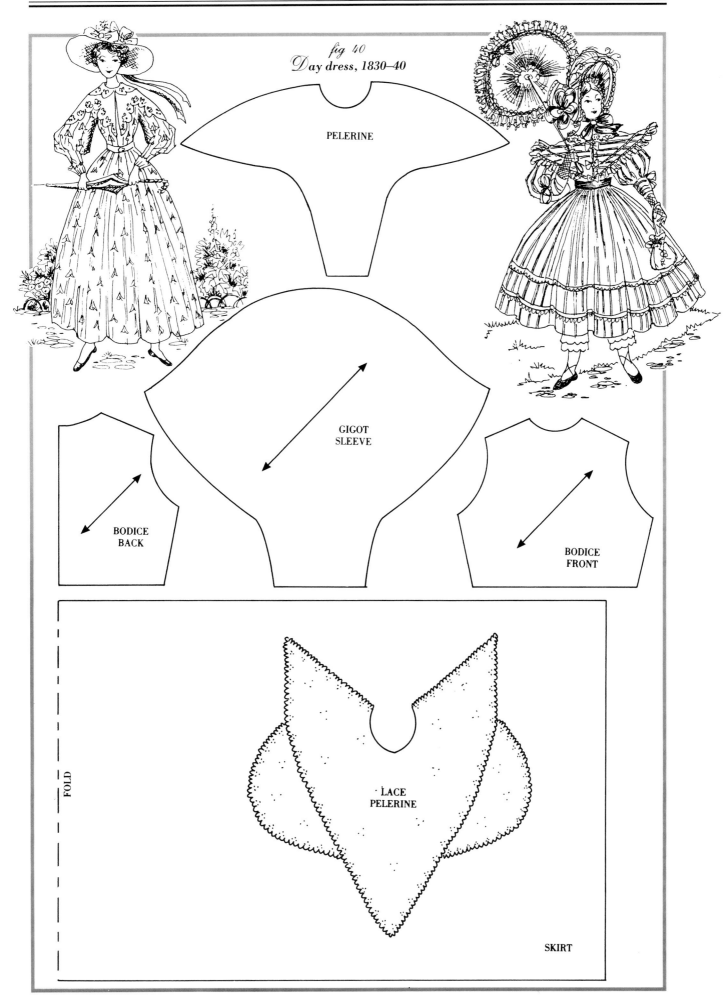

fig 40
*D*ay dress, 1830–40

PELERINE

GIGOT
SLEEVE

BODICE
BACK

BODICE
FRONT

FOLD

LACE
PELERINE

SKIRT

before. Rows of the same ribbon at the hem look particularly effective.

- **ALTERNATIVE BODICE**

An alternative pattern is given for a plain low-necked bodice (Fig 39c) shaped with darts, but these must be fitted and sewn accurately. Cut the bodice back and front in bonded silk and stitch shoulder and side seams. While still inside-out, fit onto the doll and mark where the front darts should be. Tack, stitch and press the darts, stitch the bodice to the skirt and add trimmings. Fit short or long sleeves as described below.

- **HIGH-NECKED BODICE**

(Fig 39d)

To make the high-necked long-sleeved bodice stitch the shoulder and underarm seams. Clip around the neckline, fit onto the doll and slip stitch the back seam, concealing the opening with a short length of braid and tiny bead buttons. Dart or gather the bodice as above and fit to the skirt. Finish the neckline with a narrow stand-up frill of lace, trimming the join with braid. Gather the lower edge of the upper sleeves to fit the top of the lower sleeves and seam them right sides together. The sleeves fit tightly and should be slip stitched on the doll and finished with lace or braid cuffs. Gather the top of the sleeves and stitch to the armholes.

- **HAIR**

Either drawn back into a Grecian bun, softened with tiny tendrils around the hairline and nape of the neck, or in short curls, decorated with a ribbon bandeau.

- **HAT**

High poke-bonnet and parasol.

- **ACCESSORIES**

As dresses were generally flimsy, shawls were worn for warmth. Use either a straight piece of softly draping fabric, frayed to fringe the ends, or a large Paisley-patterned triangle.

DAY DRESS, 1830–40

(Fig 40 – shown in colour on pp102/103)

- **FOOTWEAR AND UNDERWEAR**

Flat slippers, pantaloons and two full petticoats.

- **DRESS**

Make dress in plain, sprigged or striped cotton or silk. Cut the skirt and make up to ankle length as described for the basic pattern (see p60). Cut the bodice front and backs in bonded fabric and make up as described for the basic pattern. Cut the gigot sleeves in unbonded fabric; stitch the upper part of the underarm seams and gather the sleeve tops. Slip stitch the sleeves to the armholes and slip stitch the lower part of the sleeve seams tightly onto the arm. Make a ribbon or fabric belt fastened with a buckle.

- **PELERINE**

Cut the lace pelerine so that it is pointed at both back and front waist. Suitable large-scalloped lace is manufactured for lingerie or the shape can be built up in pieces of ³/₄-1in (1.9-2.5cm) wide lace cut diagonally at the ends and seamed to form a point at the centre back; add extra width by attaching another slightly pleated layer at the shoulder. Good lace is very easy to build up into the shape shown on the pattern, as stitching in matching thread will be invisible. Fold in and slip stitch the front edges together, with a few pearl beads as a button fastening and add a neat lace collar.

Cut the fabric pelerine back and front in bonded or double-bonded fabric to match the dress, and trim with braid. Stitch the shoulder seams, slit down the front or back just far enough to slip the pelerine over the doll's head, and slip stitch closed.

- **HAIR**

Elaborate side curls and fringes; the back hair should be drawn up into a high bun.

- **HAT**

Large-brimmed hat with a soft crown, decorated with bows of ribbon and feathers, worn at a slight angle, or a high-fronted poke-bonnet.

CRINOLINE DRESS, 1840–60

(Fig 41 – shown in colour on pp102/103)

The 'crinoline' was actually a flexible hooped cage designed to replace some of the many petticoats worn to support the immensely full skirts of the Victorian period, but it has come to refer to the skirt itself. It is not practical to make a crinoline cage in this scale, but the effect can be achieved by making a very full skirt by one of the following methods:

1 Use very fine fabric gathered as tightly as possible to fit the waist. Use two gathering threads slightly apart and pull them up together to obtain the neatest finish. If the extra bulk of lining would be too much, the hem should be neatly sewn and covered by trimming, which could be quite elaborate.

2 Cut a semi-circular skirt so that the waist is much smaller than the hem. It is difficult to turn up a curved hem neatly, so this shape is best finished with lace, a self-ruffled or pleated trimming, or fully lined.

3 Make a tiered skirt. This looks pretty, especially if a bordered fabric or wide lace over fine silk is used.

4 Make a bell-shaped skirt, with the fullness drawn to the back (from about 1863).

Pleating in self fabric is an excellent trimming to add controlled fullness. The neatest method is to use doubled fabric; when used single, the edge must be finished before pleating. On some fabrics it may be sufficient to paint the edge with Fray Check or to fold it under once –

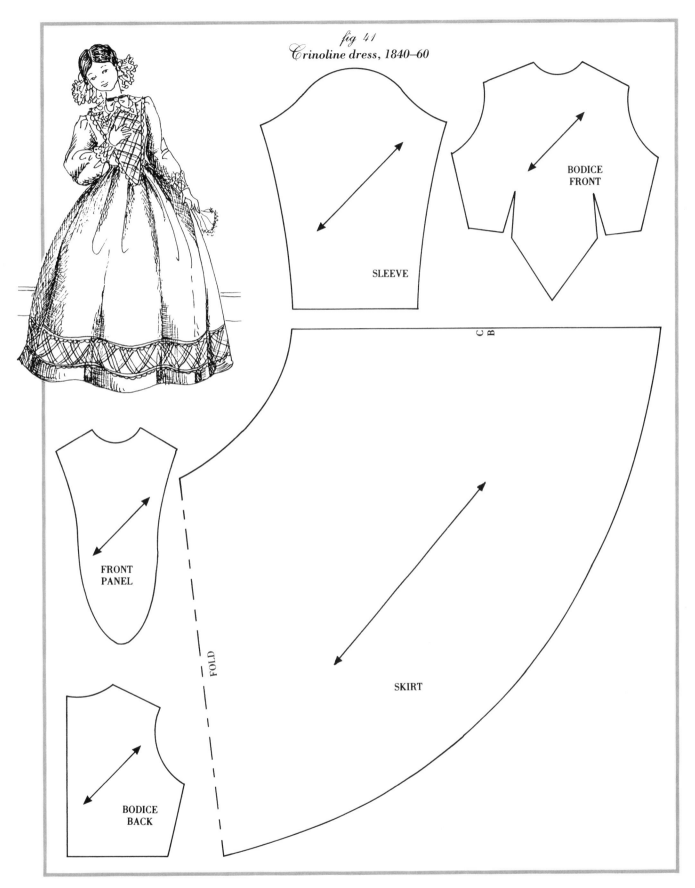

fig 41
Crinoline dress, 1840–60

SLEEVE

BODICE FRONT

FRONT PANEL

SKIRT

FOLD

C B

BODICE BACK

the pleating will hold it in place – or to sew on a lace edging.

The line of the full skirt is echoed by sloping shoulders, with tight sleeves and a tight-fitting V-shaped bodice, accentuated by trimming. The choice of skirt rather depends on the design and thickness of the fabric, but a shaped skirt cut on the bias will look very effective.

■ FOOTWEAR
Neat leather buttoned boots.

■ UNDERWEAR
Lace-trimmed drawers and at least two petticoats, full or tiered, to support the skirt.

■ DRESS
Cut the skirt in bonded fabric and in lining. Stitch the centre-back seams and, with right sides facing, stitch the skirt to the lining around the lower edge. Clip the curve, trim, turn through and press. Add the trimming, which could be contrast fabric cut on the bias, pleating or rows of braid. Stitch the skirt to the waist, pleating in any fullness.

Cut a bodice front in interlining and trim to the stitching line at either side of the bottom V. Iron this to the wrong side of the fabric bodice front. Fold back the seam allowance to make a crisp V-shape which will fit over the skirt. Stitch the darts. Cut the bodice back in bonded fabric and stitch the shoulder and side seams. Fit the bodice onto the doll and close the back opening, making sure that the bodice fits as tightly as possible, and insert extra bust padding if required. Slip stitch around the waistline. Long tight sleeves should be left open at the bottom and slip stitched on the doll. Although there is very little fullness at the top of the sleeves, ease with a gathering thread and slip stitch the sleeves to the armholes, lower on the shoulder than is normal to make the sloped-shoulder effect. This can be further accentuated (and any slight puckering concealed) by adding a cord or picot-braid trim to represent a piped seam. Finish the sleeves with neat cuffs or tiny frills, and add a matching collar.

The dress can be elaborated by the use of braid or lace trimming, especially to accentuate the sloping-shoulder line. The front panel is made by cutting the pattern shape in lace or fabric, trimming the edge, and tacking it over the bodice. If the panel is of a contrasting fabric such as tartan, add a band or two around the skirt, edged with the same trimming.

■ HAIR
Centre-parted and drawn smoothly back into a bun or snood worn on the nape of the neck.

■ ACCESSORIES
Any ladylike occupation such as needlework or watercolour painting.

BALLGOWN, 1840–60
(Fig 42 – shown in colour on p78)

Dresses for evening wear were very elaborate, with low necklines and short puffed sleeves. This style is only suitable for a doll with long porcelain arms, preferably wired onto the shoulder-plate (the wires will be covered by the top of the sleeves). For shorter arms, the sleeves could be lengthened. Use pastel-coloured silk or satin. The underskirt could be made in a deeper shade, echoed in the sash or trims.

■ FOOTWEAR
Silk or kid slippers or painted shoes to match the dress.

■ UNDERWEAR
Ankle-length pantaloons, one straight gathered and one tiered petticoat in cotton lawn or silk, prettily trimmed.

■ DRESS
An underskirt is needed as a firm foundation and should be cut on the bias in bonded silk. Seam the centre back, leaving the top open for fitting. Cut the bottom edge to ankle length. Pleat or gather a strip of silk, folded lengthwise, to fit around the line marked on the pattern and stitch this to the underskirt so that it just clears the floor. Neaten the top edge of the pleats with lace or braid.

Cut the overskirt on the bias in the thinnest unlined silk and mark the gathering lines. Stitch the back seam and finish the lower edge with narrow lace edging. At each of the marked points, run a neat gathering thread and draw up to 1in (2.5cm). (The gathering may be adjusted for heavier fabrics until it looks right, but all ruched lines should be equal.) Decorate with small bows, ribbon or embroidered roses at the bottom of each ruched line (roses in graduated sizes are particularly effective) and continue the decoration to cover the stitching. Put the overskirt onto the doll and measure where the waist should be so that the lower edge covers the top edge of the pleating on the underskirt. Trim any surplus fabric. Gather the waist, pull up tightly and fasten off.

Cut the bodice, in double-bonded fabric, on the bias. Stitch the darts and fit onto the doll, adding a wisp of padding to provide extra shape. Pull tight to close the back seam and cover it with braid.

Cut the sleeves in unbonded silk on the bias. Stitch the underarm seams and gather the top and bottom edges. Stitch the underarm of the sleeve to the top edge of the bodice, then pull up the top gathers so that the head of the sleeve fits snugly over the doll's shoulders. Pull up the bottom gathers tightly to the arm. If the sleeves slip off the shoulders, hold them in place with the tiniest dabs of glue. Make a few stitches to draw down the centre front of the bodice and cover with a ribbon rose. The neckline

Her First Ball (pp78/79)
Overcome by shyness, the girl in her white-silk Ballgown (1840–60) is invited to dance by the ambassador, watched by his wife in a beaded pink-taffeta evening gown variation of the Walking Dress (1860–70). The ladies wear Evening Toilette in blue silk with long sleeves and Bustle Dresses, in pink silk with short sleeves, and the chaperone is in black silk with a lace yoke. The gentlemen wear Evening Dress Suits and Military Uniforms

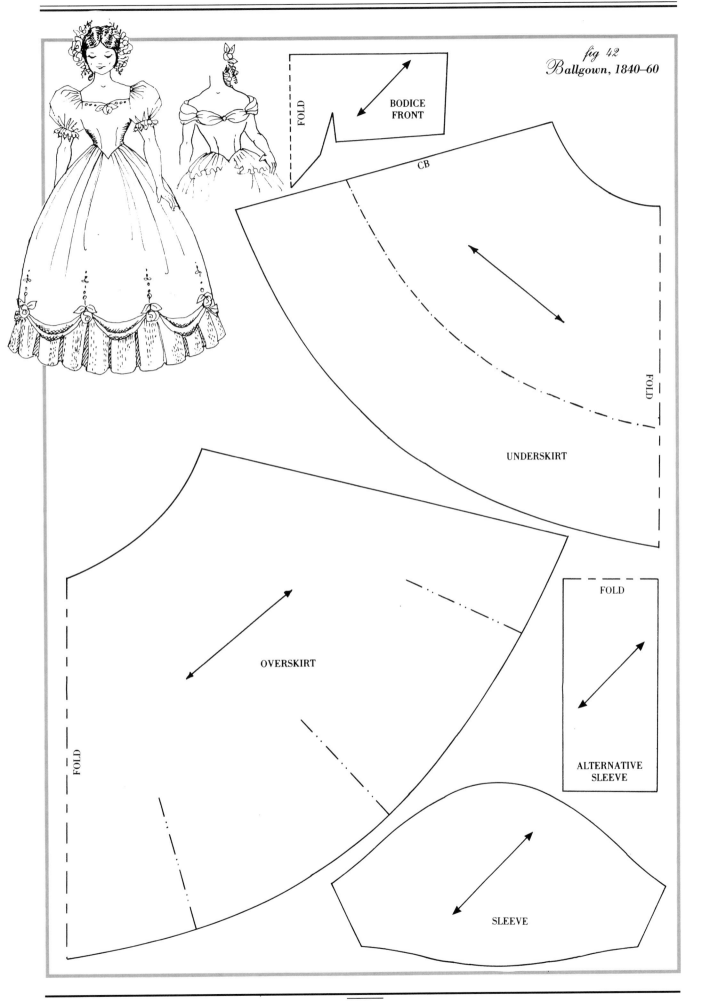

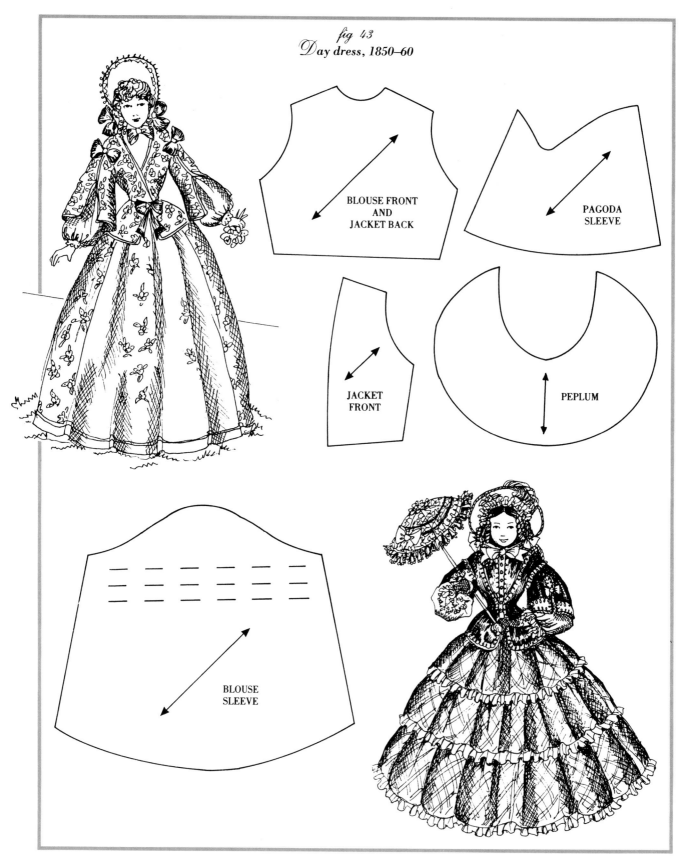

fig 43
Day dress, 1850–60

BLOUSE FRONT
AND
JACKET BACK

PAGODA
SLEEVE

JACKET
FRONT

PEPLUM

BLOUSE
SLEEVE

and sleeves can be trimmed with narrow lace, picot or flat grosgrain braid, or tightly gathered narrow silk ribbon. The V-front of the bodice could be outlined in braid or bunka. Add a large ribbon or self-fabric bow at the back waist.

■ ALTERNATIVE SLEEVES
Before making up, the sleeves can be overlaid with lace to about halfway down, which makes an attractive epaulette effect.

Instead of puffed sleeves, a pretty ruched finish can be

made using a piece of silk cut on the bias 4¼ x 1in (11 x 2.5cm). Seam the short ends together to form a loop. Press this seam, turn in and press both long edges. Slip the loop over the doll's shoulders so that the seam is just behind the left arm. Gather through the loop over the seam, pull up tightly and stitch to the top edge of the bodice. Repeat at the back of the right arm, at the front of both arms, and at the centre front and centre back. Cover the gathering points with ribbon bows or roses.

These classic styles could be used for a ballgown or wedding dress right up to the present day, although for Edwardians a slimmer skirt with a small train would be more fashionable.

■ **HAIR**
Elaborately dressed in ringlets, trimmed with matching ribbon and roses.

■ **ACCESSORIES**
Jewellery, a ribbon choker, matching fan or reticule, or a small bouquet of flowers.

_____ DAY DRESS, 1850–60 _____
(Fig 43 – shown in colour on pp102/103)

This style features three-quarter-length pagoda sleeves which fit tightly at the armhole and flare over full under-sleeves, gathered at the cuffs. It was a fashionable style during the 1850s and 60s for boleros, hip-length jackets and dresses.

This version looks very attractive made in contrasting colours – perhaps white lawn or silk for the blouse, tartan silk for the skirt and black velvet for the jacket with pagoda sleeves. The skirt may be made as a simple full skirt from the pattern in Fig 41, or as a tiered skirt as described.

■ **FOOTWEAR**
Ankle-length boots over plain or striped stockings.

■ **UNDERWEAR**
Drawers and several petticoats trimmed with lace.

■ **TIERED SKIRT**
Cut a foundation skirt using the pattern in Fig 34. Cut the tiers in bias silk (lace-edged or double if the fabric is fine enough). The finished width should be about 2in (5cm) and the length of the three tiers about 12, 15 and 18in (30, 38 and 46cm). This will make a dress with the fashionable outline, although more fabric could be used if a very wide skirt is required. Plan where the frills are to be sewn and mark them on the foundation skirt so that each layer will be even. Gather each tier and stitch to the foundation skirt, starting with the bottom tier first, so that it covers the foundation and will hang just above floor level. Work upwards to the waist, which should be pulled in tightly. Alternatively, make a full skirt from the pattern in Fig 41 and trim with a row of braid just above the hem.

■ **BLOUSE**
Cut the blouse front and sleeves in fine lawn or Jap silk. Pull up the lines of gauging shown on the pattern to fit the top of the arms. Stitch the underarm seams and tack the sleeves to the top of the doll's arms. Gather the lower edges into cuffs. Fit and tack the blouse front onto the doll at the shoulders and waist.

■ **JACKET**
Cut the jacket back and fronts in bonded fabric and trim the front edges with braid. Stitch the shoulder and side seams, press open and fit onto the doll. Slip stitch around the waist. Cut a pair of pagoda sleeves on the bias in bonded fabric and trim the lower edges with braid. Make gathering threads and stitch the sleeves to the armholes so that the open edges meet to the front of the shoulder seams and the undersleeve is exposed. Add a ribbon bow at the top of each sleeve opening. Cut the peplum in double-bonded fabric, trim the lower edge with braid and fit and stitch around the waist so that the fronts just meet. Finish with a bow.

■ **HAIR**
Centre parting with ringlets.

■ **HAT**
Any Victorian bonnet.

■ **ACCESSORIES**
Matching parasol and reticule.

_____ WALKING DRESS, 1860–70 _____
(Fig 44 – shown in colour on pp154/155)

By the 1860s, skirts, although still very large, were flatter at the front and longer and fuller at the back. Braiding, in straight rows or elaborate patterns, was a fashionable trimming. The bolero and jacket in this pattern have simplified pagoda sleeves, cut in one piece with the front, and are typical of the period. The bolero is worn over an underbodice front which, with undersleeves stitched to the bolero sleeves, represents a blouse.

The skirt must be stiff to hold its shape, so use bonded silk or cotton fabrics and lining. The underbodice should be in lightweight fabric and the bolero or jacket in bonded fabric to match or contrast with the skirt.

■ **FOOTWEAR AND UNDERWEAR**
Make as the previous fashion.

■ **SKIRT**
Cut the skirt in bonded fabric and in lining. Stitch the front to the back at the side seams on both pieces, press the seams open and stitch the fabric and lining together around the hem; turn through and press. Add trimming to the skirt. Fit, pleating the fullness at the back and stitch the waist edge to the doll.

■ **UNDERBODICE**
Cut the underbodice and undersleeves in matching fabric and trim the front with lace and bead-buttons. Fit the

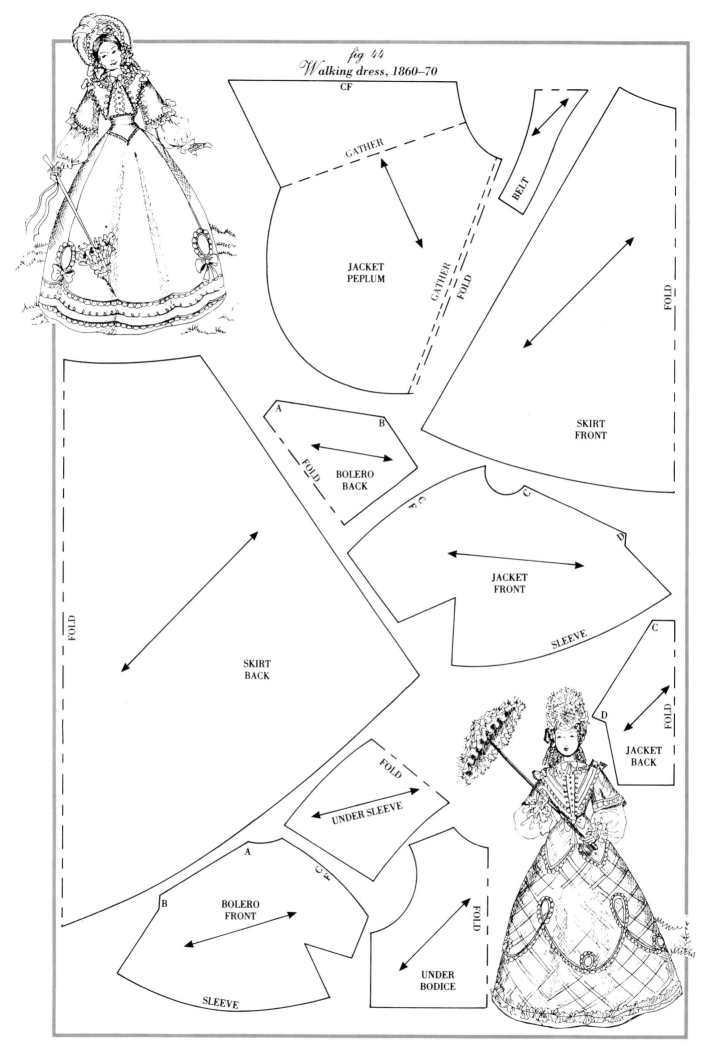

fig 44
Walking dress, 1860–70

CF

GATHER

JACKET
PEPLUM

GATHER

FOLD

BELT

FOLD

SKIRT
FRONT

FOLD

A

B

BOLERO
BACK

FOLD

C
F

C

D

JACKET
FRONT

SLEEVE

C

D

FOLD

JACKET
BACK

SKIRT
BACK

FOLD

UNDER SLEEVE

FOLD

A

B

BOLERO
FRONT

C
F

FOLD

UNDER
BODICE

SLEEVE

underbodice onto the doll, over the skirt, and lace securely in place across the back.

- **BELT**

Cut the belt in double-bonded fabric, trim both edges with braid and fit around the doll's waist with the point downward at the centre front.

- **BOLERO**

Cut two fronts and one back in bonded fabric and stitch the shoulder seams from A to B. Place the bolero sleeve ends over the top edges of the undersleeves and stitch together. Trim with braid to cover the seam. Stitch the underarm seams from the sleeve ends to the waist, clip the curves, turn through and press the seams open. Trim the edges with braid, adding small bows at the top of the sleeves. Fit the bolero onto the doll and tack the fronts together at the neckline. Add a lace collar and bow. Gather the sleeve ends to the wrists and finish with lace cuffs or frills.

ADAPTATION FOR 1870 STYLE

The later version of this style uses the jacket pattern with its peplum, gathered at the back to make a small bustle.

Cut and make up the skirt as before. Omit the underbodice but cut the undersleeves as before. Omit the belt.

- **JACKET**

Cut jacket fronts, back and peplum in bonded fabric. Make up as the bolero (above), including the undersleeves. Trim with braid, fit onto the doll and slip stitch the fronts closed. Trim the lower edge of the peplum and gather as shown on the pattern to make a graceful bustle. Fit the peplum onto the doll and join the edges at the centre-front waistline. Make a fabric or ribbon bow and stitch to the back waist to cover the gathers.

ADAPTATION FOR EVENING GOWN

(shown in colour on pp78/79)

Any of the Victorian bodice patterns may be used with this skirt and peplum to make an evening gown. This dress was made in rose-pink taffeta, embroidered with pearls and crystals. To make a similar effect more simply, apply cut-out lace motifs. Instructions for making the mittens, fan and jewellery can be found in Chapter 11, Accessories.

- **HAIR**

Centre parting and ringlets for the earlier style dress, drawn up into a chignon for the 1870s, and with more elaborate styles for evening wear.

- **HAT**

Victorian bonnet for earlier styles, small bonnet or hat worn tilted forward for the 1870s, lace and flowers for evening wear.

- **ACCESSORIES**

Small parasol; jewellery and fan for evening.

BUSTLE DRESS, 1875–80

(Fig 45 – shown in colour on pp154/155)

When the supportive crinoline cage was abandoned in the early 1870s, the fullness at the back of the skirt was drawn into a bustle. Dresses of this period were usually made from at least two fabrics with gathered, pleated and fringed trimming, although on a small doll this can be overwhelming unless the fullness is controlled.

- **FOOTWEAR**

Small boots or shoes with heels and front trimming.

- **UNDERWEAR**

Drawers and slim-fitting petticoat with lace trim at the hem.

- **DRESS**

The underskirt is pleated in one piece on a 10½in (27cm) pleater board which will give pleats up to 4in (10cm) long. The bottom edge of the fabric must be finished before pleating by using the selvage (if it is good enough), treating with Fray Check or sewing on lace – several overlapping layers of lace look very pretty. Pleat enough fabric to make the whole skirt; approximately 18in (46cm) will be needed to fill the board. Before removing the fabric from the pleater, measure the length required to reach from waist to floor, and draw a pencil line across the pleats at this level. Use the line as a guide to run a gathering thread to pick up each pleat. Stitch the back seam so that it is concealed under a pleat. Fit the skirt onto the doll and pull up tightly at the waist. To make the skirt more elaborate, a second, slightly shorter, layer of pleats can be added over this using another fabric. If a pleater is not available, the skirt can be cut in bonded fabric using the underskirt pattern (see Fig 38). The lower edge can be trimmed with layers of lace or a ruffle of self fabric.

Cut the train in bonded fabric and the facing in unbonded fabric. With right sides together, stitch the facing to the end of the train, clip the curve, turn through and press. With matching thread run neat gathering lines across the train as shown in Fig 45 and pull up a little to give a slight pouched effect. Trim around the train with medium-thick lace – guipure is excellent – one layer facing inwards, and one or two layers overlapping the edge outwards, or use finer lace slightly gathered. Pleat the top edge and stitch the train to the back of the waist.

Make up (optional) tails and trim around the edge with lace. Stitch to the waist to fall either side of the train.

Cut the apron in bonded fabric and trim to match the train with some lace facing inwards and one or two layers around the edge, with the inner edge covered in braid. Fit around the waist and stitch in position.

A plain tight-fitting bodice is needed to contrast with this elaborate skirt. Cut the bodice in bonded fabric, stitch the shoulder and side seams and fit onto the doll,

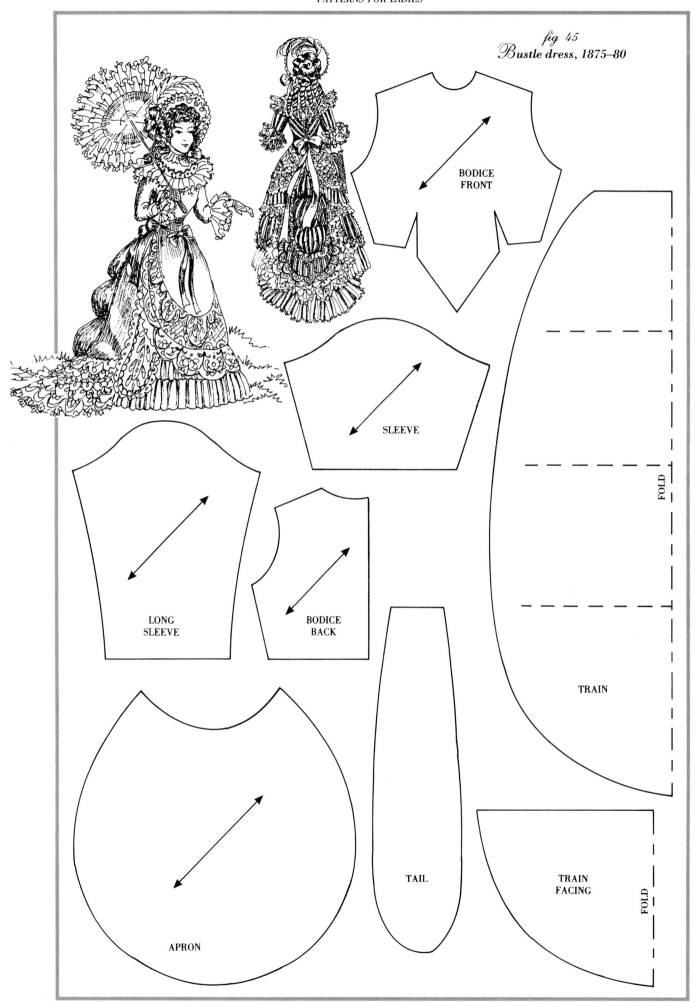

fig 45
Bustle dress, 1875–80

BODICE
FRONT

SLEEVE

LONG
SLEEVE

BODICE
BACK

FOLD

TRAIN

APRON

TAIL

TRAIN
FACING

FOLD

inserting extra padding for the bust. (If it is not a really tight fit, make darts.) Slip stitch the back seam and around the waist and cover with braid. Cut three-quarter-length sleeves and stitch the underarm seams, run gathering threads around the tops, pull up slightly to fit and stitch in place. Make mittens from fine lace stitched around the hands and wrists. Pleat the lower ends of the sleeves to fit tightly, and cover with frills of lace.

Using the same lace as for the train and apron, gather a piece around the neck to make a yoke, covering the join with braid. Add a ribbon sash with a bow at the back, and bows on the sleeves.

■ **HAIR**

A softly curling style, with chignon and long ringlets at the back.

■ **HAT**

Make a half-moon-shaped bonnet in matching fabric and laces, and trim with ribbons and feathers.

■ **ACCESSORIES**

Use the same lace and ribbon to make a matching parasol and tie it to the doll's hand with ribbon.

LATE-VICTORIAN BRIDE

(Fig 46)

Any of the late-Victorian patterns can be used to make a wedding dress, although for an antique look use ivory rather than white silk with muted pale colours for the flowers, and the finest tulle for a veil.

To make the dress shown in colour on pp86/87, adapt this pattern. Make long tight-fitting sleeves and add a peplum (see Fig 50). Stitch several rows of lace to the underskirt before pleating. Add more lace and decoration to the long train and gathered ribbon trimming to simulate a jacket. Make the veil from 8 x 3½in (20 x 8.9cm) of net folded 2½in (6.5cm) from one end, slightly gathered and stitched to the head. Use tiny ribbon rosebuds, with cream and green gathered ribbon to make the head-dress and bouquet; the flowers should be mounted on a piece of lace-trimmed ribbon cut to shape.

_____ EVENING TOILETTE, 1875–85 _____

(Fig 47 – shown in colour on p118)

Although many dresses of the period were made with a separate bodice and skirt, when a really slim shape was desirable, the one-piece 'Princess' style was used. This pattern requires smooth seams and accurate fitting and is recommended for experienced mini-dressmakers. The sleeves are made authentically in two parts. The dress could be made in one fabric, but is particularly effective in striped and toning plain silks. The lace is an important part of the design and should be carefully chosen for size and design – a small scalloped edge looks best. The pleating is made in a half-inch-size pleater.

■ **FOOTWEAR**

Silk stockings and dainty slippers or evening boots.

■ **UNDERWEAR**

Bustle petticoat and a bustle pad to give extra support to the dress.

■ **DRESS**

Cut a piece of plain silk about 4 x 8in (10 x 20cm) and press into the pleater about seventeen pleats. Cut the centre-front panel in iron-on backing and place it onto the pleated silk so that the pleats run on the bias across the bottom half of the panel. Steam press this part firmly, but press the top part only lightly to prevent the silk from becoming marked with unwanted pleater lines. When the pleats are set, remove the fabric from the pleater and cut out around the backing. Press the pleats flat so that they turn up towards the top of the panel. Stitch a row of lace facing upwards inside every third pleat.

Cut the centre-back panel in bonded plain silk. Cut the side fronts, side backs, and sleeves in bonded striped silk (remember to reverse the patterns for the left and right sides). Stitch the curved darts on the side backs; press open as far as possible, then press the seam towards the back. Stitch the side backs to the centre-back panel; press the seams open and snip at the waist. Stitch the back to the front side pieces and press the seams open. Stitch the right front side to the front panel and press open.

Face the hem with a 2in (5cm) bias strip of silk, catching it in position invisibly at the seams. Stitch the left side front to the front panel from the hem to X. Stitch the shoulder seams and press open.

With right sides together, stitch the outer to the inner sleeves at the front seams. Face the lower edges with narrow bias strips of silk and attach lace trim for the cuffs. Stitch the back sleeve seams, press open and turn right side out. (The pressing can be done over a pencil or chopstick – use tweezers or forceps to turn the sleeves.) Insert the thick end of a seam ripper or pencil into the top of a sleeve and set the sleeve into the dress armhole, matching the marked points; stitch all round. Alternatively, turn in the seam allowance on the top of the sleeve and stitch the sleeve to the outside of the armhole.

Trim the top of the centre-front panel with lace, edge

The Wedding ▸

The wedding party assemble on the lawn to receive the first guests. The bride wears a Bustle Dress in ivory silk and lace and her groom wears Military Uniform. The bride's mother and her aunt wear Edwardian Dresses in blue and green silk and the lady guest wears an Edwardian Suit in pink and cream. The gentlemen wear Lounge Suits and Frock-coat. The bridesmaids and the little-girl guest wear Regency Dresses, the brother wears a Skeleton Suit

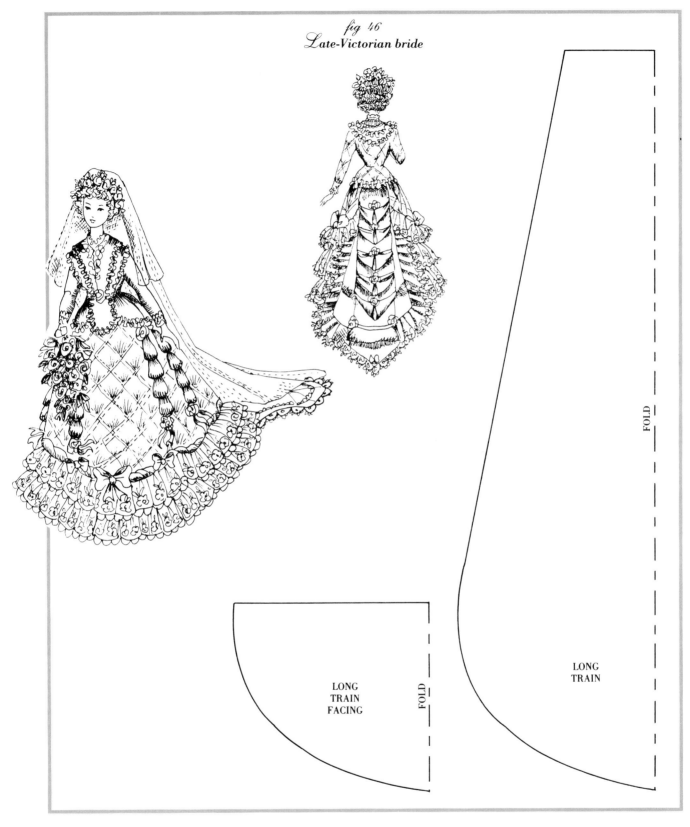

fig 46
Late-Victorian bride

FOLD

LONG
TRAIN

LONG
TRAIN
FACING

FOLD

upwards. Fit the dress onto the doll and slip stitch the opening on the front panel. Stitch lace all around the front panel and neckline from hem to hem with the edge facing outwards.

■ TRAIN

Cut one piece in plain silk, and one in lining, 2¼ x 11½in (5.7 x 29cm). Stitch the pieces together, leaving the top edge open, turn through and press. Trim with lace to overlap the edge of the silk. Fold in and press the top raw edge, make six rows of gathers close together and pull up tightly. Stitch the train to the back panel as shown in Fig 47. Starting from the bottom, gather the train into four puffs so that it falls gracefully. Hover the steam iron over it to 'set' the folds.

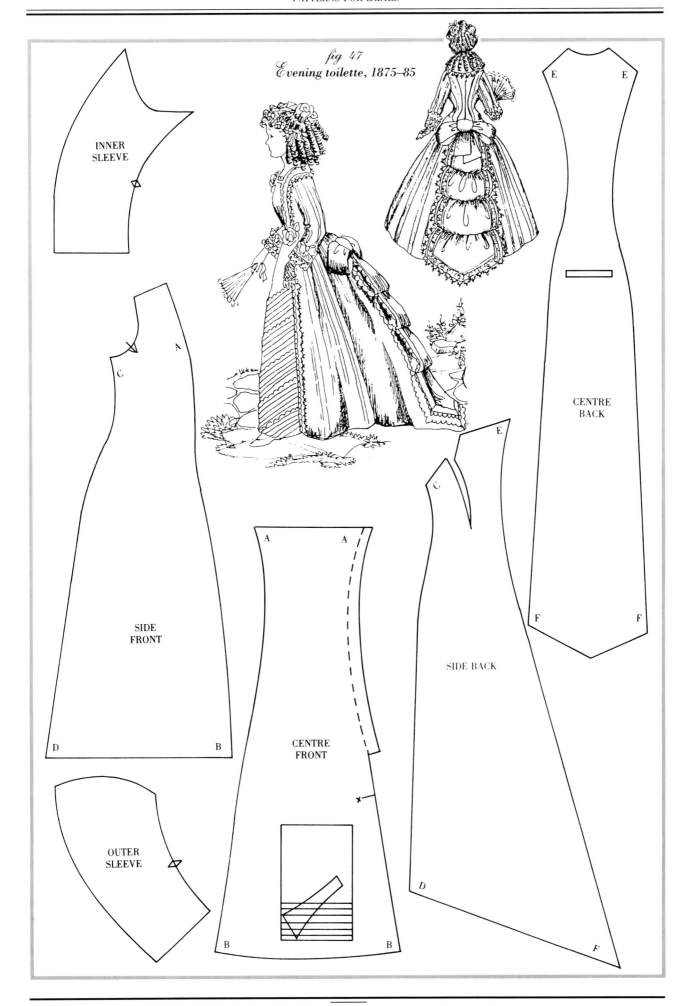

fig 47
Evening toilette, 1875–85

INNER SLEEVE

OUTER SLEEVE

SIDE FRONT

CENTRE FRONT

CENTRE BACK

SIDE BACK

■ HAIR

A soft up-swept style, with long ringlets at the back, possibly falling over one shoulder. As this is evening wear, decorate with a scrap of lace, roses or ribbons.

■ ACCESSORIES

A fan, reticule or small bouquet of flowers.

VISITING TOILETTE, 1875–80

(Figs 48 and 49 – shown in colour on p159)

This is another elegant Princess-style pattern which requires careful sewing and fitting by an experienced mini-dressmaker. It is designed for plain and striped silks. The skirt has a bustle and flounce trimmed with piping and pleats, and a bias frill around the hem. The separate overdress is trimmed with piping and pleats, although the piping is optional and the pleats could be replaced by pleated lace.

■ FOOTWEAR

Pale coloured stockings and dainty boots or shoes with small heels.

■ UNDERWEAR

Lace-trimmed drawers, bustle pad and the petticoat designed for this dress. Make a bustle pad in felt, stuff lightly and stitch to the doll just below the waist. Stitch the petticoat centre-back seam and press. Turn up a narrow hem and whip on the lace trimming. Run rows of gathering thread where indicated, draw up to about 2½in (6.4cm) and fasten off. Whip a frill of gathered lace over the stitches. Gather the top of the petticoat, put onto the doll and draw up tightly over the bustle pad with most of the fullness to the back.

■ DRESS

Use the smallest size pleater (¼in (6mm)) and plain silk folded in half lengthwise to make the pleating for the skirt and overdress – about 11in (28cm) of ¾in (1.9cm) fine pleats will be needed for the skirt flounce and the same for the overdress. To make the piping, cut bias strips ⅜in (9mm) wide. Lay thick crochet thread or similar down the centre, fold over and stitch as close to the thread as possible – approximately 25in (64cm) of piping will be needed.

Cut the skirt in bonded plain silk. Make up the back panel first: cut the flounce in striped silk and in lining. Edge the flounce with piping, sewn right sides together and raw edges even. Tack on the pleats, easing around the curves and exactly following the line of piping. Stitch to the lining, clip curves, turn through and press carefully. Gather along the top edge, pulling up to fit the curved line shown on the skirt pattern and stitch in position. Tack the raw side edges of the flounce down to each side of the skirt panel.

Cut the bustle in striped silk, gather the curved edge from X to X, and pull up to fit the top edge of the flounce.

With right sides together, stitch the gathers to cover the raw edge of the flounce. Gather the top of the bustle to fit the top of the skirt and tack in position. Make small upward tucks in the sides of the bustle where shown so that it will fit the back panel smoothly. Stitch the skirt side panels to the front and back panels, matching the letters, then press the seams open.

Cut the skirt lining in plain silk and make it up to match the skirt. With right sides together, stitch the skirt lining to the skirt around the hem. Clip the curves, turn through and press the hem. Catch the lining to the top of the skirt at the waistline.

Cut a strip of silk on the bias and seam the long edges together to make a tube which is at least 1½ times the skirt hem circumference and a finished width of ⅞in (2.2cm). Press, then run two gathering threads along one side (the first ⅛in (3mm) from the edge); draw up to fit the skirt with only slight fullness at the front. Stitch the frill to the skirt, just above the hem as shown in Fig 49 and cover the gathering with a narrow bias strip of striped fabric or ribbon.

On the inside of the skirt, stitch 1½in (3.8cm) of narrow ribbon or tape, from one back-side seam to the other, 1¼in (3.2cm) up from the hem. This will keep the fullness of the skirt to the back.

Run a gathering thread around the waist, put the skirt onto the doll and draw up tightly with most of the fullness at the back. Hover a steam iron over the bustle to set it in a pleasing arrangement. Make a small inverted pleat on the lower part of the skirt under the flounce and catch firmly with two or three stitches to help the set of the skirt.

For the overdress, cut the bodice side fronts, backs and side backs in bonded striped silk, the cuffs in striped silk, and the front panel and sleeves in bonded plain silk. With the raw edges together, stitch piping to the sides of the front panel. With right sides together, seam the side fronts to the front panel, following the piping accurately. Clip and press seams towards the sides.

Stitch the side backs to the back, easing the curve, clip and press the seams open. Stitch the backs to the side fronts at the side seams, clipping the seams at the waist and press open. Stitch the shoulder seams. Stitch the piping all around the lower edge. With right sides together and the raw edges even, stitch the pleats over the piping, easing the fullness around the curves. Turn to the right side and press gently. Catch the pleats and piping to the seam allowances on the wrong side at each seam.

Pipe the top edge of the cuffs. Turn the raw edges under, press and stitch to the outer sleeves. With right sides together, stitch the outer to the inner sleeves at the front seams, clip and press open. Stitch piping to the wrist edges, turn the raw edges under and press. Whip gathered lace frills just inside the sleeves. Stitch the back sleeve seams, press open and carefully turn

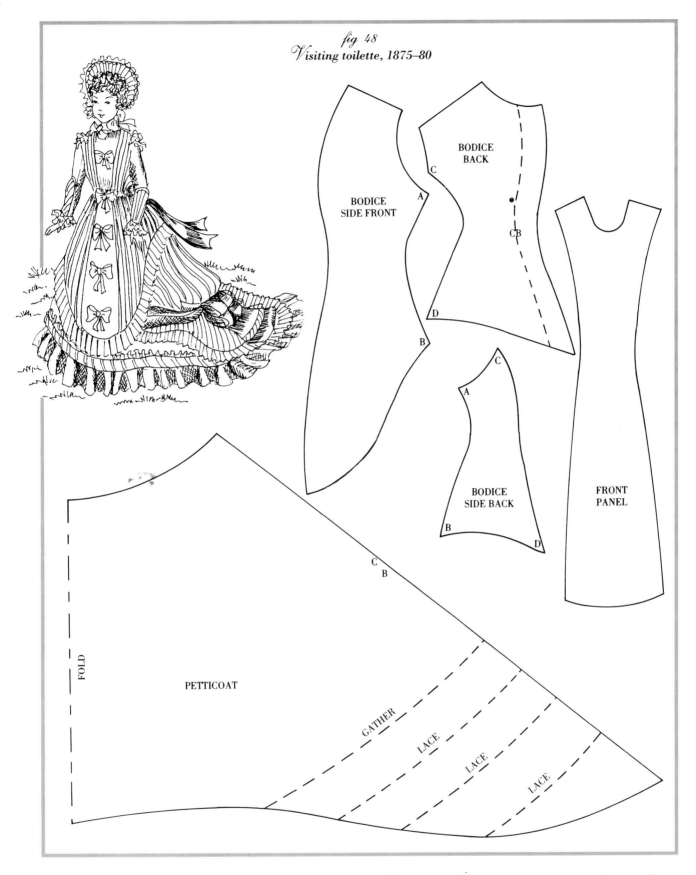

fig 48
Visiting toilette, 1875–80

BODICE SIDE FRONT

BODICE BACK

BODICE SIDE BACK

FRONT PANEL

PETTICOAT

FOLD

GATHER

LACE

LACE

LACE

through. Put a pencil through the sleeve to hold it in place while stitching the sleeves into the armholes, matching the back sleeve seam to the side back bodice seam. Avoid gathers by easing any fullness over the top of the sleeve.

Pipe the neckline, snip and turn in the raw edges, catching to the underside at the shoulder seams. Tack a small lace frill inside the neckline. Press under the back facing. Make small bows of ribbon and stitch them to the dress front.

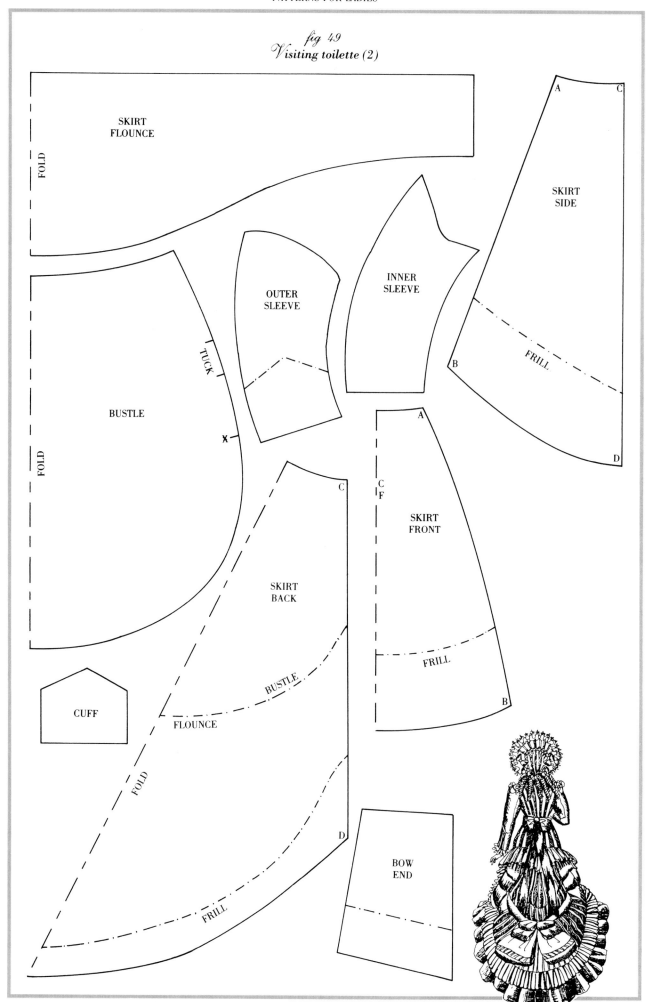

fig 49
Visiting toilette (2)

SKIRT
FLOUNCE

FOLD

SKIRT
SIDE

A   C

OUTER
SLEEVE

INNER
SLEEVE

B

FRILL

TUCK

BUSTLE

FOLD

X

A

C
F

SKIRT
FRONT

C

SKIRT
BACK

BUSTLE

FLOUNCE

FRILL

B

CUFF

FOLD

D

BOW
END

FRILL

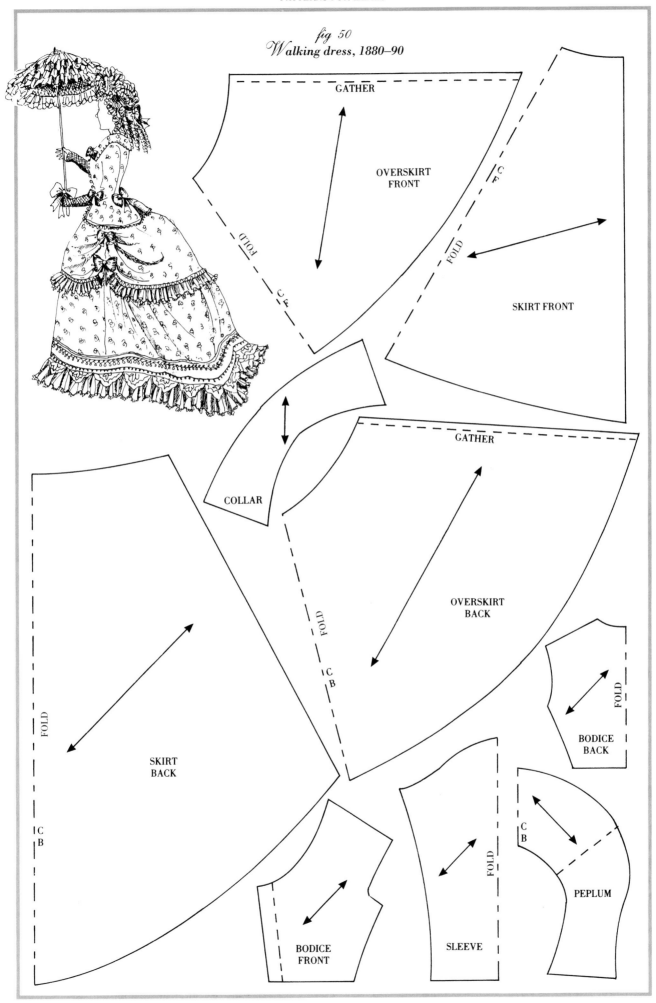

fig 50
Walking dress, 1880–90

GATHER

OVERSKIRT
FRONT

C F

FOLD

FOLD

C F

SKIRT FRONT

COLLAR

GATHER

FOLD

C B

OVERSKIRT
BACK

FOLD

BODICE
BACK

FOLD

C B

FOLD

SKIRT
BACK

C
B

FOLD

C
B

PEPLUM

BODICE
FRONT

SLEEVE

Fit the dress onto the doll and slip stitch the centre back seam closed. Cut a strip of plain silk, about 12in (30cm) long, fold, seam and turn through so that the finished width is about ½in (1.3cm). Cut 7½in (19cm) and fit it around the bustle, between the bustle and the flounce, stitching to either side under the overdress on the skirt side seams. Cut four bow ends in plain silk. On two pieces stitch or glue a band of striped fabric cut on the bias (or use contrast ribbon) about ½in (1.3cm) from the bottom edge. Face each decorated piece with a plain piece. Turn and press. Stitch to the centre back over the flounce. Make two double loops of the remaining ribbon and stitch these over the bow ends. Neaten the raw edges, although they will be covered by the bustle.

■ HAIR

Centre parting or a small fringe, with upswept sides, and loose ringlets at the back.

■ HAT

Either a half-moon bonnet worn at the back of the head, or a small hat tilted forward. Trim with lace and ribbon to match the dress.

■ ACCESSORIES

A small bag, parasol, gloves, etc, or a bunch of flowers.

WALKING DRESS, 1880–90

(Fig 50 – shown in colour on p95)

This costume has a very simple draped front and bustle effect, which can be varied by the choice of fabrics and trims.

■ FOOTWEAR

Neat walking boots.

■ UNDERWEAR

Lace-trimmed drawers and at least two full petticoats.

■ DRESS

Cut front and back skirts, and bodice in bonded fabric; the collar and peplum in double-bonded fabric; the sleeves, front and back skirt lining and back and front overskirt in unbonded fabric.

Seam front to back on skirt and lining, clip, press seams open and stitch together around the hem. Clip, turn and press exactly on the stitching line. Add decoration or a pleated or gathered ruffle. Fit the skirt onto the doll, pleating the back to fit the waist.

Seam the front to the back overskirt, finish the lower edge with ruffled lace and cover the join with braid. Fit onto the doll, pleating at the back to fit the waist. Run gathering threads up both side seams, pull up so that the fabric drapes gracefully, and add one or two bows. Hover a steam iron over the dress to set the folds.

Trim all around the peplum with one or two bands of braid. Make a box pleat at the centre back, but do not press. Fit around the waist, joining at the centre front, adjust the box pleat to fit and stitch to the waist.

Stitch the bodice shoulder and underarm seams and press open. Fold in the right-front edge. Fit onto the doll, slightly lapping the front edges, and slip stitch together, adding bead buttons. Slip stitch the waistline.

Run a gathering thread around the top of the sleeves, ease slightly and stitch to the armholes. Slip stitch the underarm seams to make a tight fit and finish with lace cuffs.

Trim the outer edge of the collar with braid, clip the inner edge, turn under, and stitch a ruffle of gathered lace to just peep out. Fit the collar around the neck to form revers, and finish with a bow at the front.

■ HAIR

Drawn back from the face in soft waves, with ringlets at the back.

■ HAT

A small prettily trimmed hat, tipped well forward, or a high-crowned hat or small bonnet.

■ ACCESSORIES

Parasol, gloves.

EVENING GOWN

The dress bodice (see Figs 42 or 53) can be used with this draped skirt to make an elegant evening gown. Add lace mittens and flowers or jewellery in the hair.

EDWARDIAN BLOUSE AND SKIRT

(Fig 51 – shown in colour on pp182/183)

The era of the tailored skirt and blouse or jacket with 'leg o' mutton' sleeves is usually considered Edwardian, although it is actually late Victorian.

Patterns are given for a well-shaped hip-hugging five-piece skirt typical of the later Edwardian period and a simpler, looser three-piece skirt typical of the 1890s (Fig 52), which can be made in practical dark colours, or in pastels for summer wear in silk or firm cotton fabrics. Sleeves during this period were large and puffy at the top, tight below the elbow. Three shapes are given for these in the Edwardian patterns. The high-necked blouse could be made in fine striped shirting for everyday wear for a business lady or governess, or more elaborately in silk trimmed with lace and ribbon.

FOR ALL EDWARDIAN FASHIONS

■ FOOTWEAR

Boots, high-laced walking shoes, or lighter shoes with rosettes, buckles or several buttoned straps.

■ UNDERWEAR

Knee-length drawers and lace-trimmed petticoats with fullness to the back. A small hip pad to accentuate the figure (this may need adjusting to fit the skirt).

■ BLOUSE

The blouse should be tight-fitting and look as if it is worn

Time Passes

Three elegant ladies stroll in the garden, wondering if it is time for tea. The lady on the left wears a Walking Dress (1880–90), the lady in the centre wears a Bustle Dress and on the right is an Edwardian Dress

be the same as the suit or a contrast. Add trimming to the outside edge to match the peplum. Snip the inside edge and press under. Fit the collar around the neck and tack it in place, joining at the centre-front waistline.

Stitch the sleeve seams, gather the top of the sleeves, pull up and stitch the sleeves to the armholes, stitching twice if necessary. Finish the sleeve ends with cuffs to match the collar. Add a neat buckled belt or ribbon bow.

EDWARDIAN DRESSES

(Fig 53 – shown in colour on p95)

■ HIGH-NECKLINE DRESS

Make bodice and skirt in the same fabric, using fine cotton or silk. The bodice might have a decorative yoke or trimming – guipure lace cut to shape is excellent for this. The sleeves may be cut from the other Edwardian patterns and the three- or five-piece skirts used as alternatives to the trained skirt. Use soft unbonded fabric for the pouched bodice front and upper sleeves, and bonded fabric for the bodice back and skirt.

Make three- or five-piece skirts as described above, or cut the skirt front from Fig 52 and trained-skirt backs in bonded fabric on the bias. Make up the skirt as before and add trimming. Run a gathering thread across the back waistline, fit the skirt onto the doll and pull up the gathering, concentrating the fullness at the centre back, and stitch in place.

Cut the bodice backs and lower sleeves in bonded fabric, the front and upper sleeves in unbonded fabric. Stitch shoulder and side seams, fit onto the doll and close the back opening. Run a gathering thread around the lower front edge and pull up to the waistline to make a

pouched effect and fasten off. Make up sleeves as described for the blouse and add trimming. Make belt as shown in Fig 51 or add a ribbon sash.

■ LOW-NECKLINE DRESS

Make bodice and skirt in the same fabric, using fine cotton or silk. Use delicate lace, applied lavishly for trimming. Cut the skirt front panel (see Fig 52) in lace over bonded fabric and the trained-skirt backs in bonded fabric. Make up the skirt as described above. Add a pleated ruffle in doubled fabric at the hem, and a gathered lace ruffle above, covering the top edge of the fabric ruffle. Add lace trimming to either side of the skirt front panel. Gather the waist edge and fit the skirt onto the doll, drawing all the fullness to the centre back.

Cut the bodice front and backs in bonded fabric. Stitch the darts and shoulder and side seams. Treat the neckline edge with Fray Check and add a narrow lace edging. Fit the bodice onto the doll and close the back opening so that the bodice fits tightly. Cut the (upper) sleeves in unbonded fabric, stitch the underarm seams and gather the tops. Stitch the sleeves to the armholes. Gather the lower edges to fit the arms and add gathered lace frills. Add gathered lace frills over the shoulders. Cut the belt (see Fig 51) in bonded fabric, trim and fit onto the doll, closing at centre back. Add ribbon roses and bows to neckline, sleeves and skirt. Make lace mittens if required (shown in colour on p95).

■ EVENING DRESS

Use delicate silk, chiffon or lace over silk fabrics in pastel colours or black. Make the trained skirt and a bodice from this pattern or the Ballgown, 1840–60, pattern (see p77). Add plenty of decoration, ribbon flowers, lace or beading. (Shown in colour on pp78/79.)

7

Patterns for babies and girls

BABY GOWNS

(Fig 54 – shown in colour on p151)

BABIES ARE A DELIGHT TO DRESS, especially if you use delicate lace – preferably antique – with white or ivory lawn or silk to tone.

■ UNDERWEAR
Make a nappy (diaper) from wide cotton tape or a scrap of lawn, and stitch in position around the waist.

■ DRESS
Decide the length of the skirt – a long flowing gown could be up to 3½in (8.9cm) long and 5½ (14cm) wide, and will look better cut on the bias as shown on the pattern. Make a lace-trimmed cotton petticoat slightly shorter than the finished dress length, gather and fasten firmly under the arms with long stitches as shoulder straps to keep it in place.

Stitch the lace decoration to the skirt – this might be a flared front panel, rows of frills, or a combination of both – finishing with a slightly gathered frill around the hem. Complete the decoration before stitching the back seam. Gather the top edge and fasten off firmly under the baby's arms, with extra stitches over the shoulders.

The bodice can be made in fabric, but this is fiddly, especially if the baby has bent arms. Cut the piece, seal the neckline with Fray Check and snip the back opening just far enough to put over the doll's head. Stitch the underarm seams and fit onto the doll. Close the back opening. Gather the sleeve ends and pull up to fit the arms, tucking in the raw edges. Turn in the lower edge and slip stitch over the skirt gathers.

A simpler and very pretty bodice can be made from 5 or 6in (13 or 15cm) of ⅝in (1.6cm) lace – wider lace can be cut down to size. Seam the lace ends into a loop, gather the top edge around the doll's neck and pull up tightly. Arrange the gathers evenly and pin to the front and back of the skirt.

Starting at the centre back, gather and stitch the lace over the raw edge of the skirt, working to the underarm. Gather the edge of the lace around the arm, pulling tightly, and stitch to the underarm. Gather and stitch across the front to the second underarm, gather around the second sleeve and gather and stitch to the starting point. You will then have a bodice with puffed sleeves, which can be trimmed with tiny ribbon bows. More bows, ribbon roses and streamers can be added to trim the skirt.

SHORT BABY DRESS
The method described above can be used to make a shorter, fuller petticoat and skirt. Matching knickers can be made from the toddler pattern (see Fig 55).

■ HAIR
A tiny wisp to show at the bonnet front, or painted hair.

MATCHING BONNET
Make the bonnet in delicate lace to match the gown. For the bonnet cap, gather the plain edge of 1¾in (4.5cm) of lace ½in (12mm) wide. Pull up tightly and fasten off. Tuck in the raw edges and fit to sit well back on the head. Hold in place with a thread sewn under the chin. Gather about 3½in (9cm) of the same lace and arrange as a frill, stitch to the front of the cap and oversew the raw ends. Gather down the centre of a 6in (15cm) piece of narrow silk ribbon, pull up tightly, and arrange this to frame the baby's face inside the bonnet frill. Add two or three loops of ribbon to either side of the cap and tie in a bow under the chin or to one side.

■ ACCESSORIES
A rattle made from a pretty bead on a short length of toothpick, or a tiny pipe cleaner teddy tucked into one arm (for dolls later than 1903).

Early-Victorian Style (1830–60) ▸
Admiring the new baby, the proud papa wears a Frock-coat with trousers and mama wears a Crinoline Dress. The baby's godmother wears a Day Dress (1850–60) with tiered skirt and her aunt wears a Day Dress (1830–40) with a lace pelerine. Big sister wears a white broderie-anglaise Victorian Summer Dress, big brother wears an Early-Victorian Suit and their cousin is dressed in a tartan Victorian Winter Dress

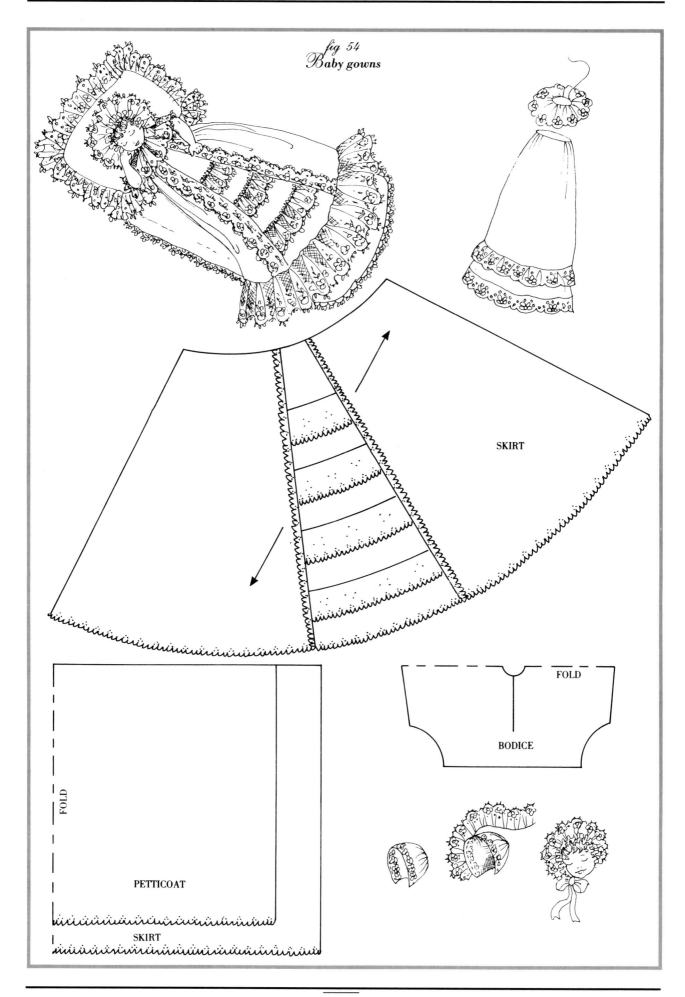

fig 54
Baby gowns

SKIRT

FOLD

BODICE

FOLD

PETTICOAT

SKIRT

■ PILLOW

A pillow is a good way to display a baby in a long gown. To make the pillow, cut a piece of thin foam or wadding about 6 x 2½in (15 x 6.4cm). Cut off 1¼in (3cm) for the head pillow and lay it over one end. Make a silk case just large enough to enclose the foam. Tack through at the base of the head pillow to hold it in position. Trim all around the edge of the pillow with slightly gathered lace edging.

TODDLER DRESS AND ROMPERS

(Fig 55 – shown in colour on pp166/167 and 182/183)

These little dolls are well displayed with bare feet and short modern clothes. The pattern is for a very simple dress which is open at the back to show frilly knickers, and one-piece rompers for a baby boy. Use fine silk or cotton fabric trimmed with lace and narrow silk ribbon.

■ KNICKERS

Cut the knickers and check that they fit neatly. Slightly gather narrow lace and stitch to the lines marked on the back. Snip the curve around the legs, turn under and whip on slightly gathered lace. Stitch the side seams, catching in the lace frills. Run a gathering thread around the waist. Fit onto the doll, tucking in the raw edges and fasten off securely. (If necessary, make long stitches over the shoulders to hold the knickers in place.)

■ DRESS

Cut the dress twice in fabric so that it will be fully lined and, with wrong sides facing, stitch together from X to X. Trim, clip curves and turn. Press carefully on the line of stitching. Thread 2mm silk ribbon through the lace for the edging trim and stitch the lace all around the hem so that it overlaps the edge – the ribbon should be pulled up slightly around the curve. Alternatively, ribbon can be threaded through very narrow, straight-edged insertion lace, sewn flat, with slightly gathered lace whipped to the edge.

Treat the armholes with Fray Check and snip through both layers of fabric just far enough to accommodate the doll's arms. Sew the shoulders together with a few stitches. Snip the curve of the neckline and fit the dress onto the doll with the opening at the back, tucking in the raw edges around the neckline. Slip stitch the back edges together from the neck to the top of the knickers. Add

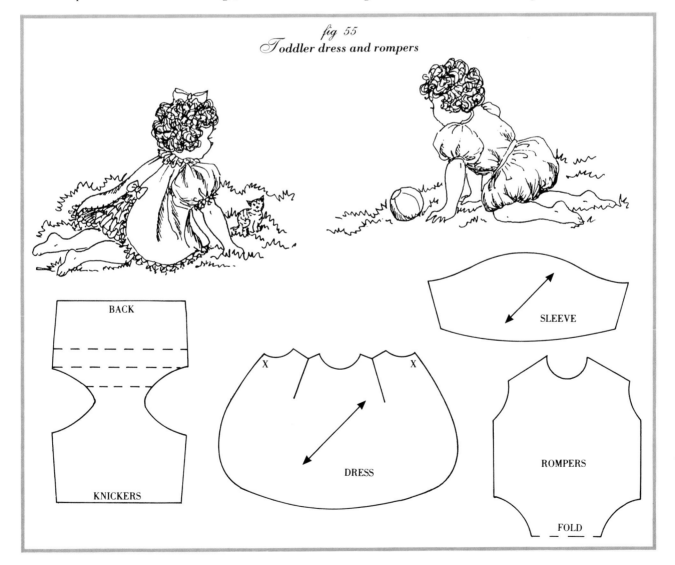

fig 55
Toddler dress and rompers

BACK

KNICKERS

X   X

DRESS

SLEEVE

ROMPERS

FOLD

fig 56
Simple dresses and pinafores

FOLD

SKIRT

FOLD

BODICE

FOLD

PINAFORE

FOLD

SKIRT

FOLD

PINAFORE

COLLAR

tiny bead buttons.

Cut the sleeves on the bias. Run a gathering thread around the top and bottom edges. Stitch the underarm seams and fit onto the doll. Pull up the top gathers and stitch the sleeves to the natural armholes. Pull up the lower gathers tightly to the arm, tucking in the raw edges, and fasten off securely. Trim with small bows on the dress and legs of the knickers.

■ ROMPERS

Cut the pattern with the crotch to the fold of the fabric, check the length and treat the neckline and armholes with Fray Check. Turn in the edges around the legs (adding lace if required) with gathering threads. Stitch the side seams and fit the rompers onto the doll. Pull up the gathering threads around the legs to fit tightly and fasten

off. Slip stitch the shoulder seams. Snip the neckline, turn under and finish with a tiny lace collar. Make a gathering thread around the waist, pull up and cover with a ribbon sash. Make puffed sleeves as for the dress above.

■ HAIR

Soft curly hair, finished with a bow to match the dress.

■ ACCESSORIES

Any soft toy, teddy, etc, or building blocks made from small square beads.

SIMPLE DRESSES AND PINAFORES

(Fig 56 – shown in colour on p159)

The simplest dress has a bodice and sleeves cut in one

fig 57
Simple dresses (2)

BODICE FRONT

BODICE BACK

SLEEVE

YOKE

UPPER SLEEVE

PUFFED SLEEVE

LOWER SLEEVE

piece with a straight or flared gathered skirt. Different fabrics, trimmings, sleeve and skirt lengths will make endless variations.

Cut the bodice, skirt and skirt lining. Seam short edges on both skirt and lining and press open. With right sides together, seam the lower edges of the skirt and lining, trim, turn and press. Adjust the length at the waist. Run two gathering threads around the top edge, fit onto the doll, distributing the gathers evenly, and pull up, fastening off securely (The seam may be at the centre back or to one side.)

Cut the bodice open from neck to waist on one side – the opening can be at either the front or the back. Stitch the underarm seams, clip and press open. Snip around the neckline so that it will fit closely – very little snipping is required as a child's neck is small. Fit the bodice onto the doll. Turn under and lap one edge of the opening over the other and slip stitch closed. Turn in the bottom edge and slip stitch over the skirt gathering.

Pleat or gather the ends of the sleeves and trim with strips of folded fabric, braid, lace or broderie anglaise. With the point of a needle, tuck in the raw edge around the neckline and finish with a little collar of lace or braid. Cover the bodice closure with braid and bead-buttons. Add a sash and trimmings to suit the period.

- **FITTED BODICE**

(Fig 57)

For more style and a better fit, cut the bodice front and backs in bonded fabric on the bias. Stitch the shoulder and side seams and snip around the neckline. Fit the bodice onto the doll, over the skirt, and slip stitch the back opening closed. Use a needle to tuck in the raw edges around the neckline.

Cut plain sleeves, gather the tops and stitch the seams. Pull up the gathers and stitch the sleeves to the armholes. Cover the sleeve ends with lace or braid cuffs. For an Edwardian look for an older girl, use the gigot sleeve pattern. Cut upper sleeves in unbonded fabric and lower sleeves in bonded fabric. Gather the bottom edge of the upper sleeve and stitch to the lower sleeve, press the seam upwards. Stitch seams, gather sleeve tops and stitch to the armholes as before and add cuffs.

VARIATIONS

The yoke can be cut in lace or contrasting fabric and applied to the bodice front before making up. Alternatively, make a pinafore bib from bonded fabric and use with the pinafore skirt (Fig 56) and a waistband. Stitch ribbon straps to the shoulder edges to cross at the back. The Alice in Wonderland costume shown in Fig 58 is made from this bodice pattern. Use the puffed sleeve pattern and add ruffles to the yoke to make shoulder-straps. The Quaker costume (Fig 58) is also made from this pattern. Cut the collar (Fig 56) in bonded white cotton fabric, snip the neckline edge to fit and turn in. Fit the collar onto the doll over the bodice and close at the centre-front top edge. Variations of the pattern can be used for eighteenth-century girls' clothing, which should be made in plain drab fabrics for poor or country children and rich silks with lace for wealthy girls. A simple, short version in cotton or silk can be used for little girls up to the present day (shown on p115).

fig 58
Alice in Wonderland and Quaker girl

EDWARDIAN PINAFORE

This was one of the most popular and practical styles for girls of all ages through a long period from Victorian to 1914. To wear over a dress of dark, plain or printed cotton, make the pinafore in fine white cotton trimmed with lace or wide broderie anglaise edging with a small design. Use the shaped pattern for the best results with cotton fabrics. Use the straight pattern for broderie anglaise and neaten both short edges (Fig 56).

Cut one piece in cotton, trim one long and both short edges with narrow lace edging. (A fancy machine-embroidered edge could also be used.) Run a gathering thread through the top edge and pull up to fit neatly, right under the arms, meeting at the centre back, and stitch in position. To make the yoke, gather 8in (20cm) of lace, about ¼in (6mm) from the edge. Starting at the centre back, stitch the lace to the bodice to form a round or square frill, allowing plenty of fullness over the shoulders. Finish off at the centre back. Gather and draw up the top edge of the lace and stitch it to the dress to form a yoke. Unless the lace is wide enough to reach the neckline, gather a second piece, about 4in (10cm) long, and pull it up to fit around the neck, arranging it evenly over the first layer. Trim the neckline and the overlap of lace with narrow braid to tone with the dress fabric. (Shown in colour on pp182/183.)

YOKED DRESS
(Fig 59 – shown in colour on p115)

These comfortable loose-fitting dresses have been worn by girls for the last hundred years. Use pastel-coloured or white silk, muslin or broderie-anglaise edging for sum-

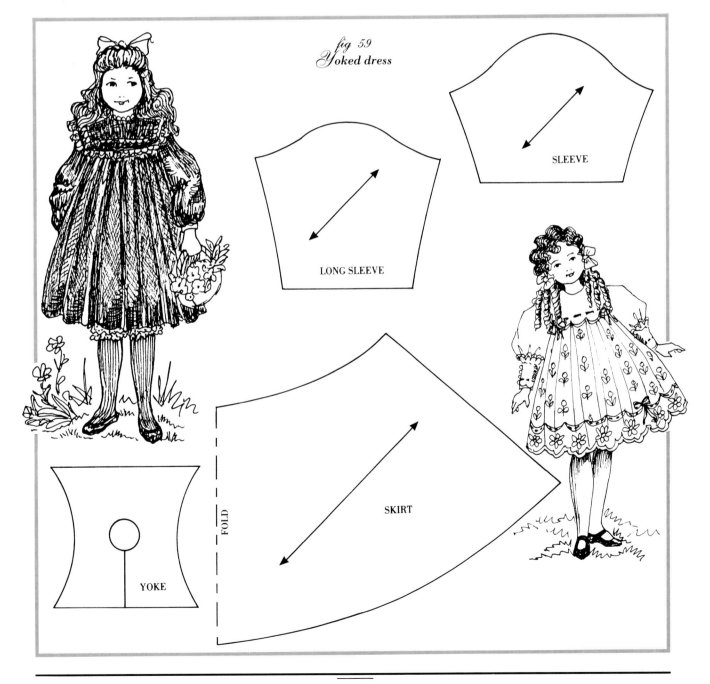

fig 59
Yoked dress

LONG SLEEVE

SLEEVE

FOLD

SKIRT

YOKE

mer dresses and darker colours and slightly heavier fabrics for winter clothes. Dresses should be worn over drawers and one or two lace-trimmed petticoats appropriate for the period.

■ DRESS

Cut the skirt in bias fabric and in lightweight fabric for lining. (Broderie anglaise should be cut as a straight length and unlined.) Stitch the back seams on skirt and lining and, with right sides facing, stitch skirt to lining around the hem. Clip the curve, turn and press. (Trim Edwardian winter styles with two bands of braiding at the hem.) Run a gathering thread around the top edge and fit onto the doll as high as possible under the arms. Pull up the thread and arrange the gathers between the back and front with little fullness under the arms. For extra security make tacking stitches over the shoulders.

Cut and fit the sleeves next. Cut long or short sleeves in unbonded fabric and stitch the underarm seams. Run gathering threads around the top of the sleeves and pull up to fit the armholes, with the gathers to the top. Stitch in position on the skirt and use long tacking stitches to join the sleeves across the body, back and front.

Cut the yoke in double-bonded fabric to match or contrast with the dress, or in lace bonded over dress fabric. Cut the back of the yoke open and try on, snipping around the neckline to obtain a neat fit. In order to make a crisp outline to the yoke there are no turnings, so trim to the exact size required. When the yoke looks right, lay it over the raw edges of the skirt and sleeves and stitch neatly in position. Slip stitch the back opening closed and cover with narrow braid and bead buttons.

Trim the edge of the yoke with narrow gathered lace or flat braid (or both). Gather or pleat the sleeve ends and trim with cuffs to match the yoke and add a small lace collar.

LOW-WAISTED DRESS
(Fig 60 – shown in colour on p127)

These styles have been worn since the mid-nineteenth century, made in fabrics and trimmings reflecting the fashion of the period, from white muslin to dark woollens. The skirt looks best pleated, but can also be made from a strip of fabric folded lengthwise and gathered. Interesting effects can be made by using two complementary fabrics, such as a dark wool for the bodice with matching satin or a print for the skirt, sash and cuffs. Large lace or broderie anglaise collars were usually worn with this style of dress.

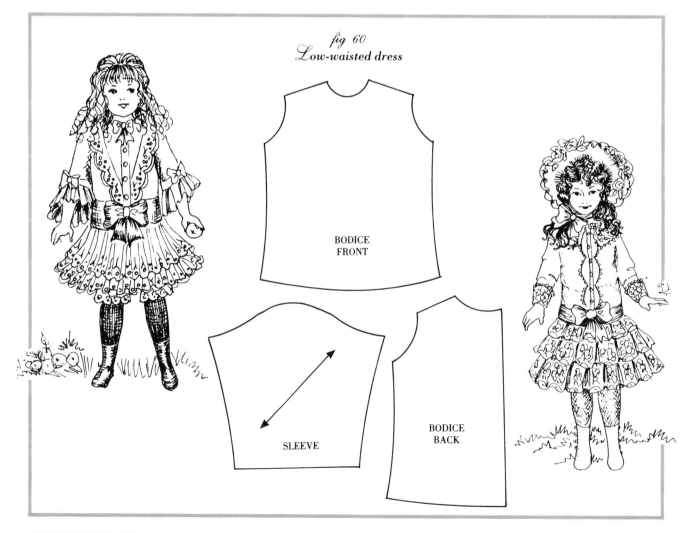

fig 60
Low-waisted dress

BODICE FRONT

SLEEVE

BODICE BACK

The Quarrel

Teased beyond endurance by her brother, the little girl bursts into tears and her older sister tries to make peace. Big sister wears a Regency Dress, the little girl a Georgian Gown and her brother a variation of the Early-Victorian Suit with a lace collar

■ DRESS

Cut the bodice in bonded fabric and stitch the side seams. Make the pleated skirt from a strip 2½ x 9in (6.4 x 23cm) folded lengthwise, so that no hem is required. Tack the raw edges together and pleat. Remove from the pleater and press flat. (As this pattern is suitable for a girl of three to fifteen years old, adjust the length for the individual doll. For older girls, two overlapping layers of pleating, using thin silk, would be fashionable.)

Make a neat seam at the centre back, concealed in a pleat. Check the length and stitch the skirt to the bodice, at a slightly dropped waistline. (The skirt should be short for young girls and longer for older girls.)

Stitch the bodice shoulder seams and fit the dress onto the doll. Slip stitch the back opening closed and add bead buttons.

Cut the sleeves, make gathering threads around the tops and stitch the underarm seams. Pull up the gathers and stitch to the natural armholes. Make a softly pleated, bias cut, fabric sash, pressing under the raw edges, or use ribbon. Stitch the sash to the side seams of the dress and join at the centre back. Make a large bow to cover the join. (For a white dress the sash would be pretty in pastel silk.)

Pleat the fullness at the end of the sleeves into lace cuffs. Add a wide lace collar, gathered slightly at the neck so that it will lie flat. Join at the front with a small bow or make a tiny brooch from beads and jewellery 'findings'.

SMOCKED DRESS

(Fig 61 – shown in colour on p115)

As smocking takes considerable width, the fabric should be fine silk or cotton. The smallest scale tartans and checks look delightful and avoid the need for marking rows of dots to keep the gathering even. If you have never tried smocking, experiment first on a piece of similar fabric until you get the stitching even and the tension right. Use embroidery silk, in a colour which will show up well on the fabric – white, yellow or red on tartan, deeper self-shades on checks, or white on dark grounds. The pattern is given in two sizes.

■ DRESS

Cut out the dress and mark the smocking dots in pencil or tailor's chalk on the wrong side. This can be done by measuring, or by marking a grid, but ensure that the dots are exactly in line vertically and that they will not show through the fabric. Using a separate thread for each row, pick up each dot as a small running stitch. Leave the thread ends loose. Make four rows for the small pattern and at least five rows for the large one. Pull up all the threads together, stroking the pleats smoothly into line with the point of a needle. (They should be pulled up

fairly tight, but slack enough so that you can stitch into each pleat.) Tie the thread ends together in pairs.

Use one or two strands of embroidery silk and secure to the back of the left-hand side of the work. With the right side of the work toward you, bring the needle up to the left of the first pleat. Take a small stitch through the edge of the pleat from right to left, with the thread below the needle, and pull up. Pick up the next pleat in the same way, but with the thread above the needle, and pull up. Repeat across the first row and fasten off. Start the second row, again at the left, securing the thread. Stitch as before, but starting with the thread above the needle, then below, to form a mock honeycomb pattern. Repeat for the required number of rows. This will make the simplest of smocking patterns, which is quite sufficient in $1/12$ scale. Remove the gathering threads and check that the dress will fit around the doll. If it is loose, a gathering thread run through the back of the bottom row will keep it in shape.

Apply Fray Check and cut out the front and back neckline, noting that the seam is to the side (where it will show least). Run a line of Fray Check where the armhole is marked. Snip open just enough to allow for the arm and stitch the side seam to armhole level. Turn up the hem. Gather the shoulders and seam together so that they fit the doll.

Cut long or short sleeves and run gathering threads around the top edges. Stitch the underarm seams, pull up the top gathers and slip stitch to the natural armhole. For short puffed sleeves, gather the lower edge tightly to the arm, tucking in the raw edges. Pleat long sleeves neatly into lace cuffs. Add a narrow lace edging at the neckline, with a ribbon bow at the join. Beads can be sewn to the back for buttons. Add a ribbon sash if required.

GEORGIAN GOWN

(Fig 62 – shown in colour on pp42/43)

This dress has a low neckline, so the doll should have a deep shoulder-plate. If not, the neckline can be filled with a fine muslin or lace fichu. Use stiff silk or cotton fabrics in plain pastel colours or striped or sprigged patterns. The underskirt can be made in a contrasting fabric or decorated as for the Georgian lady (see Fig 38). Use lightweight silk or cotton for lining.

■ FOOTWEAR

Silk or cotton stockings and buckled shoes.

■ UNDERWEAR

Simple drawers and one or two full petticoats.

■ DRESS

Unless the fabric is very stiff, cut the underskirt in bonded fabric and in lining. Decorate the front panel, stitch the back seam and stitch the skirt to the lining around the hem. Clip, turn through and press. Gather the

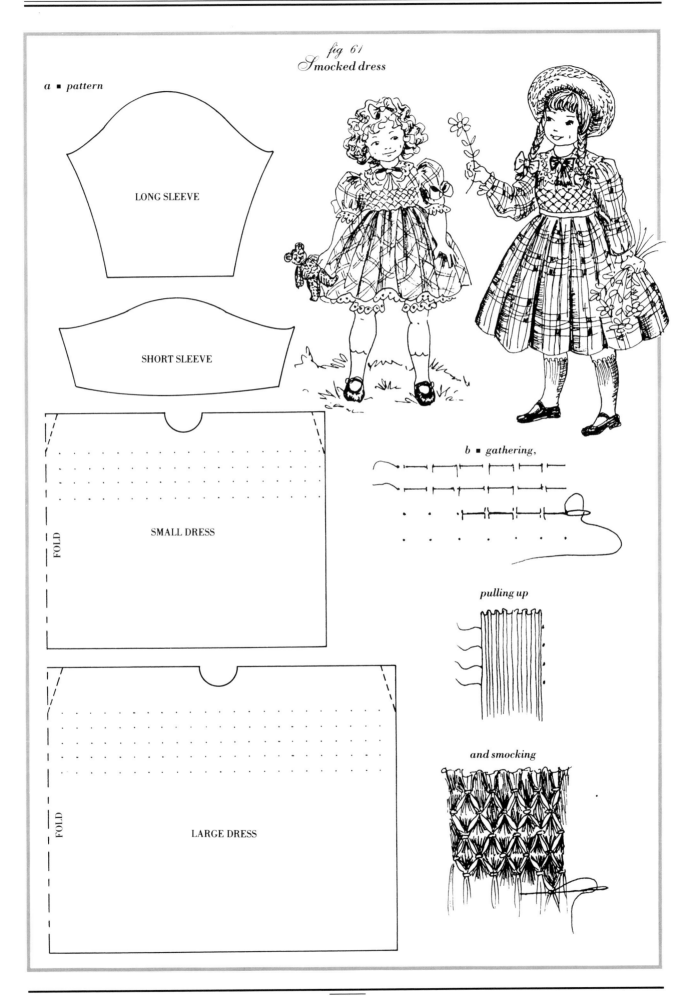

fig 61
Smocked dress

a ▪ *pattern*

LONG SLEEVE

SHORT SLEEVE

FOLD

SMALL DRESS

FOLD

LARGE DRESS

b ▪ *gathering,*

pulling up

and smocking

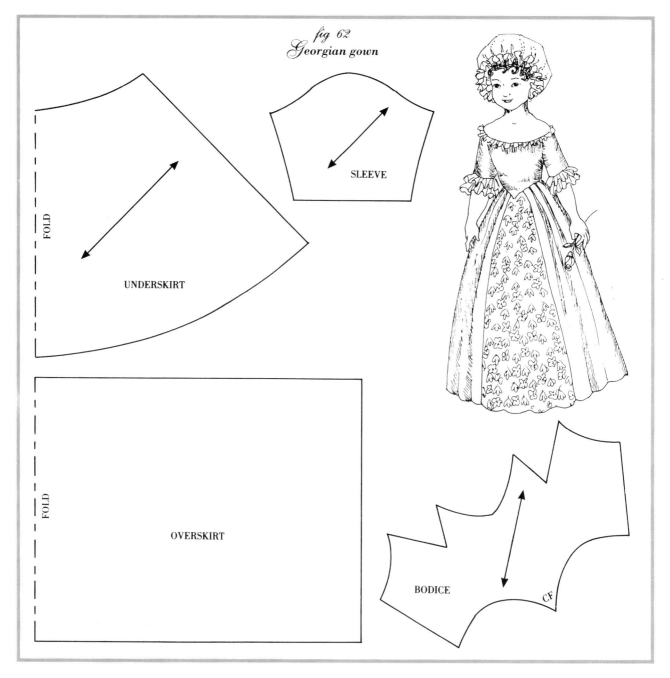

fig 62
Georgian gown

SLEEVE

FOLD

UNDERSKIRT

FOLD

OVERSKIRT

BODICE

CF

waist edge and fit onto the doll, drawing any fullness away from the centre front so that the skirt is ankle length. Cut the overskirt in bonded fabric and in lining, and seam together down the front edges and around the hem. Turn through, press and decorate the front edges if required. Fit the skirt onto the doll, taking in the fullness at the waist with even, flat pleats, working away from the centre fronts, which should just meet.

Cut the bodice in double-bonded fabric, check that the neckline will cover the lower edge of the shoulder-plate with the points meeting on the shoulders, and stitch the points together. Trim the neckline with fine braid and a ruffle of narrow gathered lace to cover the stitching. Fit the bodice onto the doll over the skirts, trim the lower edge with braid to define the pointed waistline and close the bodice back, adding 'lacing' if required.

Cut the sleeves to fit tightly to the elbow. Run gathering threads to ease around the top edges and stitch the underarm seams. Slip stitch the sleeves to the bodice, without gathers, at the armholes. Finish the sleeve ends with lace ruffles and add ribbon bows or roses as trimming.

■ SKIRT VARIATION

The overskirt can be drawn up at the sides in 'Bo-Peep' style if it is made in a fabric which is not too stiff. Seam the overskirt to the lining as before, snip the curves, turn and press. Fit onto the doll, arranging the pleats around the waist. Run gathering threads at each side and pull up until the skirt loops gracefully. Trim over the gathers with ribbon roses or bows.

■ HAIR

Soft curls with a fringe or drawn up into a small bun.

The Birthday Party

The hostess and the little girl offering her gift both wear Simple Dresses. The hostess's best friend wears a Bustle Dress. One girl playing oranges-and-lemons wears a tartan Smocked Dress, the other wears a Yoked Dress and her little sister wears a Simple Dress with sash. The girls helping themselves to cakes wear a Yoked Dress in dark print and the Alice-in-Wonderland variation of the Simple Dress

■ HAT

A mob-cap or wide-brimmed straw-hat trimmed with ribbon and roses.

■ ACCESSORIES

A wooden toy or doll, or a basket of flowers.

REGENCY DRESS

(Fig 63 – shown in colour on pp54/55)

The simple high-waisted muslin gowns of the Regency period are not easy to make in miniature as it is difficult to find fabric that is soft enough to drape properly. The short-sleeved version of this pattern is only suitable for a doll with long porcelain arms, as the sleeves are very short. Plain or sprigged silk or lawn in white or a pastel shade would be suitable. The dress could be either ankle length or, from 1803, short enough to display pantaloons. The pattern can be used for a Kate Greenaway costume, and would also make a charming bridesmaid's

dress up to the present day.

■ FOOTWEAR

Silk or lace stockings with flat slippers to match the dress.

■ UNDERWEAR

Long drawers, decorated with several rows of frilled lace if they are to show below the dress, and a slim petticoat.

■ DRESS

Cut on the bias in bonded fabric and in lining. This is a one-piece dress so when the armhole slits are cut and the top edge is folded under, it should fit smoothly around the doll's shoulder-plate under the arms. Stitch the back seams on fabric and lining, taking care not to stretch the fabric. Make any adjustment for length before stitching the fabric and lining together around the hem. Clip the curve, trim, turn and press. Decorate the hem. Snip the armholes to allow for the doll's arms and seal with Fray Check. Snip the curved top edge and turn under to form a low square neckline. Fit onto the doll and hold in place with tacking threads over the shoulders.

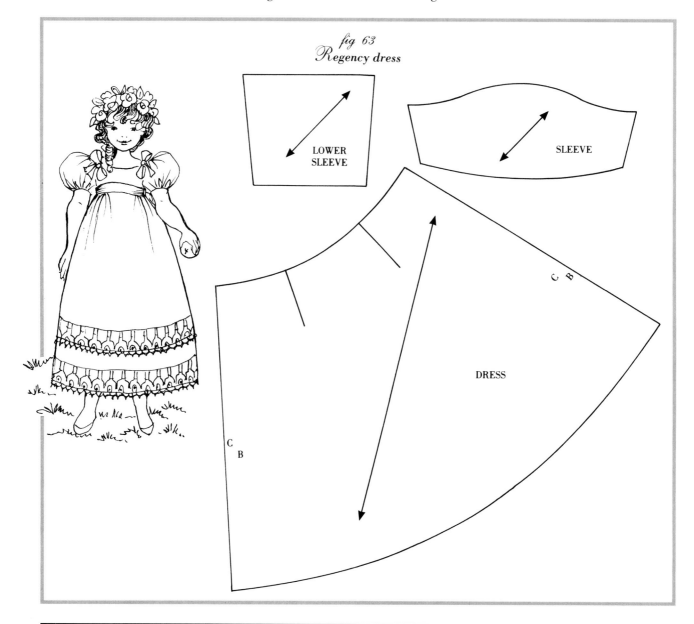

fig 63
Regency dress

LOWER SLEEVE

SLEEVE

DRESS

Cut the sleeves in fabric and run gathering threads along the top and bottom edges. Stitch the underarm seams. Pull up the top gathering threads, fit the sleeves onto the doll, arranging the fullness to the top, and stitch the underarm to the bodice armhole, pulling up the thread so that the sleeve sits neatly on the shoulder. Fasten off securely. Pull up the lower thread tightly to the arm, tucking in the raw edge. Using 7mm ribbon, stitch bows over the shoulders to form the sides of the square neckline. Tie a sash of matching ribbon above the natural waistline with a bow and streamers at the back.

- **LONG SLEEVES**

Make the dress as described above. Cut the lower sleeves in fabric and slip stitch the seams on the doll. Make up the sleeves and fit as before, over the lower sleeves. Trim the sleeve ends with lace cuffs.

- **HAIR**

Short curls look best.

- **HAT**

A small ribbon-trimmed muslin mob-cap, a poke-bonnet or a chaplet of pastel-coloured silk-ribbon roses.

- **ACCESSORIES**

A toy or a tiny basket of flowers to match the chaplet.

VICTORIAN SUMMER DRESS

(Fig 64 – shown in colour on pp102/103)

White broderie anglaise dresses were fashionable girls' wear from about 1830 to the Edwardian period. Use broderie anglaise edging with a small design on good quality cotton. For a 3½in (9cm) doll it should be at least 1½in (4cm) wide and for a 4in (10cm) doll it should be 1¾in (4.5cm) wide. Alternatively, use strips of muslin or similar lightweight fabric with narrow lace trimming stitched to one edge. Trim with pastel-coloured silk ribbon.

- **FOOTWEAR**

Lace socks and cream or pastel-coloured slippers to match the dress trim, or dainty boots.

- **UNDERWEAR**

Pantaloons, mid-calf or ankle-length, and one or two full petticoats.

- **DRESS**

Cut overskirt and underskirt and stitch the seams on both pieces. Place one over the other, the raw edges together, and run a double gathering thread through both. (For a

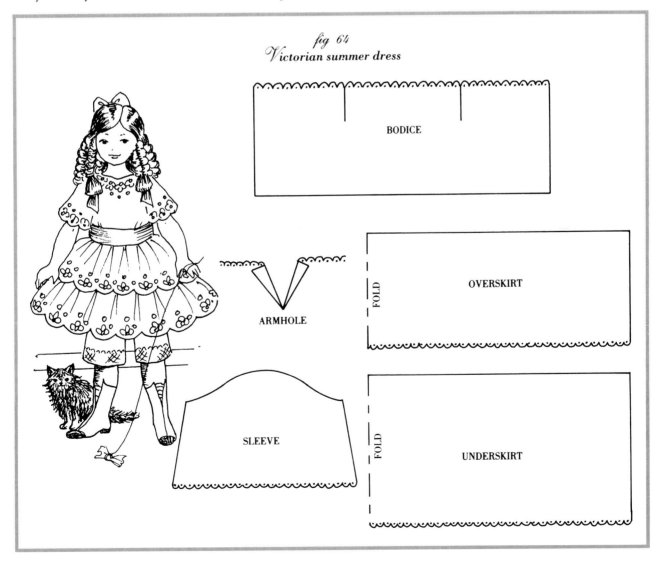

fig 64
Victorian summer dress

BODICE

ARMHOLE

OVERSKIRT

FOLD

SLEEVE

FOLD

UNDERSKIRT

In The Conservatory

The boy from next door comes to call with his papa so mama offers a
glass of wine. Mother's Evening Toilette and daughter's Princess-style
Dress are made in matching fabrics. The boy wears a Skeleton Suit
and his father wears the blazer and flannels variation of the
Lounge Suit

small doll it may be possible to fold a double-edged design.) Fit the skirt onto the doll and pull up the threads, distributing the gathers evenly, with the seams to one side or at the centre back.

Cut the bodice, treat with Fray Check and cut slits to take the doll's arms so that the top edge of the fabric is straight across at the neck. Fit the bodice tightly around the body, trimming any surplus fabric to leave just enough to turn under at the waist. Slip stitch the back edges closed and around the waist over the skirt gathers. Secure the top edges of the bodice with tacking threads over the shoulders.

Cut the sleeves and run gathering threads around the tops. (For a soft-bodied doll, ensure that the sleeves are long enough to cover the cloth arms.) Stitch the underarm seams. Pull up the gathers and, tucking in the raw edges,

stitch the sleeves to the bodice. Cover the top of the sleeves with large silk-ribbon bows over the shoulders and add a matching sash with a bow and streamers at the back.

- **HAIR**
Centre parting and ringlets.

- **HAT**
A simple flat-crowned, wide-brimmed straw-hat trimmed with a ribbon and streamers.

- **ACCESSORIES**
A doll, toy or posy of flowers.

VICTORIAN WINTER DRESS
(Fig 65 – shown in colour on pp102/103)

This costume looks particularly attractive made in the

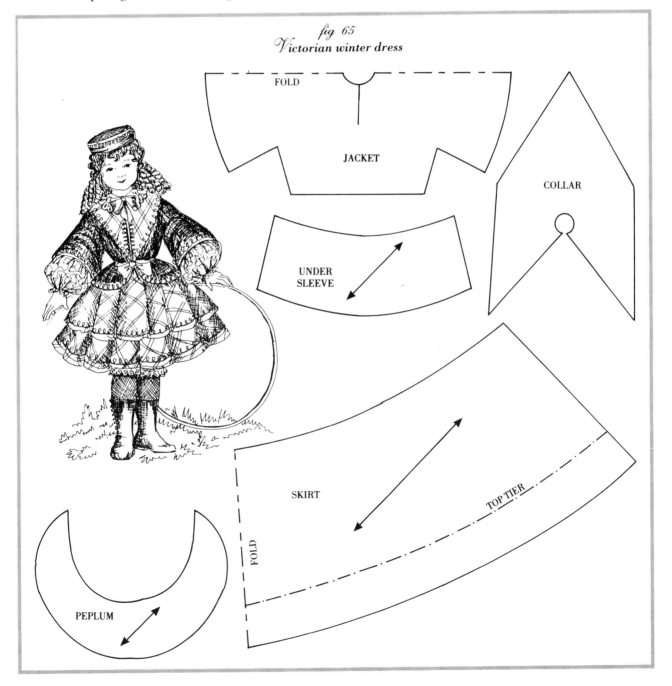

fig 65
Victorian winter dress

tartans and dark colours which were popular with the Victorians. Use silk or lawn for the skirt, which can also be made in two tiers, and fine velvet plush or taffeta for the jacket. The undersleeves may be made in lace, fine silk or muslin. Trim the skirt with dark-coloured braid to match the jacket.

■ FOOTWEAR

Black or white jersey stockings and short leather boots.

■ UNDERWEAR

Mid-calf or ankle-length drawers, with several lace-trimmed petticoats.

■ DRESS

Cut the skirt (or skirts) and lining in bias fabric. Stitch the back seams and, with right sides facing, seam together around the lower edge, turn and press. Trim with rows of braid at the hem. Run two rows of gathering around the top edge (with both tiers together) and fit onto the doll. Pull up the gathers, distribute evenly and fasten off.

Cut the jacket in bonded fabric and cut an opening at the back far enough to slip over the doll's head. Lap the sleeve ends over the undersleeves, stitch together and cover the join with braid. Stitch the underarm seams, clip the curve and press. Fit the jacket onto the doll, slip stitch the opening closed, and slip stitch the waist edge over the skirt gathers. Gather the sleeve ends to fit the wrist and finish with neat cuffs.

Cut the collar in double-bonded skirt fabric, trim the edge with braid and stitch in position – the points should just meet at the waist. Stitch the fronts together and trim with braid and bead-buttons. Add a neat lace collar and small ribbon bow.

Cut the peplum in double-bonded jacket fabric. Trim the edge with braid and slip stitch around the waist, adding a ribbon bow at the front.

■ HAIR

Centre parting and ringlets.

■ HAT

A small pillbox hat trimmed with a perky little feather worn well forward.

■ ACCESSORIES

A small muff hung from the neck on a ribbon or crochet-thread cord.

DRESS AND JACKET, 1870–85

(Fig 66 – shown in colour on p159)

This is a very simple, easy-fitting outfit. The lace-trimmed jacket fits over a pleated skirt and sleeveless bodice. Fine silk or cotton fabrics would be suitable; the dress could be made in two toning fabrics, or wide ribbon could be used for the skirt. Trim with narrow insertion lace or flat braid.

■ FOOTWEAR

Stockings and boots or neat slippers.

■ UNDERWEAR

Mid-calf-length drawers and two lace-trimmed petticoats, with gathers to the back.

■ DRESS

Cut the bodice in bonded fabric. Cut the skirt in fabric, approximately 2½ x 9in (6.4 x 23cm), fold lengthwise and tack the raw edges together. Alternatively, use 1¼in (3cm) wide ribbon. Pleat the skirt to make a finished length of 3½in (9cm).

Stitch the skirt to the bodice waistline and press the seam upwards. Stitch the back skirt seam so that it is concealed in the pleats. Stitch the shoulder seams. Snip around the neckline, turn under and catch down. Fit the dress onto the doll and stitch the back seam, which will be covered by the jacket.

Cut the jacket in bonded fabric and in lining. Stitch the centre-back seams on both and press open. With right sides facing, stitch the fabric to the lining, down the fronts and around the hem to the side seams, across the back lower edge and the sleeve ends. Turn through and press carefully so that the lining will not show. Stitch frilled lace and trimming to the sleeve ends. With right sides together, stitch the side and sleeve seams. Press, snipping the underarm where necessary, and turn through. Trim the jacket with flat trimming and pleated or gathered lace at the hem. Neaten the neckline with narrow self-bias, or a tiny lace collar. Stitch bead-buttons to the front. Fit onto the doll and slip stitch the front closed. Make a bow of 7mm silk ribbon and stitch it to the back of the jacket.

■ HAIR

Centre parting and ringlets.

■ HAT

A prettily trimmed bonnet or a flat straw-boater.

■ ACCESSORIES

A doll, toy or posy of flowers.

'RENOIR'-STYLE VARIATION

A copy of the costume worn by the little girl with a hoop in Renoir's painting *Les Parapluies* can be made using this dress and the alternative ('Renoir') jacket pattern. The doll should wear black stockings with black strap shoes and a lace-edged petticoat which just shows below the skirt hem. Make the dress in pale greyish-blue silk and the jacket in dark brown or black velvet. Make up the dress as described above. Cut the jacket in fabric and lining and cut the centre front open. Make the box pleat at the centre back as shown on the pattern. Make up the jacket as described above. Use two rows of five cream bead-buttons to fasten the front as a double-breasted closure and add a large collar and cuffs in heavy cream lace. The hair should be fair, wavy and shoulder-length and the bonnet made of straw or gathered lace trimmed with two or three rows of

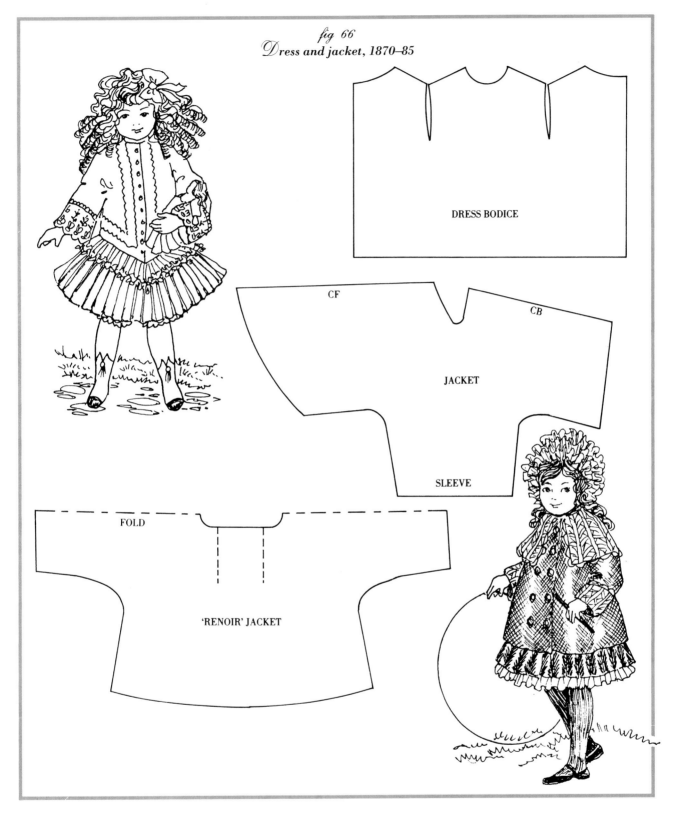

fig 66
Dress and jacket, 1870–85

DRESS BODICE

CF · CB

JACKET

SLEEVE

FOLD

'RENOIR' JACKET

gathered silk ribbon and a pale blue feather. Glue a hoop and stick to the doll's hand. (Shown in colour on pp154/155).

BUSTLE DRESS, 1875–85

(Fig 67 – shown in colour on pp154/155)

This fashionable style was used extensively by famous French dollmakers of the period, particularly Jumeau. It is doubtful if any but the wealthiest children actually wore the exaggerated styles shown in fashion plates, although simpler versions can be seen in contemporary photographs. However, the style looks delightful on dolls and there are endless variations of detail. Essentially it is a low-waisted dress with a pleated or gathered skirt, and a jacket with a small bustle. The dress bodice could be made in contrasting fabric, lace or very fine silk gathered into lines of ruching. Lace edging and braid around the jacket makes a nice finish. Any rich-looking silk, satin or brocade would be suitable, with delicate lace and trimming. Approximately 1in (2.5cm) wide lace is used to overlay the skirt. This can be cut from a wider piece or narrow lace could be overlapped to make up the width. Good fitting is essential.

■ FOOTWEAR

Fine lacy socks or stockings and dainty boots or strap shoes in colours to tone with the outfit.

■ UNDERWEAR

Knee-length lace-trimmed drawers, with one or two lace-trimmed petticoats.

■ DRESS

Cut the dress bodice in bonded fabric and check that it will fit tightly. Lay lace over the front and tack in place. Cut a strip of silk approximately 2½ x 9in (6.4 x 23cm) for the skirt, fold in half lengthwise and lay the lace over it to just clear the fold. Tack the raw edges of fabric and lace together, and pleat. Alternatively cut the skirt in fabric and lining, stitch the back seams, stitch together around the hem, turn through, press, and gather the top edge.

With right sides facing, stitch the skirt to the lower edge of the bodice, clip and press the seam upwards.

fig 67
Bustle dress, 1875–85

DRESS BODICE

JACKET FRONT

JACKET SLEEVE

JACKET BACK

FOLD

DRESS SKIRT

Stitch the (pleated) back skirt seam, so that it is concealed in the pleats. Stitch the shoulder seams to include lace on the bodice front. Apply Fray Check around the armholes, snip the neckline, turn in the raw edges and neaten with narrow braid or lace. Fit onto the doll and stitch the back seam, which will be covered by the jacket.

Cut the jacket fronts, backs and sleeves in bonded fabric. Stitch the centre back, side and shoulder seams, clip curves and press open. Check the fit and if necessary make a gathering stitch or small pleat at the centre-back waist. Trim the edge with braid. Fit the jacket onto the doll and tack it to the bodice at the front edges.

Run gathering threads around the top of the sleeves, pull up slightly to fit and stitch to the armholes. Slip stitch the underarm seams so that the sleeves fit tightly. Finish with narrow lace cuffs.

Gather a few inches of wide lace tightly and stitch it to the centre back waist, tucking in the raw edges. Cover with a bow of 7mm ribbon with streamers. Stitch a bow to the centre front at the top of the skirt.

- HAIR

Ringlets with a ribbon bow to match the dress.

- HAT

An elaborately trimmed Breton bonnet.

PRINCESS-STYLE DRESS, 1875–80

(Fig 68 – shown in colour on p118)

This dress is designed to complement the lady's outfit shown in Fig 47 and if the same fabrics are used they will make a delightful 'mother and daughter' pair. Use either striped and toning plain silks or all one fabric. The pattern is designed for a 4in (10cm) doll, but, if lengthened, would be suitable for a teenager. It is a shaped Princess-

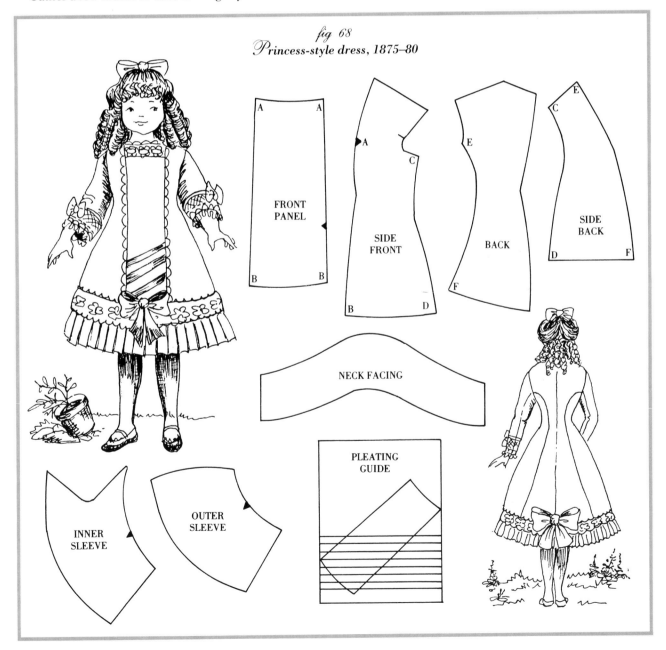

fig 68
Princess-style dress, 1875–80

FRONT PANEL

SIDE FRONT

BACK

SIDE BACK

NECK FACING

PLEATING GUIDE

INNER SLEEVE

OUTER SLEEVE

style with two-part sleeves and the fit is very important, so the pattern is not recommended for beginners.

- FOOTWEAR

Dainty boots or strap shoes.

- UNDERWEAR

Lace-trimmed drawers and one or two petticoats with fullness at the back.

- DRESS

Cut the side fronts, side backs and backs in bonded striped silk; cut the outer and inner sleeves, and the neck facing in striped silk (remember to reverse the pattern for the right and left sides). Cut a strip of plain silk 1½ x 16in (3.8 x 40cm) for the skirt pleats, fold in half lengthwise, tack the long edges together and pleat to make a 6-7in (15-18cm) finished length. Secure with a very narrow strip of iron-on backing. Press the pleats flat.

To make the centre-front panel, cut a piece of plain silk 2½ x 3½in (6.3 x 9cm) and press in the pleater for seven pleats. Cut a front panel in iron-on backing and lay this on the pleats, on the bias as shown on the pattern and press. Remove from the pleater, press to fix the pleats to the backing and cut the front panel.

Stitch the centre-back seam, stitch the side backs to the back and the side fronts to the side backs. Stitch the front panel to the side fronts, leaving one side open, as shown on the pattern. Clip the curves and press the seams open. Tack lace to the hem, easing it to fit. Tack, then stitch the pleated piece around the hem, easing it on, and seam neatly either at the centre back or to one side. Cut a bias facing strip of 1in (2.5cm) wide thin silk, stitch it over the previous line of stitching and turn the seam upwards. Press carefully so that the pleats hang well. Catch the facing to each seam.

Stitch the shoulder seams. Stitch the front sleeve seams, clip and press. Face the lower edges of the sleeves with strips of bias silk, turn to the wrong side and press. Attach lace trim for cuffs. Stitch the back sleeve seams, clip, press open and turn through. Run a gathering thread around the top of each sleeve. The sleeves should be smooth fitting, so pull up the gathering threads a little to ease the sleeves onto slightly dropped armholes and stitch in place so that the sleeve seams correspond to the front and back dress seams.

With right sides together, stitch the neck facing to the back of the neck. Clip, turn and press. Catch the facing to the shoulder seams and trim if necessary.

Fit the dress onto the doll. Slip stitch the front panel opening closed. Trim the top edge of the panel with lace, then stitch lace all around the front panel.

Cut a strip of striped silk 5 x 1½in (13 x 3.8cm). Fold in half lengthwise, seam, turn through and press. Cut 3in (7.6cm) to make a bow and cut the rest in half for bow tails. Stitch the bow and tails to the centre back just above the pleating. Make a bow of 7mm silk ribbon and stitch it to the bottom of the front panel.

- HAIR

For a little girl, a fringe and ringlets would be suitable. For an older girl, pull the front hair upwards with ringlets at the back. Add ribbon bows to match the dress.

SAILOR DRESSES, 1880–1920
(Fig 69 – shown in colour on p150)

Use fine, closely woven cotton in any combination of white, blue and navy, plain or striped – all white or all navy – for example, white top with navy skirt, navy top with white skirt, or stripes with plain, and a contrasting collar. Trim with narrow braid – red is very attractive. Patterns are given for a blouse and skirt, a small dress and matching knickers.

- FOOTWEAR

Black stockings and boots or shoes.

- UNDERWEAR

Fairly plain, but a full petticoat will hold out the pleated skirt.

- MATCHING KNICKERS

Cut the knickers (in the appropriate size) in white cotton or fabric to match the dress. Stitch the centre front and back seams, clip the curves and press open. Stitch the inside leg seam, clip the curve and press open. Run gathering threads around the legs and the waist edge. Put the knickers onto the doll and pull up gathering to fit, tucking in the raw edges, and fasten off securely. Make long tacking stitches over the shoulders to hold the knickers in place if necessary.

- SKIRT

Cut a piece of fabric 2½ x 11in (6.5 x 28cm), fold in half lengthwise and tack the raw edges together. Pleat, press the pleats flat, and stitch the back seam so that it will be concealed in a pleat. Fit onto the doll and tack firmly in position. (On an all-bisque doll, make long tacking stitches over the shoulders.)

- BLOUSE

Cut in one piece and cut open down the centre back just enough to slip over the doll's head. Make very small snips around the neckline. Check the sleeve length. Stitch the underarm seams, clip the curves and press open. Run a gathering thread around the bottom edge. Fit onto the doll, tuck in the raw edges at the neckline with the point of a needle and close the back opening. Pull up the bottom gathering thread, tucking in the raw edges. Arrange the gathers evenly to make a bloused effect and fasten off. Trim the neckline with braid if required.

Cut the collar in bonded fabric and in lining. (White or a contrast colour looks best.) With right sides facing, seam the fabric to the lining, leaving most of the straight bottom edge open. Press back the seam allowance on the straight edge to give a guideline for closing. Trim, clip

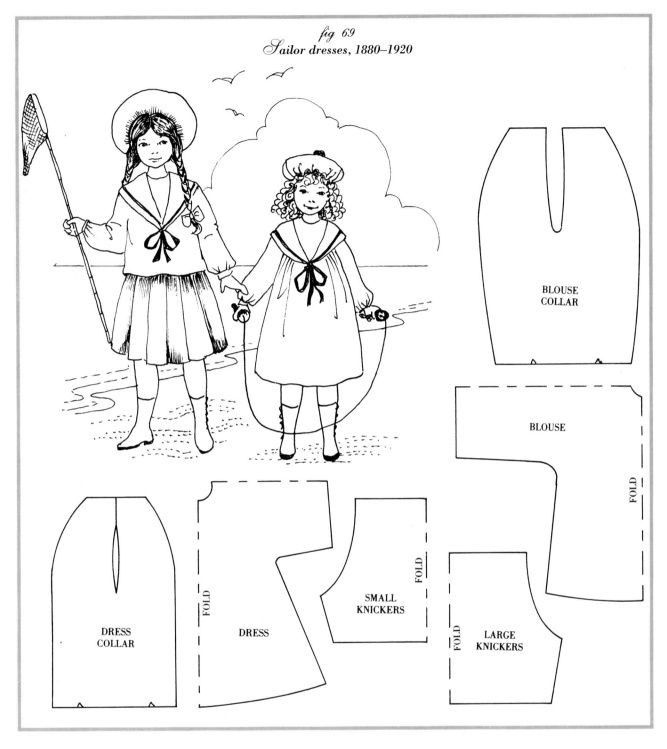

fig 69
Sailor dresses, 1880–1920

BLOUSE
COLLAR

BLOUSE

FOLD

DRESS
COLLAR

FOLD

DRESS

FOLD

SMALL
KNICKERS

FOLD

LARGE
KNICKERS

the corners and curves, and carefully turn through. Push out the corners and seams fully so that they can be pressed on the exact seam-line. Slip stitch the straight edge closed. (If this proves too fiddly, the collar can be cut in double-bonded fabric. Trim the seam allowance, clip the neck edge and turn under.)

Trim the collar with braid, close to the outside edge, and fit onto the doll, with pointed ends meeting. Tack in place and add a bow of braid. Pleat or gather the sleeve ends to fit the wrist and cover with braid cuffs.

■ DRESS

Use the simple A-line dress pattern for a small doll

($3\frac{1}{2}$in (9cm)). Make up in the same way as the blouse, but apply Fray Check to the bottom edge and turn a small hem. Make the collar as described above.

■ HAIRSTYLE

Short curls, loose waves or plaits.

■ HAT

A slightly upturned straw-hat with matching ribbon or a beret with pom-pom.

■ ACCESSORIES

Bucket and spade, shrimping-net or skipping-rope.

__ ELABORATE EDWARDIAN DRESS __

(Fig 70 – shown in colour on p35)

Edwardian girls usually wore simple styles for everyday clothing, although dresses for grand occasions could be very elaborate. This style would be particularly attractive made in fine lawn or silk and lace in white or pastel colours – perhaps to complement an elegant Mama, dressed in the same fabric.

- ■ FOOTWEAR

Lace socks or stockings in white or cream, and dainty slippers trimmed with rosettes.

- ■ UNDERWEAR

Knee-length lace-trimmed drawers and two petticoats.

- ■ DRESS

To make the skirt, cut a strip of fabric 3 x 9in (7.6 x 23cm) and fold in half lengthwise. Lay wide lace edging threaded with ribbon over it to just clear the fold or use narrow lace sewn in rows. Tack the raw edges and lace

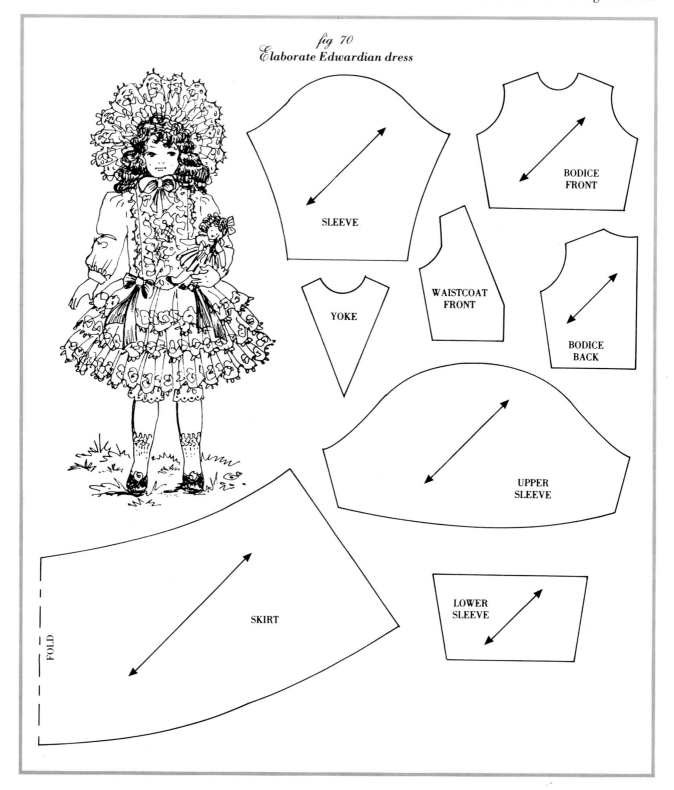

fig 70
Elaborate Edwardian dress

A Posy From The Gardener
The gardener is busy weeding but he stops to pick a posy for the little miss. Mama wears an Edwardian Suit, the little girl wears a Low-waisted Dress and the gardener wears Working Clothes

$\mathscr{P}$atterns for men

Men's clothes are undoubtedly the most difficult to make in miniature, and it is not possible to obtain crisp tailoring without great care, accuracy in fitting and constant pressing. The width of shoulder and size of the neck on each doll will vary, so collars must be fitted individually. The basic essential is a man-shaped body and padding is very important – without shoulders any coat will hang badly (see Chapter 1).

Pad the body to look right for the man you wish to portray. Use shoulder pads and probably extra chest padding, but avoid too much bulk at the waist unless he is to be portly. Pad the bottom, otherwise the trousers will droop; for breeches it may be necessary to add extra padding to the legs before fitting the stockings. Tack all padding in place so that it will not slip when the clothes are fitted. The shirt is laced tightly over the padding to make a smooth foundation for the suit.

Press every seam on both sides using a cloth. Clip curves and points right to the stitching line, and trim any surplus fabric. If the collar does not fit, make another one – this is usually quicker than trying to make alterations. Adjust the collar length from the centre to fit the individual neck, working it around to make a good curve.

Check that hands and feet will pass through sleeves and trouser legs before completing the seams – they may need to be left open and finished after fitting. The lengths of the crotch and trouser leg are critical and must be adjusted until they look right. Stitched hems can be avoided by pressing iron-on backing over the turned edge (see Chapter 3). Do not press the centre-front and back creases on trousers worn before 1906.

The patterns are designed for slim men 6in (15cm) tall, so make adjustments for larger men as required. For trousers, allow a little extra at the waist, tapering below the hips. Coats can be widened at centre-back and side seams – very little added at each seam will make quite a difference. Adjust sleeve and trouser lengths at hems.

GEORGIAN SUIT

(Fig 72 – shown in colour on pp42/43)

Full-skirted coats, long waistcoats and knee breeches were worn, with minor variations, throughout the eighteenth century. The waistcoat was usually made in brocade or beautifully embroidered silk, which can be reproduced by using wide jacquard ribbon with a suitable design. Make the breeches in cream fabric or to match the coat, in plain or patterned silk, taffeta or brocade. Use plain cottons for lawyers, clerics, merchants and countrymen. This style does not need a shirt.

■ FOOTWEAR

Thick silk or cotton stockings and shoes with high tongues, decorated with buckles. Country gentlemen wore knee-length boots.

■ BREECHES

Cut in fabric bonded to muslin interlining. Stitch the front and back seams, clip and press open. Stitch the inside-leg seam and press open. Turn through and fit onto the doll, adjusting the length to just below the knee. Take up any fullness with a small pleat on the outside of the leg, trim with braid and add two or three bead-buttons or a ribbon bow. Stuff the breeches lightly – take up any fullness with pleats and stitch to the waist.

■ WAISTCOAT

Cut waistcoat fronts in bonded fabric and in lining (the same fabric or toning silk). With right sides facing, stitch each front to the lining from A around the neckline, down the front edge, the bottom and up the side to B. Trim, turn and press. Lap the left front over the right and stitch together with bead-buttons at regular intervals from neck to waist. Continue the buttons on the right-hand side almost to the bottom and make corresponding small horizontal stitches on the left-hand side to represent buttonholes. Lace the waistcoat onto the body with long stitches around the back and from the shoulders to the back waist. (The waistcoat back is omitted under a coat.)

■ STOCK

Cut a bias piece of white silk or fine lawn $1\frac{1}{2}$ x $\frac{3}{4}$in (3.8 x 2cm). Press in the raw edges. Wind the stock tightly around the neck and fasten at the back. Stitch a short length of gathered lace to the centre of the stock, as a jabot, to fall over the waistcoat.

■ COAT

Cut back, front, sleeves and cuffs in bonded fabric, and the front and lower back lining in the same, unbonded, fabric. The upper back is unlined. With right sides facing, stitch the side seams on both coat and lining. Clip

The Letter
The old gentleman and his wife, wearing Regency Suit and Dress,
enjoy the weekly letter from their married daughter

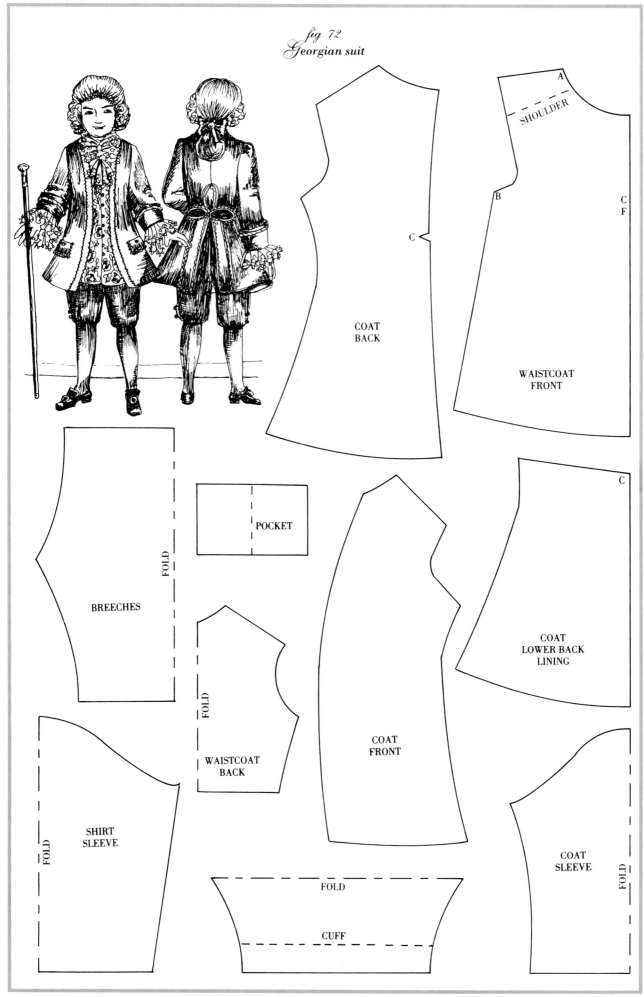

fig 72
Georgian suit

COAT
BACK

A

SHOULDER

B

C
F

C

WAISTCOAT
FRONT

C

BREECHES

FOLD

POCKET

COAT
LOWER BACK
LINING

FOLD

WAISTCOAT
BACK

COAT
FRONT

SHIRT
SLEEVE

FOLD

COAT
SLEEVE

FOLD

FOLD

CUFF

the curves and press. Clip the centre back at C. With right sides facing, stitch each half of the coat to the lining to C. Clip the curves and corners, turn through exactly on the stitching line and press. Stitch the centre-back seam. Stitch the shoulder seams.

Although the coat can be left plain, it looks splendid with plenty of braid trimming, especially around the back vent, with a loop at the waistline. Pocket flaps can also be added. Fit the coat onto the doll and tack it in position so that the fronts lie flat on the waistcoat.

Stay stitch all around the sleeves to prevent stretching. (A pattern is given for large cuffs, but these can be omitted and the sleeve ends turned under.) Adjust the sleeves for length. Fold the cuffs in half, then fold again at the lower line and trim with matching braid. Lay the cuffs over the sleeve ends with the raw sleeve edge in the fold. Tack the angled edge of the cuff to the sleeve so that the cuff will stand away from it. With right sides facing, stitch the sleeve seams as far as the cuffs. Turn through and stitch the rest of the seam from the outside to avoid turning the cuff, and press.

Add frills of gathered lace inside the sleeves to hang over the wrists. The sleeves should fit smoothly, so use gathering to ease the top, and slip stitch to the natural armholes. Any ·puckering can be concealed with braid trim around the armhole.

- HAIR

Wigs were worn for most of this period in white or natural hair colour, with rolled curls at the sides and a queue at the back tied with a black ribbon bow.

- HAT

A tricorn hat.

SERVANT

A working man or servant might wear a waistcoat over full shirt sleeves, gathered into narrow wristbands, without a coat. The stock should be plain, untrimmed in white or cream cotton to match the shirt sleeves.

Make the waistcoat in grey or brown 'homespun' fabric to match or complement the breeches and line with light-weight silk. Cut the waistcoat fronts and back in bonded fabric and fronts in lining. Make up the fronts, as described above, and stitch fronts to back at shoulder and side seams, turning up the lower back edge, and press. (Note that the back is waist length.)

Snip around the back neckline and fit onto the doll, tucking in the raw edge, over the stock. Slip stitch the front closed, adding buttons and buttonholes as before. Stitch sleeve seams, gather sleeve tops and stitch to the armholes. Gather sleeve ends to the wrists and add wristbands or frills.

- HAIR

Natural hair, tied in a queue with black ribbon or cut short.

REGENCY SUIT

(Fig 73 – shown in colour on pp54/55)

The full-skirted coat of the previous century is replaced by a tailcoat cut short at the front to display a decorative waistcoat worn over tight breeches, which later became trousers. Breeches (or trousers) can be made in silk or firmly woven cotton in a pale colour, or to match the coat. Use silk or cotton fabrics in plain colours for the coat – blue, green and dark red were fashionable. The waistcoat can be made to match the coat, but a patterned silk fabric in a complementary colour would be more typical of the period.

- FOOTWEAR

Silk stockings and black slippers, or riding boots.

- SHIRT

Cut the shirt in white silk and the collar in bonded silk. Fit the shirt front onto the doll and lace firmly across the back. Fold the collar in half lengthwise, and seam the two short ends, clip and turn. Snip the raw edges, fit onto the doll and stitch the ends together at the front. The collar should stand up with the points under the chin and not lie flat.

- CRAVAT

Cut on the bias in white or coloured silk. Seam into a tube, clip and turn. Tuck in the raw edges and close neatly. Start with the centre of the cravat at the front of the neck, cross at the back and knot in front. (Wide ribbon could be used as a simpler alternative.)

- BREECHES

Cut in fabric bonded with muslin interlining. Make up breeches as for the Georgian man or make trousers as for the Victorian man (Fig 74), but taper the legs slightly to the ankles. Fit onto the doll and secure to the waist, pleating any fullness to each side of centre front.

- WAISTCOAT

Cut in bonded silk and in matching lining. With right sides facing, seam from A to B. Trim the corners, turn and press carefully. Press back the lapels on the fold marks. Lap the left side over the right, and stitch together with bead-buttons. Fit the waistcoat onto the doll over the breeches, and lace tightly across the back to fit snugly. (The waistcoat back is omitted to avoid bulk.)

- COAT

Cut fronts, back, collar, tails and sleeves in bonded fabric. Cut front and collar linings in unbonded fabric. Stay stitch the neckline to prevent stretching. Stitch the fronts to the back at the side seams and press open. With right sides facing, seam the coat tails from C to E, clip the curves, turn and press. With right sides facing, pin the tails to the coat back, matching points D. Pin the front edge of the tails C to point C on the coat front, taking up the surplus with small pleats at the back. Stitch, clip and press the seam upwards. With right sides facing, stitch

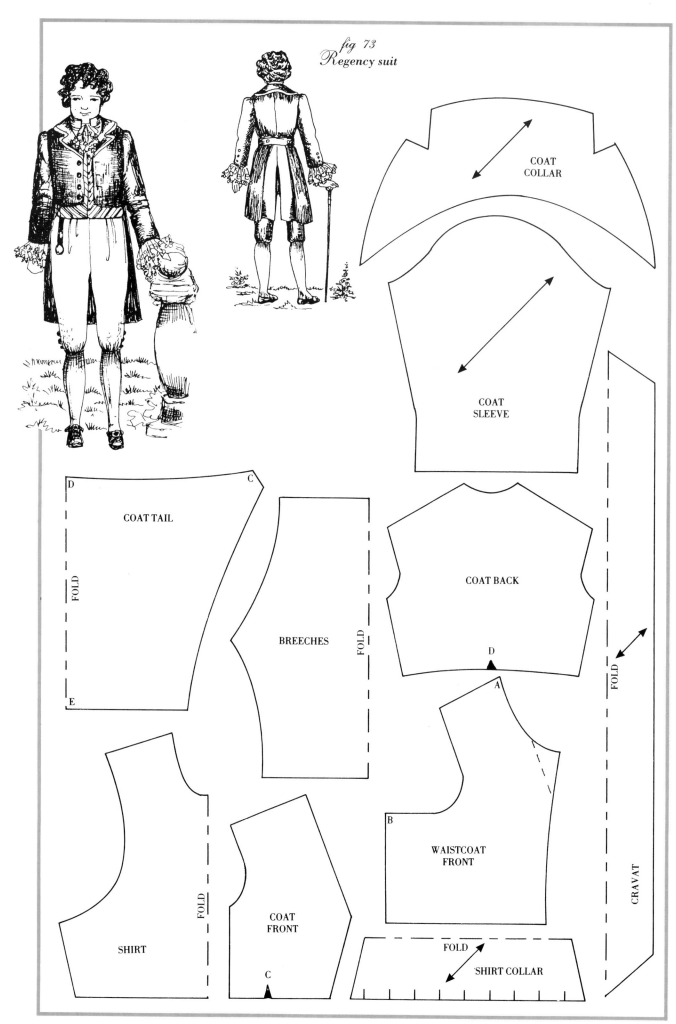

fig 73
Regency suit

COAT COLLAR

COAT SLEEVE

COAT TAIL

FOLD

D C

E

BREECHES

FOLD

COAT BACK

D

A

CRAVAT

FOLD

SHIRT

FOLD

COAT FRONT

C

B

WAISTCOAT FRONT

FOLD

SHIRT COLLAR

The Music Lesson
The Victorian music teacher, wearing a Frock-coat, often feels
there must be an easier way to earn his living. His girl pupil wears a
Low-waisted Dress *and her brother wears a* **Russian-style Suit**

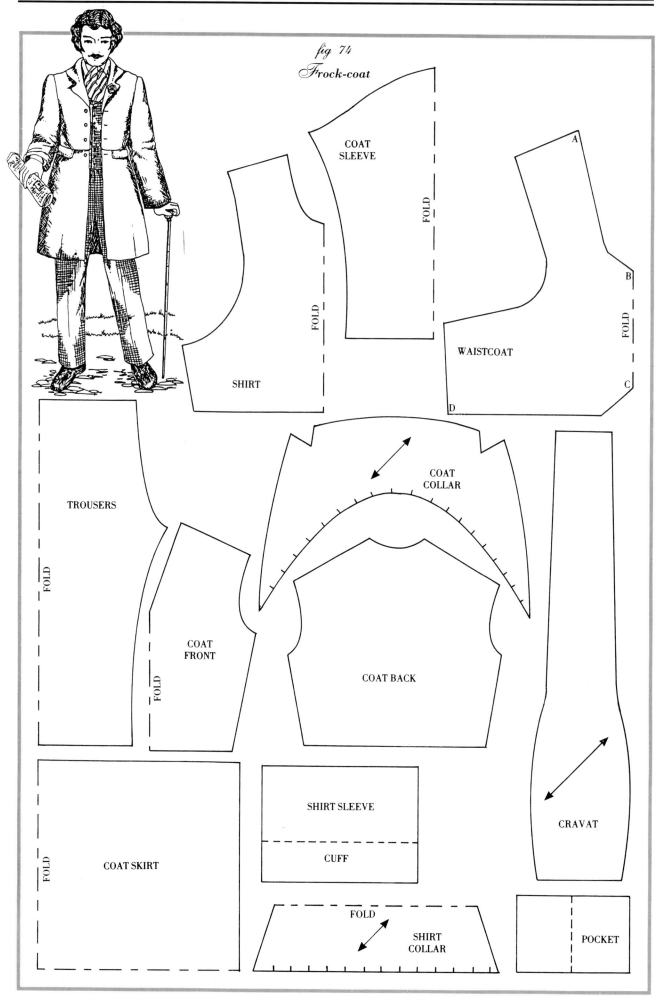

fig 74
Frock-coat

COAT SLEEVE

FOLD

FOLD

A

B

C

D

FOLD

WAISTCOAT

FOLD

SHIRT

TROUSERS

FOLD

COAT COLLAR

COAT FRONT

FOLD

COAT BACK

CRAVAT

COAT SKIRT

FOLD

SHIRT SLEEVE

CUFF

FOLD

SHIRT COLLAR

POCKET

the lining to the coat front from the shoulders and, along the previous stitching line, around the waist. Clip, trim any surplus fabric, turn and press. Stitch two or three buttons to the right coat front, with corresponding stitches to represent buttonholes on the left. Stitch the shoulder seams. (The coat back lining is omitted to avoid bulk and to allow for easing.) Press carefully, stretching and easing the curves and seams. Tack the raw edges to the lining where necessary.

Stitch the collar to the lining, clip the curve and into the notch, trimming all surplus. Turn through and press carefully. Clip the inside edge and press under. Fit onto the doll with the inside edge under the coat, curving the collar so that it will lie flat. Stitch the collar in place and tack the coat front edges to the waistcoat. Braid can be used to trim the collar and around the waist of the coat.

Stitch the underarm sleeve seams, turn and press. Turn the sleeves under at the wrist edges and stitch gathered lace ruffles to show. Run a gathering thread around the top of the sleeves and stitch to the armholes, making a wide shoulder-line. (Regency sleeves often had slight top gathering to accentuate shoulders.)

■ HAIR

Use a modern hairstyle – short curls were very fashionable.

FROCK-COAT

(Fig 74 – shown in colour on pp102/103)

About 1818 the first knee-length frock-coat appeared, a version of which is still worn for formal occasions today. For earlier periods, the coat was made in various colours, but as the century progressed, grey, brown or black were more usual. Coat, trousers and waistcoat could be of different fabrics – checks and stripes were popular – worn with a fancy waistcoat up to the end of the century. The cravat can be as decorative as modern ties. Use silk or fine cotton fabrics for the coat and trousers bonded to lightweight iron-on Vilene in preference to muslin. Avoid thicker fabrics as they are more difficult to tailor.

■ SHIRT

Cut the shirt collar in bonded fabric. Check the size: fold in half lengthwise and seam the short ends. Trim, turn through and press. Snip the raw edges and fasten around the neck as a stiff upstanding collar. Cut the shirt front in silk or fine lawn. Treat the neckline with Fray Check and add any decorative trimming before fitting onto the doll and lacing firmly across the back. Cut the shirt sleeves in bonded fabric. Press in the underarm seam allowance and fold where marked. Fit the sleeves onto the arms and stitch the cuffs together, wrong sides facing, with pearl bead cuff-links. Continue stitching up the sleeves and secure to the arms at the top. (Made this way the cuffs will stay in place and show under the coat sleeves.)

■ CRAVAT

Cut two pieces in patterned silk on the bias. With right sides facing, stitch both long sides, turn through and press, or cut one piece and hand-roll and whip the edges. It is not necessary to sew the ends as these will be tucked into the waistcoat. Arrange around the neck, bringing the wide end up under the thin end, and securing with a pearl bead. (Ribbon can be used as a simpler alternative.)

■ TROUSERS

Cut two pieces in fabric, bonded to hold the hems in place (see p32.) Stitch the centre-front and back seams, clip and press open. Stitch the inside-leg seams and neaten at the hems. Turn and press carefully. Fit the trousers onto the doll over the shirt, taking up any fullness with small pleats either side at the waist, and stitch to the doll.

■ WAISTCOAT

Cut in bonded fabric. With right sides facing, stitch from A to B and from C to D. Trim, turn through and press carefully. Lap the left side over the right, stitch together with bead-buttons, and add a looped fine gold watch-chain. Fit the waistcoat onto the doll, over the trousers and lace across the back so that it fits well. The waistcoat back is omitted to avoid bulk.

■ COAT

Cut the coat back, fronts, skirt, sleeves, collar and pockets in bonded fabric and collar lining in unbonded fabric. Open the coat front pieces and stay stitch the neckline edges to prevent stretching; fold again and press. Stay stitch the back neckline edge. Stitch the fronts to the back at the side seams. Press in the seam allowance on the pockets, fold in half as shown on the pattern, and, with raw edges together, tack the pockets to the coat fronts. With right sides facing, fold the skirt lengthwise and seam the short edges together. Clip the corners, turn and press carefully on the seam. Tack the raw edges together. With right sides facing, pin the skirt to the coat, matching at the fronts, and taking up the surplus with a flat or box pleat at the centre back. Stitch the coat to the skirt, clip the seam and press upwards. Stitch two bead-buttons at the waistline above the pleat. Stitch the shoulder seams and press flat. Fold the front lining back and stitch it to the waistline and shoulders. Stitch buttons to the right front and make corresponding stitches to represent buttonholes on the left front. Fit the coat onto the doll.

Stitch the collar to the lining around the outside edge. Clip and trim closely, especially around the notch. Turn and press out the points carefully. Clip the inside edge and press under. Fit the collar around the neck with the raw edges under the coat, tucking in the ends. Smooth the collar, working it into place, and stitch to the coat. Tack the coat fronts to the waistcoat. Make a ribbon rose and stitch it to the left lapel.

Run gathering threads around the top of the sleeves

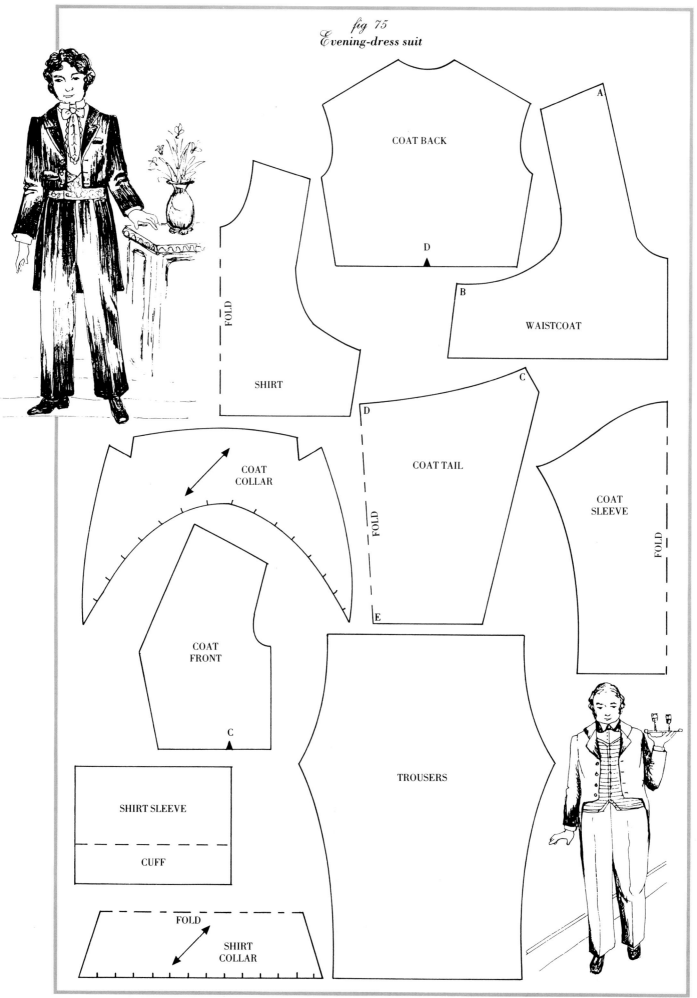

fig 75
Evening-dress suit

COAT BACK

A

D

B

WAISTCOAT

C

SHIRT

FOLD

COAT
COLLAR

D

COAT TAIL

FOLD

COAT
SLEEVE

FOLD

E

COAT
FRONT

C

TROUSERS

SHIRT SLEEVE

CUFF

FOLD

SHIRT
COLLAR

and stitch the underarm seams. Press open and turn through. Pull up the gathering slightly to ease. Fit the sleeves onto the arms, with underarm seams matching, and stitch the sleeves to the natural armholes, without gathers. Fold the sleeve ends in above the shirt cuffs and tack at the seams to hold in place. Add two or three buttons to each coat cuff.

- **HAT**

A top-hat, worn or carried.

- **ACCESSORIES**

A walking-stick, umbrella, folded newspaper or cellophane-wrapped bouquet of flowers.

EVENING-DRESS SUIT

(Fig 75 – shown in colour on pp78/79)

This formal evening-dress suit is suitable for men's wear from the mid-Victorian period to the present day. The coat and trousers should be made in lightweight black fabric, worn with a white shirt and white or brocade waistcoat and bow-tie. Use silk or cotton lawn for the shirt and silk or cotton piqué for the waistcoat.

- **SHIRT**

Cut the collar in bonded fabric, make as the previous pattern and fit under the shirt. Cut the shirt front and add a decorative panel of gathered ribbon, lace or flat grosgrain ribbon, and fit as before. Make a white ribbon bow-tie. Cut sleeves in bonded fabric and make up as the previous pattern, with pearl or gilt bead cuff-links.

- **TROUSERS**

Cut the trousers in fabric bonded to hold the hems in place. Stitch narrow flat braid to the centre of each piece to define the side 'seams'. Make up the trousers as for the previous pattern.

- **WAISTCOAT**

Cut the waistcoat in bonded fabric and in lining. Make up as for the Regency pattern (see p133).

- **COAT**

Cut back, fronts, sleeves, collar and tails in bonded fabric. Cut fronts and collar lining in unbonded fabric. (The coat collar can be made in thin satin, but the collar lining should be a lightweight fabric.) Make up the coat as for the Regency coat, omitting the lace ruffles. Add a ribbon rose buttonhole.

- **HAT**

A top-hat

- **ACCESSORIES**

A walking-stick with decorative handle.

BUTLER

This pattern can be used to dress a butler (or waiter) from the Victorian period to the present day. For a Victorian butler, make the coat and trousers in black fabric, omitting the braid stripe on the side 'seams' of the trousers. Make the waistcoat in horizontally striped fabric – for example, yellow and black stripes. For a waiter, make the waistcoat in black fabric and add a black bow-tie.

LOUNGE SUIT

(Fig 76 – shown in colour on p166/167)

Although generally associated with the late-Victorian period, suits with short jackets were worn as early as the 1850s. Use fine cotton or soft shirting with a plain, tweedy pattern or small checked designs in cotton or brushed cotton.

- **SHIRT**

Cut the shirt collar in bonded fabric and make up. Fit onto the doll as a soft turned-down collar. Cut the shirt front and sleeves in bonded fabric and make up as for the frock-coat shirt (see p137). Use a piece of ribbon, knotted under the collar, as a tie.

- **TROUSERS**

Cut the trousers in fabric bonded to hold the hems in place and make up as for the frock-coat trousers.

- **WAISTCOAT**

Cut the waistcoat in bonded fabric to match or contrast with the suit. Make up as for the frock-coat waistcoat, adding a watch-chain if required.

- **JACKET**

Cut the back, fronts, sleeves and collar in bonded fabric. Cut the front, back and collar lining in unbonded fabric. Stitch the centre-back seams on the coat and lining, clip and press open. Stay stitch the back and front neckline. Stitch the fronts to the back at the side seams on both coat and lining. Press the seams open. With right sides facing, stitch the coat to the lining from A to A. Clip, trim, turn and press. Stitch the shoulder seams. Sew buttons to the right side, with corresponding stitches for buttonholes on the left. Fit the jacket onto the doll.

Stitch the collar to the lining. Clip the curve right into the notch, trim and turn. Press carefully so that the lining will not show. Clip the neck edge and fold under. Fit the clipped edge under the jacket neckline folding the collar over and easing into position so that it lies flat. Stitch in place. Tack the jacket fronts to the waistcoat. Stitch the sleeve seams, turn in the lower ends and press. Run gathering threads around the sleeve tops. Fit the sleeves onto the doll, pull up the threads to ease and stitch the sleeves to the armholes without gathering.

BLAZER AND FLANNELS

This pattern can be made in a bold striped fabric as a blazer worn with trousers in thin cream wool. Match the blazer colours to the ribbon around a straw-boater. A tennis racquet or cricket bat would be suitably 'sporty' accessories. (Shown in colour on p118.)

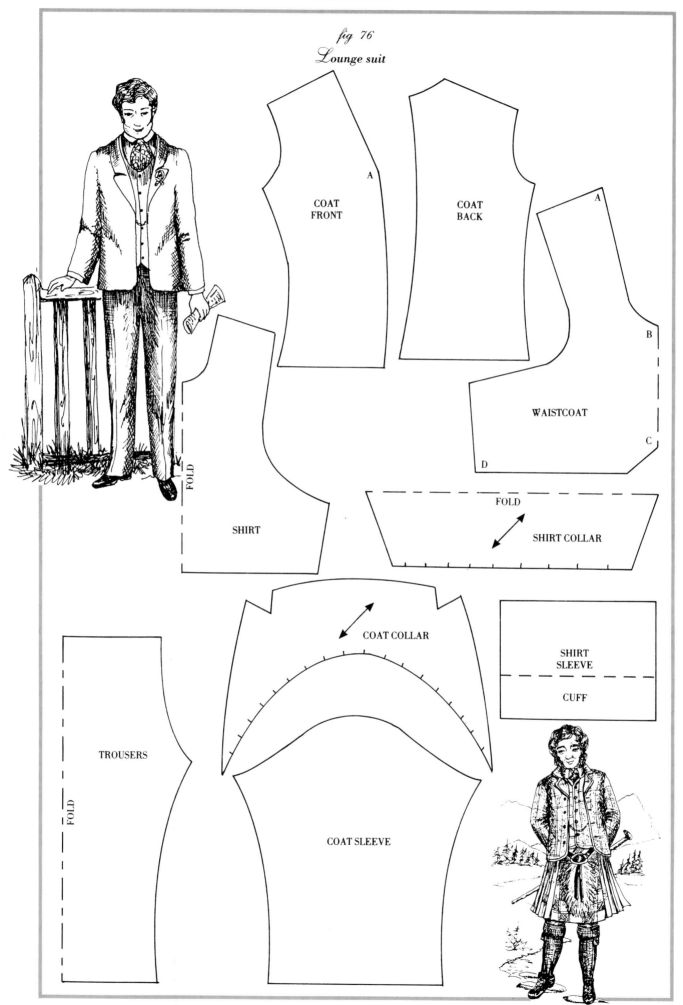

fig 76
Lounge suit

COAT
FRONT

COAT
BACK

A

A

B

C

D

WAISTCOAT

FOLD

SHIRT

FOLD

SHIRT COLLAR

COAT COLLAR

SHIRT
SLEEVE

CUFF

TROUSERS

FOLD

COAT SLEEVE

MODERN DINNER JACKET

Make in black with a black satin collar. Add a braid stripe down the side 'seams' of the trousers, and make a black waistcoat and bow-tie. The waistcoat could be replaced with a black waistband or a coloured cummerbund.

SCOTTISH DRESS

The jacket and waistcoat worn with a kilt can be used to dress a Scottish gentleman. For daywear, choose a soft tweedy fabric, worn with knee-length socks and stout shoes; for evening-wear, select a black fabric trimmed with silver buttons, worn with a lace jabot, tartan socks and black buckled shoes. The correct underwear with a kilt is a pair of matching tartan shorts.

- KILT

This is only suitable for a doll with porcelain legs which reach above the knee. Use a small-scale tartan in shirting cotton, hair ribbon or florist's ribbon.

To make the kilt, cut a piece of fabric about 2¼in (5.7cm) wide and 15in (38cm) long. Use the selvage for the hem or seal with Fray Check (or use ribbon). Pleat in a ¼in (6mm) pleater, leaving 1in (2.5cm) unpleated at one end. Secure the pleating with strips of iron-on interlining and press flat. Run a gathering thread through the pleats to secure the top edge and remove the strips. Fray the short edge at the unpleated end of the fabric, or seal with Fray Check. Wrap the kilt around the doll's waist with the unpleated panel at centre front and stitch in place over the shirt.

Make a sporran from a small semi-circle of leather and a scrap of fur. Add a silver buckle or jewellery finding clasp and fasten around the waist on a thin leather or chain strap to hang halfway down the kilt at centre front. (Shown in colour on pp182/183.)

MILITARY UNIFORMS

(Fig 77 – shown in colour on pp142/143)

Uniforms are fun to make, but it is best to avoid copying a specific regiment as the precise details of insignia, buttons and braid are difficult to miniaturise. It is easier to combine a number of features of the same period. Use cotton, velveteen or good quality felt with plenty of gold braid trimming, buttons and buckles. (Lampshade and upholstery trimmings and egg-craft supplies are a good source.)

- FOOTWEAR

Shiny black boots or shoes.

- TROUSERS

Cut in fabric bonded to hold the hems in place and make up as for the frock-coat trousers (see p137.) Alternatively make breeches as for the Georgian man. Add braid side stripes as appropriate before making up.

- COAT

The pattern shows three styles – single-breasted, double-breasted and a centre contrast panel – all with tails. Cut in bonded fabric and make as the Regency coat or evening-dress coat. Use a contrasting colour for the lining and turn up the tails. Use the same contrast fabric for collar and cuffs and apply gold-braid trimming to the tails, collar, cuffs and front of the coat. Make epaulettes in gold braid and fringe and add a sash or buckled belt and a sword.

- HAIR

Any style as appropriate for the period.

SANTA CLAUS COSTUME

(Fig 78 – shown in colour on pp166/167)

Use a doll with a jolly round face and plenty of extra body padding, especially around the waist. The hooded coat and trousers should be made in a bright red fabric which does not fray easily – for example, winceyette, brushed nylon jersey or felt. The white fur trimming could be velvet ribbon, knitting wool or trimmed fur fabric.

- FOOTWEAR

Big black boots in leather or gloss paint. Check that the trouser pattern will fit around the waist and enlarge if necessary.

- TROUSERS

Cut the trousers in bonded fabric or in felt. Stitch the centre-front and back seams, clip and press open. Stitch the inside-leg seam, clip, press open and turn through. Try the trousers on the doll and trim the leg ends so that, gathered, they will fit just above the boots. Run gathering threads around the leg ends. Fit the trousers onto the doll and stitch to the waist. Pull up the leg ends, tucking in the raw edges and fasten off securely.

- COAT

Cut the coat, hood and cape in bonded fabric or felt. Cut the coat open down the centre front. If the fabric is likely to fray, treat the edges with Fray Check.

Stitch the coat side seams. Stitch white 'fur' trimming to the right front edge from the waist, around the hem and up to the neck on the left front, and to the sleeve ends. Snip the neckline slightly and fit the coat onto the doll; lap the left front over the right and tack in place. Make a belt in black leather fastened with a buckle at the centre front. Stitch 'fur' to the outside edge of the cape, snip the

In Conference ▸
The committee meet in the library to discuss plans for the cricket club. Their host wears a Frock-coat, his brother a Military Uniform and the other gentlemen wear Lounge Suits. The butler's clothes are a variation of the Evening-Dress Suit

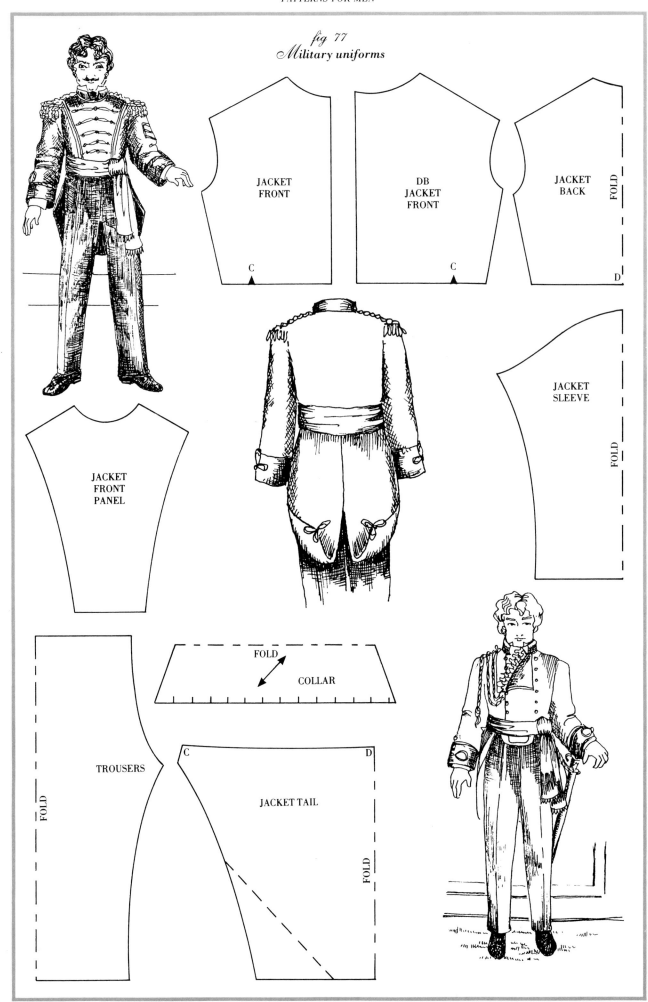

fig 77
Military uniforms

JACKET FRONT

C

DB JACKET FRONT

C

JACKET BACK

FOLD

D

JACKET SLEEVE

FOLD

JACKET FRONT PANEL

FOLD

COLLAR

TROUSERS

FOLD

C

JACKET TAIL

D

FOLD

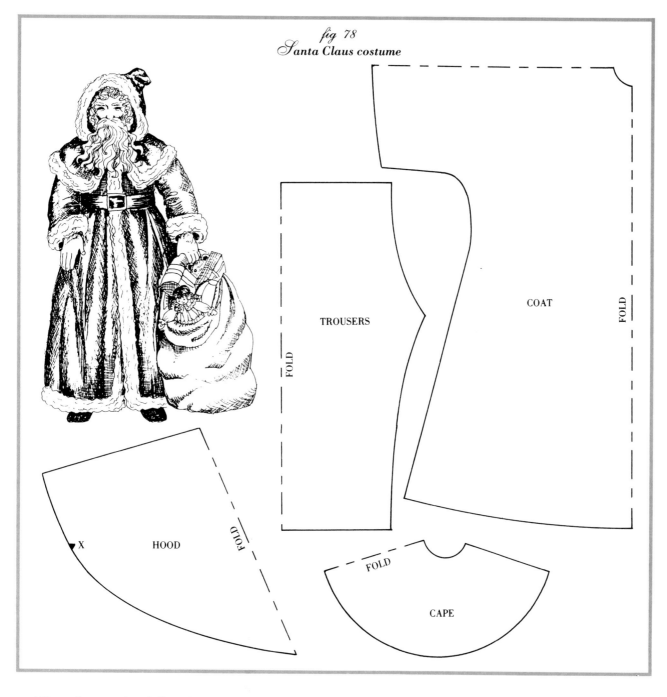

fig 78
Santa Claus costume

neckline, fit onto the doll and stitch the neck edges together at the centre front.

Make a simple wig and flowing beard (see Chapter 10) in white mohair or viscose.

Trim the straight (front) edge of the hood with 'fur' and, with right sides facing, seam from X to the point, press and turn through. Fit the hood onto the doll, trimming the neckline edge if necessary to make a good fit around the face. Stitch the hood over the cape neckline, taking up any fullness with gathers or small pleats.

MODERN ADAPTATION

Cut the coat shorter and omit the hood and cape. Trim the neckline with 'fur'. Make a cap by cutting a band of 'fur' to fit around the head and seaming the short edges. Cut a

circle of coat fabric to fit for the crown and stitch in place. Glue the cap to the doll's hair if necessary to hold it in place.

■ ACCESSORIES

A toy sack of beige cotton stuffed with cotton-wool or polystyrene beads, with toys and parcels peeping out of the top.

WORKING CLOTHES

(Fig 79 – shown in colour on pp62/63 and 127)

This pattern for a simple shirt, trousers and apron can be used to dress a variety of working men, including a gardener or shopkeeper.

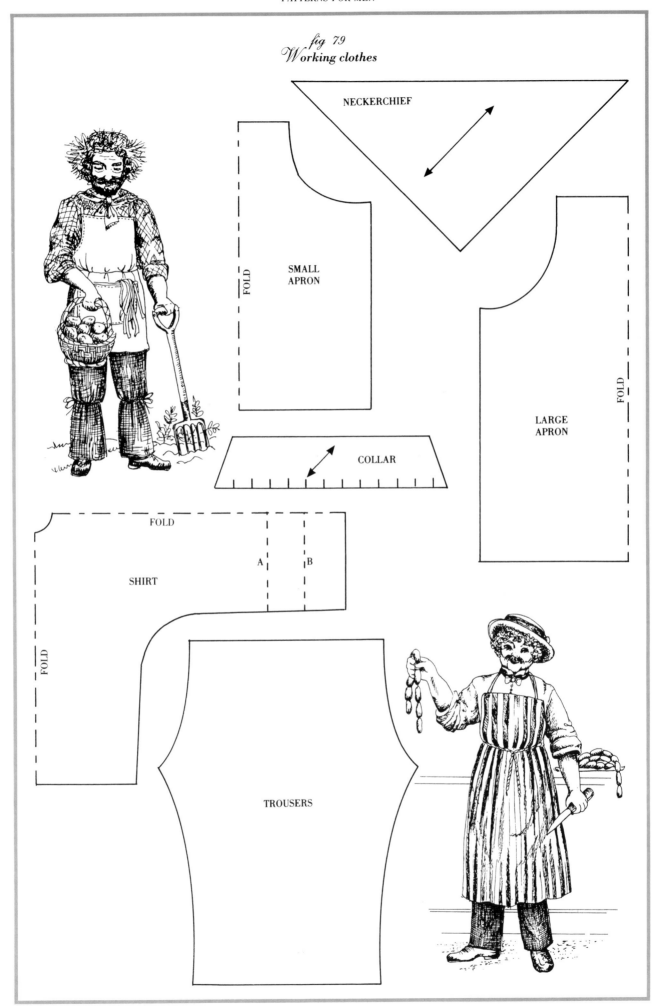

fig 79
Working clothes

NECKERCHIEF

SMALL
APRON

FOLD

LARGE
APRON

FOLD

COLLAR

FOLD

SHIRT

FOLD

A   B

TROUSERS

GARDENER

Use a soft tweedy fabric in a dark colour for the trousers and a plain or checked cotton in grey or brown for the shirt. Dark green felt is good for the apron and a bright cotton fabric for the neckerchief.

Cut the shirt in unbonded fabric and cut open down the centre front far enough to put over the doll's head. Apply Fray Check to the neckline and front edges. Stitch the underarm seams, clip the curves, press open and turn through. Fold the sleeve ends in on line A and outwards on line B to form cuffs. Fit the shirt onto the doll, fold one front edge in, over the other and slip stitch closed. Add bead-buttons.

Cut the trousers in fabric and hem the leg ends. Make up as the frock-coat trousers (see p137.) Trim any surplus fabric at the waistline and apply Fray Check. Fit the trousers onto the doll and stitch in place at the waistline. Make a leather belt and fasten around the waist to cover the raw edge. Tie the trousers below the knees with raffia or thin cord. Cut the small apron in felt. Add a pocket (or pockets) if required and make strings of thin cord or heavy thread at the bib top and waist. Fit the apron onto the doll and tie the strings. Cut the neckerchief in cotton and fray the short edges. Turn in the long edge and fit around the neck, tie the ends, stitch to hold in place and tuck inside the apron bib.

■ HAIR

Grey curly hair and a bushy beard and moustache or stubble.

■ HAT

A shapeless moulded felt or straw-hat with frayed edges would look suitably well-worn.

■ ACCESSORIES

Garden tools, potted plant or trug of vegetables; a hank of raffia in the pocket.

SHOPKEEPER

Use plain dark grey or black fabric for the trousers and white cotton fabric for the shirt. Choose apron fabric according to the trade – for example, unbleached calico for a grocer, blue and white stripes for a butcher or fishmonger.

Cut the collar in double-bonded fabric or in shiny, thin white card – for example, a postcard – to represent celluloid. Snip the lower edge as shown in Fig 79 and fit onto the doll as an upright collar, bending the top edges forward to form 'wings'. Cut the shirt, make up and fit as before and add a ribbon, tied in a bow at the front, to cover the join. Cut trousers in fabric bonded to hold the hems in place and make up and fit as before. Cut the large apron and make a small hem all around the edge. Make pockets if required and apron strings as before.

■ HAT

A straw-boater.

■ ACCESSORIES

According to the trade – for example, fruit and vegetables, a string of sausages, fish, a pot of jam or a filled paper-bag.

9

Patterns for boys

GEORGIAN SUIT
(Fig 80 – shown in colour on pp42/43)

THIS SIMPLE PATTERN designed to give an impression of the period, is based on Gainsborough's painting *The Blue Boy*. There are patterns for both 5in (13cm) and 4in (10cm) dolls. Make the suit in stiff silk, brocade, cotton or fine plush velvet in blue, green, burgundy, grey, brown or black, trimmed with braid. For the child of a wealthy family, add delicate lace collar and cuffs.

- **FOOTWEAR**

Knee-length silk or cotton jersey stockings with buckled shoes.

- **BREECHES**

Cut two pieces in bonded fabric. Check the size and adjust if necessary – the breeches should not be too full. Stitch the front and back seams, clip the curves and press open. Stitch the inner-leg seam, clip, press and turn through. Fit the breeches onto the doll, pleat to fit the waist and stitch securely to the body. (For an all-bisque body, take long tacking stitches over the shoulders.) Pleat the fullness to fit the legs just below the knee, trimming any surplus. Cover the raw edges with flat braid with a bow or rosette at the outside leg.

- **COAT**

Cut the coat and sleeves in bonded fabric. Note that no turnings are allowed for the front or lower edges. Cut the armholes just large enough to allow free movement of the arms. Stitch the shoulder seams and press open. Put the coat on the doll inside-out and pin a small pleat under each arm, which will appear as an inverted box pleat on the right side. Remove the coat, stitch the pleats down to waist-level and press. Stitch braid trimming to both fronts and around the lower edge. Stitch bead-buttons to the left front. Fit the coat onto the doll and slip stitch closed from the neckline to waist.

Stitch the underarm sleeve seams, check the length and apply Fray Check to the wrist edges. Slashed sleeves are difficult to make neatly, but an impression can be given by applying suitable narrow lace down the centre of the sleeve, drawn in tightly at regular intervals of slightly over 1/4in (7mm). Make French knots to represent buttons, or stitch beads at each of these points. The sleeves should fit smoothly, so ease slightly with gather-ing threads before stitching to the natural armholes. A perfect fit at the top of the sleeves is not essential as they will be covered by the collar. Finish the sleeves with deep lace cuffs.

Cut the collar in lace edging with a delicate design; it should be wide enough to reach from the neck to just over the shoulders. Fit the collar around the shoulders, fold-ing under the raw ends in front. Gather to fit around the neck and finish with a large bow of silk ribbon.

- **HAIR**

Soft wavy hair to the shoulders.

- **HAT**

A wide-brimmed hat made in double-bonded fabric, trimmed with a ribbon bow and a curled feather. The hat usually looks better held in the hand, but it could be made to fit the head.

VARIATIONS

For a plain suit, omit all the lace and ribbons, and trim the coat with flat braid or picot used with the loops inwards. Make a plain white collar, cut in double-bonded cotton and edge with braid. Alternatively, cut the collar in single-bonded cotton and lining (remember to add the seam allowance), seam together, turn through and press. Clip around the neckline and turn under. Tack the collar in position and finish with a braid bow or knotted cord.

'SKELETON SUIT', 1780–1830
(Fig 81 – shown in colour on pp54/55)

The high-waisted trousers of the skeleton suit are usually worn above ankle length and buttoned to the shirt. Use silk or fine cotton fabrics in cream or pastel shades. Make the shirt and trousers in the same colour or in com-plementary colours, with a contrasting ribbon sash. This pattern is suitable for a late-Victorian 'Kate Greenaway' style, or for a modern page-boy's suit for a wedding.

- **FOOTWEAR**

White socks and flat slippers.

- **SHIRT**

Cut the shirt in bonded fabric on the fold and cut open down the front. Stitch the underarm seams, clip and press open. Fit the shirt onto the doll, snipping the neckline to

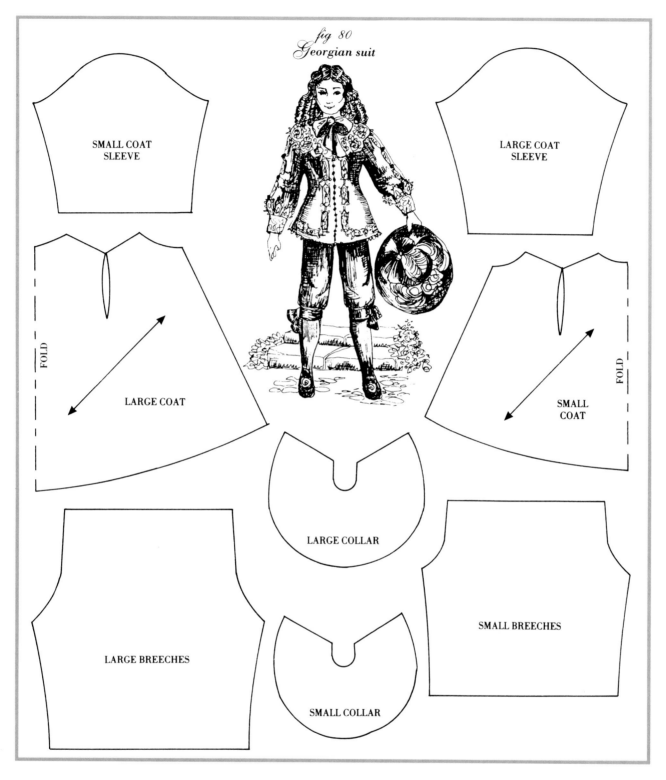

fig 80
Georgian suit

SMALL COAT
SLEEVE

LARGE COAT
SLEEVE

FOLD

LARGE COAT

FOLD

SMALL
COAT

LARGE COLLAR

LARGE BREECHES

SMALL BREECHES

SMALL COLLAR

fit. Slip stitch closed down the centre front and cover the stitching with braid and bead-buttons. Pleat the sleeve ends to fit the wrists and finish with lace cuffs. Gather a length of lace to make a wide collar, turn under both ends and finish with a ribbon bow to match the trousers.

■ TROUSERS

Cut two pieces in fabric, bonded to hold the hems in place (see p30.) Stitch the centre-front and back seams, clip and press open. Stitch the inner-leg seams, securing each end neatly. Fit the trousers onto the doll above the natural waistline, taking up any fullness with equal-sized pleats either side of the centre at front and back. Cover the join with a sash of wide ribbon tied on the left side or make a fabric waistband with bead-button 'fastening' at the front.

■ HAIR

Short hair, straight or curly.

■ HAT

A wide-brimmed straw-hat with matching ribbon or a 'baker boy' cap.

The New Hat

The little boy wearing a Victorian Velvet Suit thinks his friend's new hat would look better after a good soaking. His friends wear Victorian and Edwardian Suits, a Sailor Suit and Sailor Dresses

Playing Soldiers

The boys, wearing Victorian Suits, march to the sound of drum and trumpet and plan their next campaign while their sister, wearing a Simple Dress and Pinafore, complains to Nanny about the casualties of war. Nanny's clothes are made from the Basic Pattern, little brother wears Rompers and the baby wears a Baby Gown

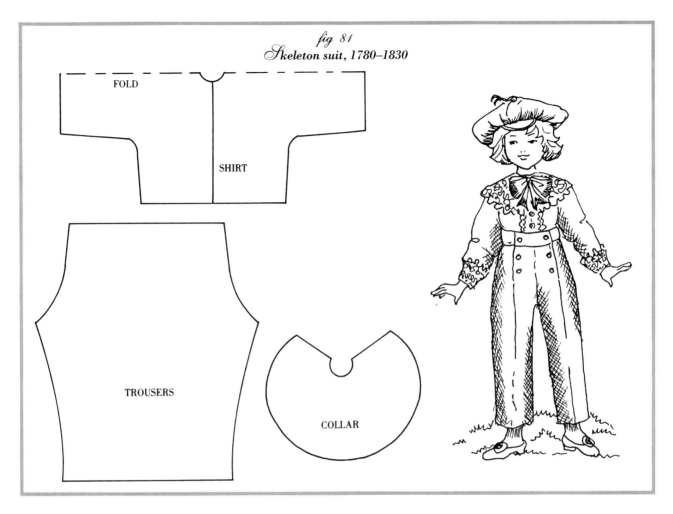

fig 81
Skeleton suit, 1780–1830

FOLD

SHIRT

TROUSERS

COLLAR

VARIATIONS

With short trousers and a natural waistline, this pattern is suitable for a young boy up to the Edwardian period. With a plain fabric collar it could be used for dress up to the present day.

_____EARLY-VICTORIAN SUIT_____

(Fig 82 – shown in colour on p27)

This suit looks best made in black or burgundy silk, trimmed with matching braid. Use fine silk or lawn for the shirt. The collar can be made in fabric or lace.

■ FOOTWEAR

Black stockings and boots.

■ SHIRT

Cut the shirt in bonded fabric and seal the neckline with Fray Check. Stitch the buttons to the front if required. Fit the shirt onto the doll and lace across the back. Cut shirt sleeves on the bias in unbonded fabric and put aside.

■ TROUSERS

Cut the trousers in fabric bonded to hold the hems in place and make up as the previous pattern. Add bead-buttons at the side 'seams' and fit onto the doll. Alternatively, cut the trousers in bonded fabric and gather the leg ends to fit below the knee, tucking in the raw edges,

as breeches. Add a ribbon or fabric band to neaten the waistline.

■ JACKET

Cut the back and fronts in double-bonded fabric and the short sleeves in bonded fabric. Stitch the shoulder and side seams and press open. The jacket should just reach the waist and hang open at the front to show the shirt. Trim all around the jacket with braid, overlapping the edge, and fit onto the doll. Place the jacket sleeves over the top edge of the shirt sleeves and stitch together. Cover the join with braid, making a little loop at the top of the V as shown on the pattern. With right sides facing, stitch the underarm seams and press open. Turn through and stitch the sleeves to the natural armholes, making sure that the braided openings are towards the front. Gather the shirt sleeve ends to fit the wrists and finish with neat cuffs. Cut the collar in double-bonded shirt fabric or lace. Fit onto the doll and finish with a ribbon bow.

■ ALTERNATIVE SLEEVES

Omit the shirt sleeves. Cut long sleeves in bonded fabric, stitch the underarm seams and stitch the sleeves to the armholes. Finish with lace cuffs to cover the sleeve ends.

■ HAT

A round sailor hat with upturned brim in straw or moulded felt, or a 'baker boy' cap.

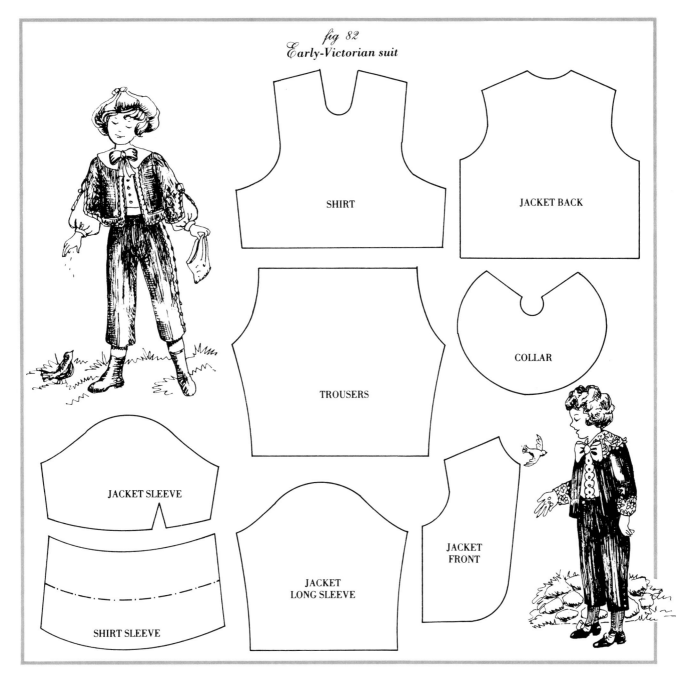

fig 82
Early-Victorian suit

SHIRT

JACKET BACK

COLLAR

TROUSERS

JACKET SLEEVE

SHIRT SLEEVE

JACKET
LONG SLEEVE

JACKET
FRONT

VICTORIAN VELVET SUIT

(Fig 83 – shown in colour on p150)

For an authentic 'Little Lord Fauntleroy' suit, use thin black non-fray velvet jersey, as real velvet is too thick, and cut with the pile downwards.

■ **FOOTWEAR**
Black stockings and flat slippers with rosettes, or black side-buttoning boots.

■ **BREECHES**
Cut in bonded fabric, stitch the centre-front and back seams, clip and press open. Stitch the inside-leg seam, clip, press and turn through. Fit the breeches onto the doll and pleat the leg ends to fit just below the knees. Finish with braid bands and bows to cover the raw edges, or gather the leg ends to fit, tucking in the raw edges.

Alternatively, cut the breeches in fabric, bonded to hold the hems in place and make up and fit as short trousers as the previous pattern.

Mid-Victorian Style (1860–80) ▸
Leaving the house to stroll in the park, mother and daughter wear matching cream lace Bustle Dresses. The friend waving and the lady on the left wear the Walking Dress (1860–70). The gentlemen wear Frock-coats and the urchin's clothes are adapted from the Victorian Suit. One little girl wears a pink Felt Coat with cape and the other wears the 'Renoir' variation of the Dress and Jacket. Nanny's clothes are made from the Basic Pattern

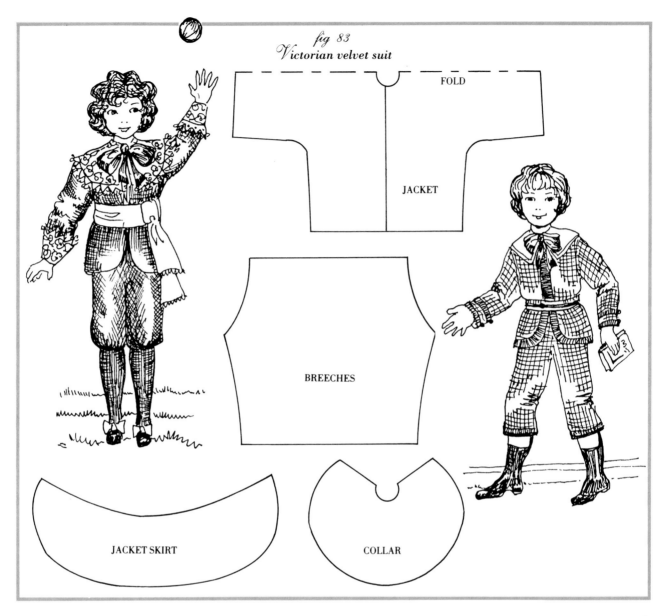

fig 83
Victorian velvet suit

FOLD

JACKET

BREECHES

JACKET SKIRT

COLLAR

■ JACKET

Cut the jacket in bonded fabric. (If there is a definite direction to the pile, cut in two pieces adding a seam allowance at the shoulders and stitch the shoulder seams.) Cut open down the centre front. Stitch the under-arm seams, clip and press open. Fit the jacket onto the doll, trimming any surplus fabric at the waistline and slip stitch the front opening closed.

Cut the jacket skirt in bonded fabric. Trim the outside edge with braid, leaving a length loose on the left side to reach from waist to neck. Stitch the skirt to the waistline, joining at the centre front. Stitch the loose braid over the front closure and add bead-buttons.

Pleat the sleeve ends to the wrists, trimming surplus fabric, treat with Fray Check and cover with lace cuffs. Cut the collar in delicate cream lace. Fit onto the doll and finish with a black ribbon bow. Add a wide ribbon sash, to match or contrast, tied on one side at the front.

■ HAIR

The original illustrations to *Little Lord Fauntleroy* show Cedric with shoulder-length ringlets, but unless you wish to be absolutely authentic, short curls look better.

■ HAT

A broad-brimmed hat in straw or felt, carried or worn.

■ ACCESSORIES

The perfect companion for Cedric would be an Irish wolf-hound, but a book, toy soldier or horse would be appropriate.

VARIATIONS

This pattern can be used to make a variety of outfits, with or without the jacket skirt. For a shirt, maybe in white cotton lawn, use the jacket pattern without the skirt. For a suit, use plain, tweedy or checked cotton fabrics in black, grey or brown and trim with flat braid. (To avoid braid trimming, the jacket skirt may be lined, but remember to add the seam allowance to the pattern.) Make plain collar and cuffs in bonded cotton and add a buckled leather belt. (Shown in colour on p150.)

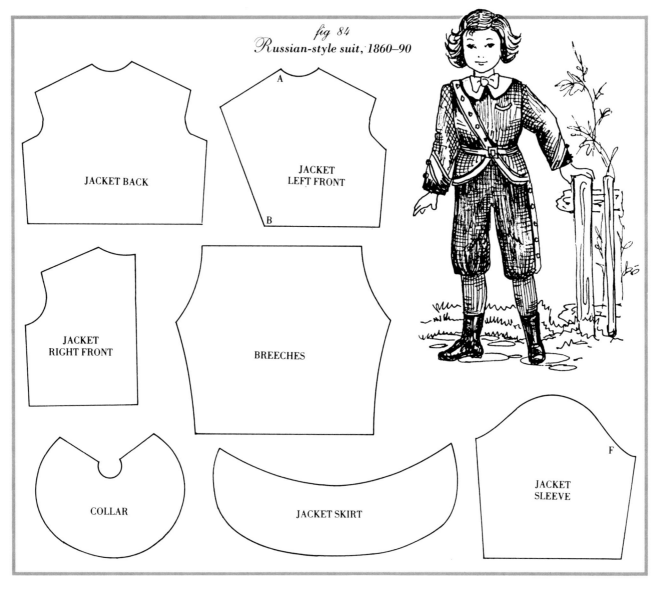

fig 84
Russian-style suit, 1860–90

JACKET BACK

JACKET LEFT FRONT

A

B

JACKET RIGHT FRONT

BREECHES

COLLAR

JACKET SKIRT

JACKET SLEEVE

F

_____ **RUSSIAN-STYLE SUIT, 1860–90** _____

(Fig 84 – shown in colour on p135)

The braid trimming and off-centre buttoning seen on Russian costumes was a popular Victorian fashion, and this pattern was inspired by a contemporary photograph. The braid and buttons are all-important, and should make a good contrast to the fabric – for example, red or burgundy on grey, blue or green, or cream on brown. Use lightweight cotton fabrics.

- **FOOTWEAR**

Black stockings and boots.

- **BREECHES**

Cut the breeches in bonded fabric. Stitch braid trimming to each piece to define the side 'seams' and add bead-buttons.

Make up and fit the breeches as the previous pattern, gathering to fit below the knees.

- **JACKET**

Cut the jacket back, fronts, skirt and sleeves in bonded fabric, and the left front in lining. With right sides fac-

ing, stitch the left front to the lining from A to B. Clip, turn and press. Trim these edges with braid and buttons as shown in Fig 84. Stitch the shoulder and side seams. Fit the jacket onto the doll and close the opening by catch-stitching the lapped diagonal edge. Stitch the jacket over the breeches at the waistline.

Stitch braid trimming to the outside edge of the jacket skirt and fit onto the doll so that the braid edges match at the centre front. Stitch the waistline edge to the jacket. Stitch the sleeve seams, fold in the wrist edges and add braid trimming and buttons. Gather the top of the sleeves to ease and stitch to the armholes.

Cut the collar in white bonded cotton, snip the neckline, fold the edge under and fit onto the doll. Secure the fronts with stitches and add a braid or ribbon bow.

Make a narrow leather belt and fasten around the waist with a small buckle at the front.

- **HAIR**

Short, straight or curly.

- **HAT**

A round felt hat trimmed with matching braid.

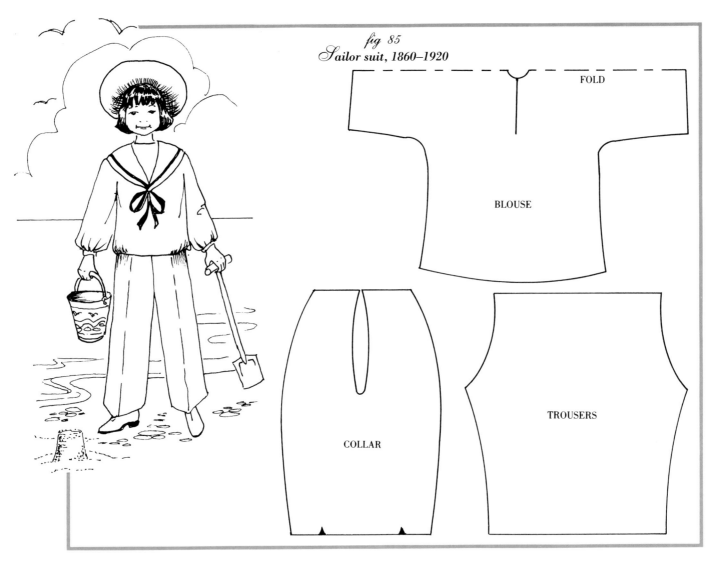

fig 85
Sailor suit, 1860–1920

FOLD

BLOUSE

COLLAR

TROUSERS

SAILOR SUIT, 1860–1920

(Fig 85 – shown in colour on p150)

Sailor suits came into fashion as boys' wear in the 1860s and are popular up to the present day. Use a closely woven cotton fabric in any combination of navy, blue, or blue stripes and white, with trimming to contrast. The trousers could be below knee length or ankle length, or above the knee for modern boys.

■ FOOTWEAR

Black stockings and boots for Victorian and Edwardian styles; white socks and shoes for modern boys.

■ TROUSERS

Cut long or short trousers in fabric bonded to hold the hems in place. (Shorten the pattern as required.) Stitch the centre-front and back seams, clip and press open. Stitch the inner-leg seam, clip and press. Fit onto the doll and stitch just above the natural waist.

■ BLOUSE

Cut the blouse in bonded fabric. Cut open down the centre back just far enough to slip the garment over the doll's head. Make small snips around the neckline and check the sleeve length. Stitch the underarm seams, clip

the curves and press open. Run a gathering thread around the bottom edge. Fit the blouse onto the doll, tuck in the raw edges around the neckline and slip stitch the back opening closed. Pull up the gathering thread, tucking in the raw edges, arrange the gathers evenly to make a bloused effect, and fasten off. Pleat or gather the sleeve ends to fit the wrists and cover with braid cuffs. Trim the neckline with braid if required.

Cut the collar in bonded fabric and in lining. (White or a contrast colour looks best.) Stitch together all around except between the points marked on the bottom edge. Press back the seam allowance on this edge to give a guideline for closing. Trim and clip the corners and curves. Carefully turn through and press on the exact seam-line. Slip stitch the bottom edge closed. Stitch braid around the collar, just inside the edge. Put the collar onto the doll, with pointed ends meeting, and tack in place. Add a bow of braid.

■ HAIR

Short, straight or curly.

■ HAT

A round straw-hat trimmed to match the suit or a beret with a pom-pom.

Sliding Down The Bannisters

To the alarm of his parents and Nanny and the amusement of his sisters, the young master demonstrates the easy way to polish the bannister rail. He wears a Victorian Velvet Suit. His sisters on the stairs wear a pale-blue Dress and Jacket and a print Simple Dress. His elegant mama wears Visiting Toilette and his youngest sister wears a Bustle Dress. Papa wears a Frock-coat and Nanny's clothes are made from the Basic Pattern

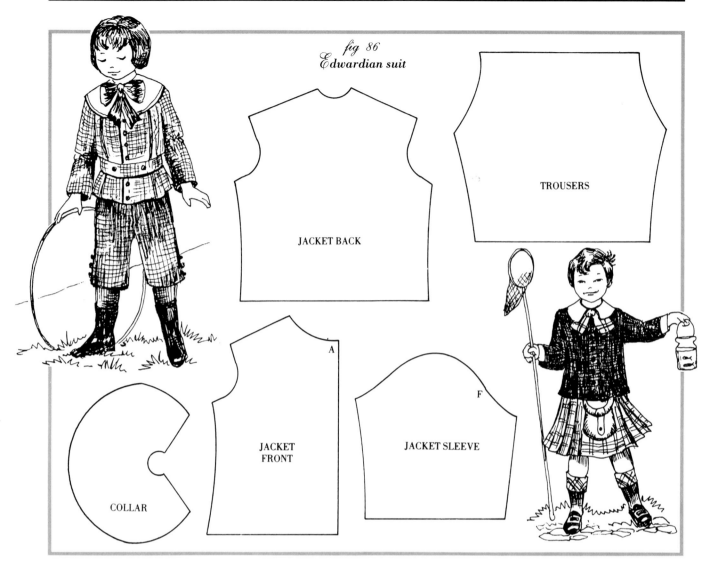

fig 86
Edwardian suit

JACKET BACK

TROUSERS

A

JACKET
FRONT

F

JACKET SLEEVE

COLLAR

- ACCESSORIES

Bucket and spade, shrimping-net, kite, or a rubber-ball.

EDWARDIAN SUIT

(Fig 86 – shown in colour on pp182/183)

This suit can be made in any plain cotton fabric, fine wool or suiting, worn with a white cotton collar. It is appropriate for boys of the late-Victorian and Edwardian periods.

- FOOTWEAR

Black stockings and boots.

- TROUSERS

Cut the trousers in fabric bonded to hold the hems in place and make up as the previous pattern, adding braid to define the side 'seams' and buttons, as required.

- JACKET

Cut back, fronts and sleeves in bonded fabric. Cut back and front in lining. Stitch the underarm seams on jacket and lining, and press the seams open. With right sides facing, stitch fronts and lower edge together from A to A. Clip corners, turn through and press so that the lining

will not show. Stitch the shoulder seams and press open. Stitch bead-buttons from the neck to the waist on the left front. Fit the jacket onto the doll and catch stitch the left front over the right from the neck to waist.

Turn up sleeve hems, stitch sleeve seams and press. Stitch two or three buttons to each cuff. Gather to ease the sleeve tops slightly and stitch the sleeves to the armholes. Cut the collar in white double-bonded fabric, snip the neckline edge and fold under. Fit the collar onto the doll and join with a ribbon bow – striped or spotted ribbon looks nice. Make a fabric or leather belt and fasten with a small buckle or two bead-buttons at the centre front.

- HAIR

Short, straight or curly.

- HAT

Cap or straw-boater.

SCOTTISH DRESS

This jacket can also be worn with a kilt (see the instructions for the man's kilt on p141). Use 1/4in (6mm) size pleater and pleat sufficient 1 1/2in (4cm) wide fabric or ribbon to fit around the body, plus 1in (2.5cm) at one end for the flat front.

10

Making wigs

H AIR MAY BE A WOMAN'S 'CROWNING GLORY', but hairstyle and colour make a major contribution to any doll's appearance. Identical heads can be made to look entirely different by changing the wig, and even varying the space between the eyes and hairline will seem to alter the facial expression. A lovely doll in an exquisite dress can be ruined by clumsy wigging and a plain doll in a simple dress can be transformed by lovely hair. To make realistic hairstyles on tiny dolls requires patience and the right materials, but good results justify the time spent achieving them.

Bought wigs very rarely fit perfectly unless they have been made for the specific head. To look realistic the hair should be styled on the doll, after the doll is dressed.

If it is essential to style the hair before dressing the doll, the wig should be made on a base so that it is removable. If the doll's head has a hole at the top, fill it with paper-tissue to complete the skull. Cover the whole head with a piece of clingfilm, smoothed down and tied tightly around the neck with thread. Make the wig on the cling film, and when the glue is thoroughly dry, cut the thread and gently ease off the film and wig. With very sharp scissors, cut the clingfilm away at the hairline, removing every scrap which might show. Save some spare curls of hair so that when the wig is later glued to the head, a few tendrils can be added to soften the hairline.

MATERIALS

Wigs can be made from a variety of fibres. The best materials to use are fine mohair (from goats) and viscose (a man-made fibre with a good sheen). Raw unspun silk or cotton, lambswool and embroidery thread can also be used, but 'theatrical hair' which is a mixture of mohair and wool available in long thin plaits, is rather too coarse for $\frac{1}{12}$ scale dolls. However, theatrical hair is tempting to use, as it forms waves when unplaited. Mohair and viscose are available in a wide range of good natural hair shades from the palest baby blonde through all the browns and greys to black. They can be obtained in small inexpensive packets from a doll supplier (see Stockists). Avoid the yellow blondes and the brightest auburns. Unless black is essential for a character, use very dark brown which looks more natural. For elderly characters,

consider using two shades of grey, with the slightly lighter shade at the temples, or a mixture of shades. If possible have a good range of colours available so that you can try them against the dressed doll to select the most suitable colour for the wig.

Before you begin, protect the doll's clothes with a small polythene bag tied at the neck, and have available a suitable sized container in which the doll can stand – for example, a mug or jam jar. You will also need:

- Small bags or boxes for storing hair
- White PVA glue – for example, Aleene's Tacky Glue, *not* Copydex
- Knitting needles, size 14 (2mm) to size 4 (6mm)
- Sewing thread to match the hair
- Pipecleaners, cut into short lengths
- Sharp scissors
- Tweezers
- A damp sponge
- An old soft toothbrush

METHOD

If the doll's head has an opening at the crown, fill the head with paper-tissue, rounded to complete the skull. Mark the natural hairline (very lightly in pencil) and cover the head to this line with a thick coating of PVA glue. The wig is made on this tacky glue base. If you are not satisfied with the wig you make, it can be peeled off and the head cleaned so that you can try again. The following methods can also be used for dolls with moulded hair – simply make the wig over the moulding but take care not to make it too thick or the head will look very large.

- SIMPLE WIGS
(Fig 87)
For a very quick simple wig, take a strand of hair long enough to reach across the head from side to side, to the required length. Tie in the centre with matching thread and fan out all around (Fig 87a). Cover the head to the hairline with glue and lay the hair in place, pulling the front hair to the side, or cutting it into a fringe. This is very rudimentary, but adequate if most of the hair is to be con-

The Wig Collection
An assortment of wig styles for ladies, girls, men and boys to
complement fashions from Georgian to Edwardian

The First Haircut
Mama watches in distress as her son's golden curls are shorn before
he goes away to school. Mama wears an Edwardian Blouse and Skirt,
her son wears an Edwardian Suit and the barber wears a
Frock-coat

fig 89
Hairstyles

a ▪ making a parting

b ▪ making a fringe   *c ▪ plaits*

d ▪ waves   *e ▪ 'Marcel' wave*

FRINGES (BANGS)
(Fig 89b)

Use a large curl so that the hair follows the curve of the head, otherwise it tends to 'fly off' in all directions. For long hair with a fringe, lay the curl from front to back, then cover with strands of hair laid from side to side. When the glue is dry, some strands can be lifted over to form a centre parting. Curly fringes can be added to other styles with individual curls well teased out.

PLAITS (BRAIDS)
(Fig 89c)

This is a very appealing style for little girls. Cover the glued head with hair, as before. If the doll is to have a fringe, bring some of the hair over her face, otherwise, make a parting and pull the hair to each side. While the glue is tacky, tie a thread around the head on the hair-line, or use a small rubber-band. When the glue is dry,

neatly plait the hair to the required length. Secure the ends with matching thread and ribbon bows. Remove the band very carefully. If the doll is to wear a hat, the parting could be omitted.

WAVES
(Fig 89d)

Soft, loose, wavy hair can be made by teasing out curled strands and is particularly pretty for little girls.

To make more formal waves for the 1930s, crimped 'Marcel' look (Fig 89e) or men's styles, use a fabric pleater (see Chapter 2). Dampen a thin strand of hair and lay it across the board. Use the two cards provided to push the hair into the grooves and slide the cards in alternate directions to make a pronounced 'S' effect. Leave the hair to dry completely. The hair can be trimmed and arranged around the head, or used for long or up-swept Edwardian styles.

STRAIGHT STYLES

Absolutely straight hair tends to look stiff and unnatural on dolls, so wind the hair on a much larger needle and then dampen all but the ends as you glue it to the head.

PERIOD STYLES FOR LADIES
(Fig 90)

To complement an authentic costume, choose the correct hairstyle for the period. Fashions in hairstyling change with fashions in clothes and the doll will not look right unless her coiffure is of the same period as her clothes. The following styles are typical of each period, but there were, of course, a number of variations. Reference to costume books, contemporary portraits and photographs will provide alternatives.

▪ GEORGIAN

(a)

Use natural colour hair or grey or white to represent powdered hair. Arrange the hair in loose waves, drawn back from the face with curls at each side, the hairline softened with curly tendrils.

▪ REGENCY

(b)

Arrange the hair in a short curly style with a ribbon bandeau.

▪ EARLY VICTORIAN

(c)

Style the hair with a centre parting arranged in coils and loops at the sides and back. In the 1830s these coils and loops were very elaborate; by the 1840s they were more modest.

▪ MID-VICTORIAN

(d and e)

Use a style which is centre parted and arranged in ringlets, or a coiled or plaited bun. The effect should be very demure.

fig 90
Period styles for ladies

■ LATE VICTORIAN

(f and g)

Draw the hair back from the face and arrange in ringlets at the back or loop into soft curls. Soften the hairline with curly tendrils.

■ EDWARDIAN

(h)

Arrange the hair in a soft, full, up-swept style with a bun, and curly tendrils at the hairline.

PERIOD STYLES FOR GIRLS

(Fig 91)

Girls' hairstyles were generally similar to their mothers', although less elaborate. In Georgian times, little girls usually wore caps, so hair was simply styled in a small bun or soft curls. Older girls wore styles similar to their mothers', but not powdered except for the most formal occasions.

■ REGENCY

(a)

Short curly hair with a ribbon bandeau was very fashionable.

■ EARLY VICTORIAN

(b)

Long hair was usually worn centre-parted and styled in ringlets at each side, or drawn back in an Alice band.

fig 91
Period styles for girls

■ **MID-VICTORIAN**

(c)

Fashionable styles were more elaborate, with long hair drawn back from the forehead in ringlets at the back and a short curly fringe.

■ **LATE VICTORIAN-EDWARDIAN**

(d)

Long hair was still usual, but was more simply styled, drawn off the face and tied with a ribbon bow. The hair was straight or curled in long ringlets.

__ HAIRSTYLES FOR MEN AND BOYS __

A handsome young man should have a good head of hair, but receding hairlines, thinning and greying temples add much character to middle-aged dolls, and blending two similar hair shades is very effective. Bald heads are only possible if the doll does not have stringing holes or painted hair. When making wigs for older men, visualise those you know, or look at newspapers and magazines, and research for periods earlier than 1900, as there was a considerable variation in styles.

The hairline is particularly important and should be well defined. One of the easiest styles to make is all-over curls, but wind the fibre on a large size knitting-needle so that the curls are more open. Arrange them to lie flat on the head, working away from either side of the parting and opening the curls so that they build up into a natural shape. Trim all stray pieces and dampen slightly. Grey curls around a bald patch are easy to make and look very effective. Add a few strands of hair spread across the front. Another method using straight or slightly curled hair is to glue short lengths from back to front and from side to side. Make a parting with a piece of thread and leave the glue to dry. Using a soft toothbrush, gently brush the surface hair, dampening slightly so that it follows the shape of the head. Trim all round, layering down the neck, and leaving a little hair in front of the ears. Use very short lengths of straight hair, glued flat to the head for a 'short back and sides'.

MOUSTACHES AND BEARDS

Cover the precise area with glue and gently press the hair in place. Make a stiff bristly moustache with short chopped lengths of hair laid flat, working out to an angle at the sides. For a big bushy curled moustache, take a strand of hair, grip it in the middle with tweezers, and dampen and twist each end to curl up the points and gently glue in place.

Hair in front of the ears, known as sideburns, was particularly popular with Victorians. One style joins a moustache, just below the cheekbones. Beards usually meet the hair, but a little pointed Van Dyck beard on the chin looks very elegant. Stubble for a workman or gardener can be made by covering the chin with a thin layer of glue and pressing finely chopped hair onto it. Brush off the surplus when dry.

fig 92
Period styles for men

PERIOD STYLES FOR MEN

(Fig 92)

Gentlemen dressed in period costume should have hairstyles of the period. Although fashions did not change as frequently as ladies' styles, hair was worn long or short, with or without beards and moustaches, at different times during the last two centuries and the correct style will complement the doll's costume.

■ GEORGIAN

(a)

Natural colour hair or white or grey to represent a wig, or powdered hair, worn long and tied back in a queue with black ribbon, with rolled curls at each side for young men; older men preferred the 'full-bottomed' style.

■ REGENCY

(b)

Natural hair worn slightly long and styled in 'Byronic' curls. Clean-shaven.

■ EARLY VICTORIAN

(c)

Hair is worn quite long with a Van Dyck beard and moustache. 'Poetic' styles were popular.

■ MID-VICTORIAN

(d and e)

Hair styled with a side or centre parting, usually waved, worn with sideburns and a small beard and moustache.

■ LATE VICTORIAN-EDWARDIAN

(f and g)

Rather more variety, including side or centre partings on straight or waved hair, and sideburns, beards and moustaches.

PERIOD STYLES FOR BOYS

(Fig 93)

Boys' hairstyles were generally similar to their fathers'. During the Georgian period, small boys wore natural long hair, although teenage boys often wore wigs, powdered for formal occasions and usually styled in a queue.

fig 93
Period styles for boys

From the beginning of the nineteenth century boys' hair was usually worn short but sometimes to shoulder length. Centre partings were fashionable with the late Victorians.

The Finishing Touch
A collection of hats and accessories ranging from elegant parasols
to children's toys

GIRL'S BRETON BONNET

(Fig 94e)

This style is particularly associated with the 1875–85 bustle dress. Cut the brim in double-bonded fabric and the crown in unbonded fabric. Gather the curved edge of the crown and stitch to the brim, allowing sufficient material at the straight back crown edge to turn under. Trim the brim with lace and braid, overlapping the edge. Gather the back edge of the crown, fit the bonnet onto the doll, pull up the gathers to fit and fasten off. Add ribbons to tie under the chin and decorate the bonnet to complement the dress. Pinch the bonnet crown so that it stands tall.

For a simple sun bonnet, cut the crown pattern to a shallower curve and make up as described without trimming.

FACE-FRAMING CAP

(Fig 95a)

This very flattering cap would be particularly suitable for eighteenth-century indoor wear, and elderly Victorian ladies.

Use fine muslin or cotton organdie. Cut one crown and two brims. Stitch the brims together around the outer edge, clip, turn through and press. Join the edges together at A. Gather the crown to fit the brim and stitch together. Clip the curve and trim any surplus. Stitch narrow gathered lace around the outer edge of the brim. Tie the cap on with a ribbon bow under the chin. (Shown in colour on pp54/55.)

BONNET WITH GATHERED CROWN

(Fig 95b)

This can be made in fabric to match the dress. Cut the brim in bonded fabric and in lining. Cut the crown in unbonded fabric. Make up as the previous pattern. Trim the brim edge with lace or braid and decorate the bonnet with flowers, feathers or gathered ribbon. Add ribbons and tie in a bow under the chin. (Shown in colour on p131.)

SOFT-CROWN PICTURE HAT

(Fig 95c)

Make this versatile and flattering hat for Victorian or Edwardian styles. Cut the brim in double-bonded fabric and cut the crown in unbonded fabric. Cut the inner circle out of the brim, and mark quarters on brim and crown. Run a gathering thread around the crown, draw up and distribute gathers evenly, match the quarters and pin the crown to the brim. Slip stitch together, tucking in the raw edges. Trim the edge of the brim with braid. Decorate the hat with ribbon, roses and feathers. Fit the hat onto the doll and gently bend the brim to a flattering shape. If very fine fabric is used, a pleated length, edged with lace, can be stitched to the gathered crown in place of the brim. (Shown in colour on pp102/103.)

MAN'S FLAT CAP

(Fig 95d)

Cut two peaks and one crown in bonded fabric. With right sides facing, seam the curve of the peak, clip, turn through and press firmly. Tack the raw edges together. Fold the crown in half, right sides facing, and stitch small darts right across. Fold the other way and repeat. From the right side this will appear as four segments stitched together. Run a gathering thread around the edge, pull up and distribute gathers evenly. Fit the cap onto the head, tucking in the raw edges and fit the completed peak under the crown. Stitch or glue in place. Add a narrow folded band of fabric between the crown and peak if required. (Shown in colour on p186.)

BAKER BOY CAP

(Fig 95e)

Cut the cap and make up as the flat cap. Add a matching tassel on a cord to hang over one side. To make the tassel, wind thread around a knitting-needle, slip the loops off carefully, press them into a small hank, and wind the spare end of thread around one end of the hank. Cut the loops at the other end. (Shown in colour on p118.)

STIFFENED FABRIC HATS

SIMPLE HALF-BONNET

(Fig 96a)

Cut in stiff bonded fabric and in lining. Seam both pieces together, leaving an opening at the back. Trim, clip the curves, turn through – preserving the shape – close the opening and press. Trim the edge with braid and lace, gathered ribbon, unravelled bunka, or use thick chenille knitting yarn for a fur effect. This is a very simple shape, so add plenty of flowers and trimming to match the costume. Add ribbons tied in a bow to one side. If this or any fabric hat needs further stiffening, paint with Fray Check, but test on a scrap first. (Shown in colour on pp154/155.)

POKE-BONNET

(Fig 96b)

This hat is a lovely shape, but is a little more complicated to make.

Cut the brim, side and top in double-bonded fabric. Snip the inner edge of the brim and glue it to the folded side, matching A to A. Snip the back edge of the side, bend in and glue on the top, matching B to B. When the glue is dry, cover the joins at the edge of the top and around the brim with narrow braid. Decorate generously with ruched ribbon, roses and feathers outside and inside the brim. Tie with a large ribbon bow to one side. (Shown in colour on p174.)

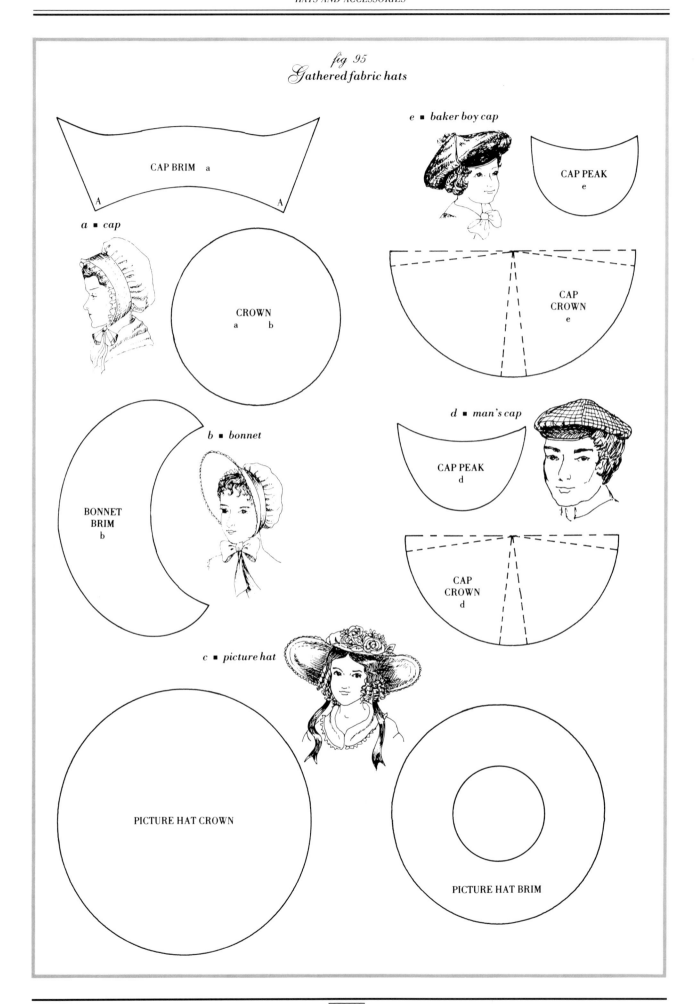

fig 95
Gathered fabric hats

CAP BRIM a

A   A

a ▪ cap

CROWN
a   b

e ▪ baker boy cap

CAP PEAK
e

CAP
CROWN
e

d ▪ man's cap

CAP PEAK
d

CAP
CROWN
d

BONNET
BRIM
b

b ▪ bonnet

c ▪ picture hat

PICTURE HAT CROWN

PICTURE HAT BRIM

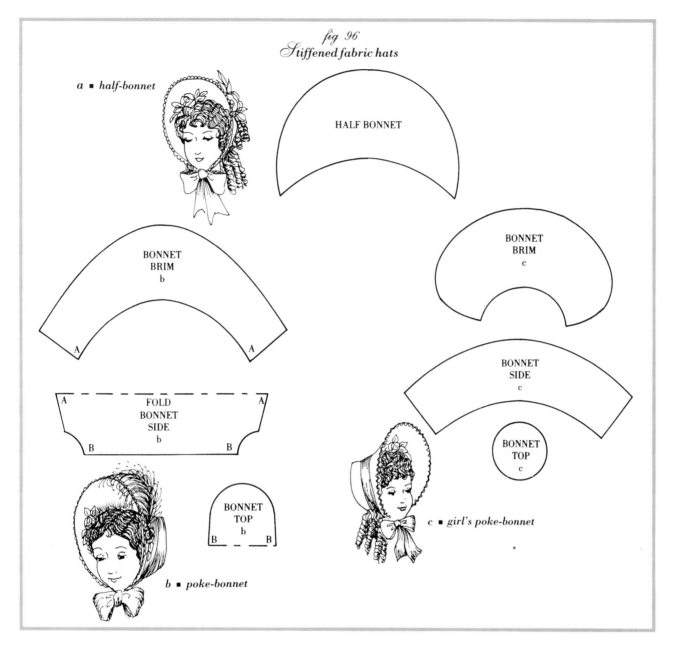

fig 96
Stiffened fabric hats

a ▪ *half-bonnet*

HALF BONNET

BONNET BRIM
b

A A

BONNET BRIM
c

A A
FOLD BONNET SIDE
b
B B

BONNET SIDE
c

BONNET TOP
c

BONNET TOP
b
B B

b ▪ poke-bonnet

c ▪ girl's poke-bonnet

GIRL'S POKE-BONNET

(Fig 96c)

This is easier to make if you have a piece of thick dowel or something similar which is the same diameter as the top pattern to use as a block. Cut the brim, side and top in double-bonded fabric. Snip the inner edge of the brim and, with centres matching, glue it to the side – the brim does not fit all the way round. Snip the back edge of the side and join it into a circle. Bend in the snipped edge over the dowel and glue on the top. Trim with braid around the brim edge and around the top. Cover the join between the brim and side with ribbon or braid. Decorate with ribbons and feathers. Tie the bonnet onto the doll with ribbons. (Shown in colour on pp154/155.)

LARGE-BRIMMED HAT

(Fig 97a)

This style is easier to make if you have a block (see previ-

ous pattern). Cut the brim, side and top in double-bonded fabric and cut out the centre of the brim. Snip the inside edge of the brim and the top curve of the side (about ¼in (3mm)). Join the back edges of the side and hold it around the block to turn in the snipped edge and glue on the top. Turn up the snipped inner edge of the brim and glue the bottom edge of the side over it. When the glue has dried, trim around the brim, side and top with braid and ribbons, and add flowers or feathers. (Shown in colour pp42/43.)

TOP-HAT

(Fig 97b)

This is very difficult to make successfully. The method for the brimmed hat above can be used, with straight sides, but the problem is making the join between the top and the crown neatly. The edge of the fabric must be cut very precisely and any white showing disguised by colouring with felt pen.

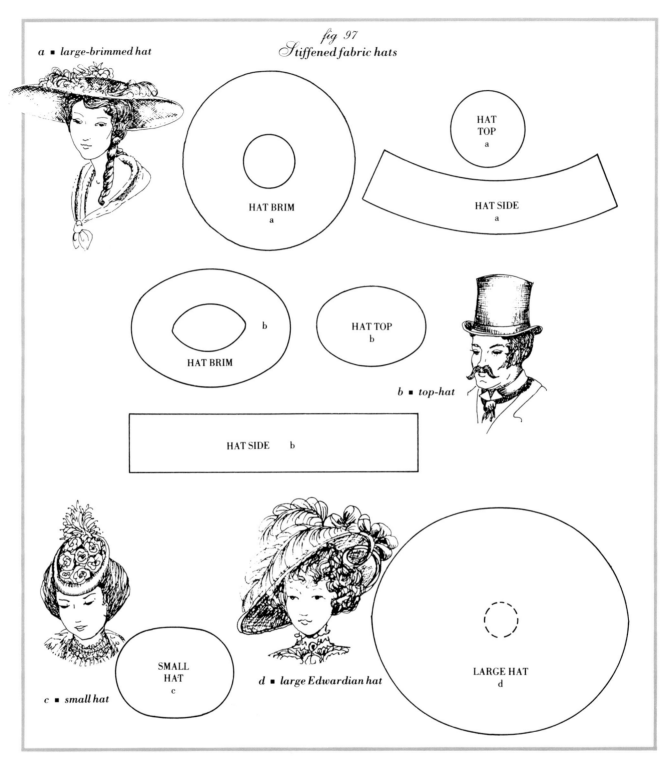

fig 97
Stiffened fabric hats

a ▪ large-brimmed hat

HAT BRIM
a

HAT TOP
a

HAT SIDE
a

HAT BRIM
b

HAT TOP
b

b ▪ top-hat

HAT SIDE   b

SMALL
HAT
c

c ▪ small hat

d ▪ large Edwardian hat

LARGE HAT
d

Because dolls' heads are large and the wig relatively thick, a top-hat made to fit would have to be rather large – a smaller one carried in the hand will look more convincing. (Shown in colour on p174.)

SMALL VICTORIAN OR EDWARDIAN HAT
(Fig 97c)
Cut in double-bonded fabric. Stiffen by painting with Fray Check. As it dries, bend the edge into a pleasing shape and allow to dry thoroughly. Glue braid around the edge and decorate generously. Place well forward on the head

and build up the hair around it. (Shown in on pp154/155.)

LARGE EDWARDIAN HAT
(Fig 97d)
Cut in double-bonded fabric and trim the edge with lace and/or braid. Pinch in the centre and with strong thread, take several stitches around the pinch, fastening off securely. This will make a slightly wavy effect at the brim. Arrange the hat to suit the doll and stitch or glue in position. Add plenty of decoration and build up the hair around the hat if necessary. (Shown in colour on pp86/87.)

The Pink Balloon
A balloon makes the daily walk in the park with Nanny more fun
for a little girl wearing a Felt Coat. Nanny and the balloon seller wear
clothes made from the Basic Pattern

STRAW-HATS

METHOD

(Fig 98)

Use 5mm fine hat-straw, which is available in natural and many other colours (see Stockists), or tightly plaited natural raffia. There is a strong cotton thread woven into the edge of hat-straw which can be pulled gently to curve it to make shaping easier. Dampen the hat-straw to soften and to make it easier to work. Frequent fitting is needed and this is easier if you have a block of the right size and shape, such as a bottle-cap or one made from Fimo or Plasticine covered in plastic film (see Fig 100a.)

The hat is made by stitching the straw braid round and round, with each layer either overlapping or butting to the previous one, as you prefer. The shaping is controlled by the tension applied as the straw is stitched – it should be tight where rounding is needed and eased where it is to be flat.

Use matching thread and begin at the centre of the crown. Secure the thread with several stitches, dampen the straw, curve it tightly and stitch into a circle with the loose end on the inside. Continue stitching round, either overlapping or butting the straw braid, pulling it into roughly the right shape. Check the size on the block frequently. Stitch round and round until the crown is deep enough. Then continue, but ease the tension so that the straw will spread out for the brim. Continue until the brim is wide enough. For an upturned brim, increase the

tension for the last round or two. Gently underlap the last quarter circle so that the edge is level with the last round. Cut the straw at an angle and fasten off neatly underneath. At this stage the hat will look more suitable for a scarecrow! Dampen it slightly and press onto the block. Apply the tip of a steam iron lightly round the crown and then press the brim flat. It will now look like a proper hat. First efforts can be disappointing, but it is a matter of practice to make the hat correctly.

The plain shape can be transformed with gathered lace over or under the brim, or both, and lots of trimming. The brim can also be dampened and moulded to make other shapes.

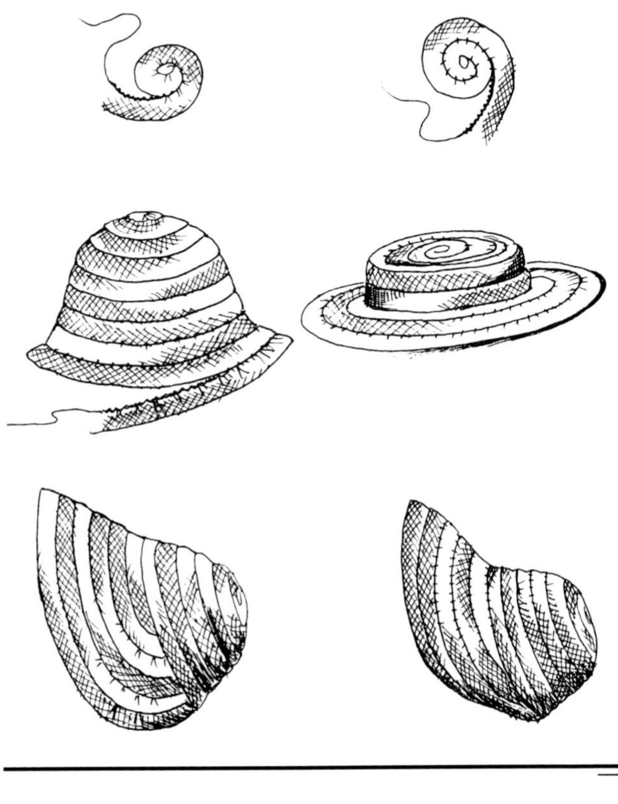

BOATER

Use the same method on an oval block with a flat top. Trim the boater with a grosgrain ribbon hat-band. (Shown in colour on pp62/63.)

STRAW BONNET

The bonnet is made in the same way as a straw-hat until the crown is completed. Then the brim is shaped by working to and fro across the front to make a curve. Stitch the final row around the whole brim and fasten neatly at one side. The tension on the straw as the brim is worked will determine the angle.

CARD 'STRAW' BOATER

(Fig 99)

Use embossed linen-weave paper or a plain postcard foundation. The pattern will fit a head circumference of about 2.5in (6.35cm) and should be adjusted for other sizes. Cut two ovals for the brim and cut out the inner ovals which will be the top. Cut the side and score the two lines shown. Snip to these lines from both edges at 1/8in (3mm) intervals. Fold the top edge inwards to support the top of the hat and the lower edge outwards to support the brim. Roll the side strip gently and fit it into one brim, securing the overlapping ends with adhesive tape. Remove the side, cover the underside of the brim with glue and replace the side. Glue the second brim to cover the snipped edge, lining up both brims and pressing firmly together. Glue one top inside the hat and one outside in line with the curve of the brim.

The plain card shape can be covered by gluing on hat-straw or crochet cotton spiralling out from the centre of the top. Neaten the brim edge by gluing on thin cord, and trim with a ribbon hat-band and a small flat bow on one side.

The method may be adapted to make hats for ladies and girls, using a circular brim and could be covered with pleated silk or lace to overlap the edge.

fig 98
Making straw-hats

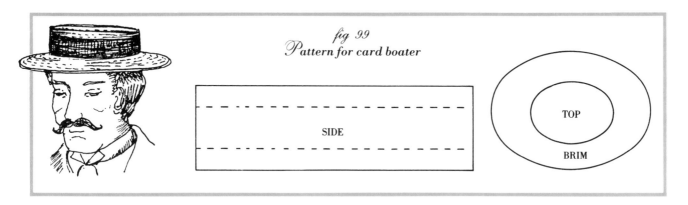

fig 99
Pattern for card boater

SIDE

TOP

BRIM

MOULDED FABRIC HATS

METHOD
(Fig 100)
Good quality felt thick enough to be stretched, buckram, or tapestry canvas can be used for these hats. It is essential to have a block exactly the right size and shape to work on (Fig 100a). Make one in Fimo, clay, wooden dowel or compressed cotton-wool stitched and tied to shape, and covered with plastic film to prevent the hat from sticking to it.

Dampen a small piece of fabric with warm water and slowly and gently ease it over the block until it is the correct depth for the crown, and tie at the base with thread. Cut the brim to size and work and curve it upwards to make the required shape. When it is nearly right, paint the hat with Fray Check and, as it dries, complete the moulding and allow it to dry thoroughly on the block. Remove the hat from the block, add a ribbon hat-band and glue narrow braid around the edge of the brim. This method can be used to make a sailor hat, flat boater, a round or flat-topped bowler (Derby), or trilby, but it is more difficult to make a top-hat.

TRICORN HAT
(Fig 100c)
This can be made in felt, as described above, but allow enough felt for the brim to allow for three shallow semi-circles. Cut these and curve the brim back over a pencil towards the crown. Secure with pins and stiffen with Fray Check. Trim the hat with braid. (Shown in colour on pp42/43.)

ACCESSORIES

OPEN PARASOL
(Fig 101a)
This looks charming and is very simple to make. Cut the cover in double-bonded dress fabric. Lap the two edges from A to B and glue. Trim the top with rows of gathered lace, adding bows and roses to match the costume. Trim both sides of the outer edge with lace, picot or grosgrain braid. Wrap a cocktail stick with spirally wound silk ribbon, secured with a touch of glue at each end. Push and

Edwardian Style (1900–10) ›
The family spend Sunday afternoon in the library. Mama, wearing Edwardian Blouse and Skirt, argues about books with her father who is wearing a Lounge Suit – her husband and son wear the Scottish Dress variation with kilts. Grandmama, wearing a dress made from the Basic Pattern with a lace yoke reads to her granddaughter wearing a Simple Dress and Pinafore and the baby wearing a Toddler Dress. The boy cousin is dressed in an Edwardian Suit

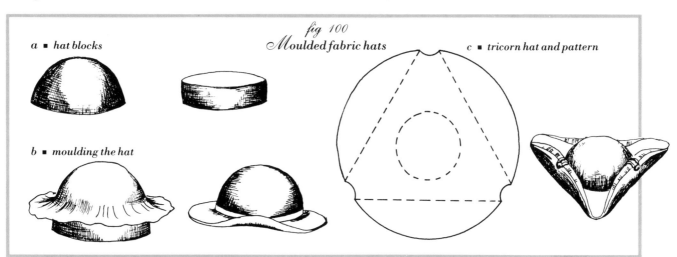

fig 100
Moulded fabric hats

a ▪ hat blocks

b ▪ moulding the hat

c ▪ tricorn hat and pattern

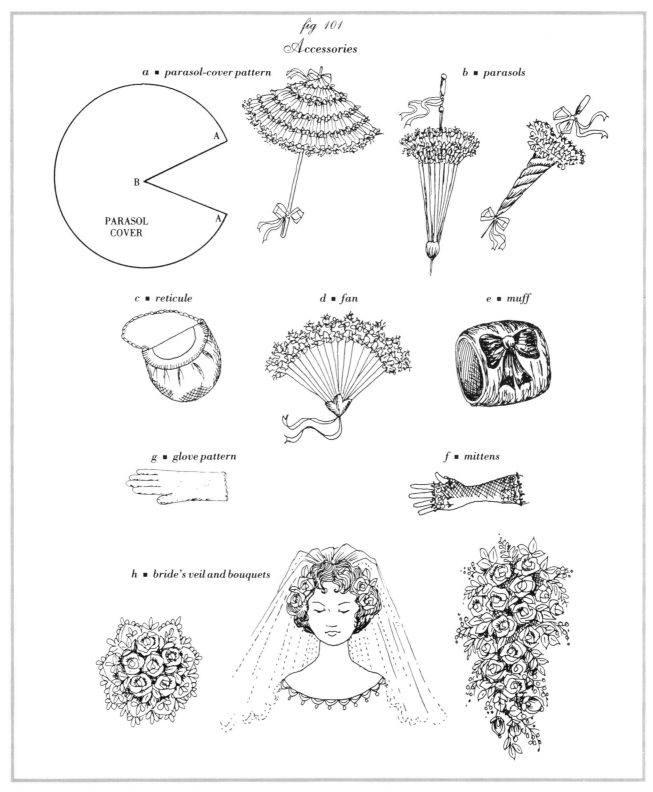

fig 101

Accessories

a ▪ parasol-cover pattern

b ▪ parasols

A

B

A

PARASOL COVER

c ▪ reticule

d ▪ fan

e ▪ muff

g ▪ glove pattern

f ▪ mittens

h ▪ bride's veil and bouquets

glue one end of the stick through the centre of the cover, and the other end into a decorative bead handle. Add ribbon streamers, bows and roses. Another method is to gather two or three tiers of lace to a similar shape and stiffen with Fray Check.

CLOSED PARASOL
(Fig 101b)
Cut the cover as a complete circle of fabric and trim the edge with ruffled lace or ribbon. Push the end of a cocktail stick into the centre, gently furl the fabric around the stick and tie ribbon just below the lace, finishing with a bow. Trim the point, and finish the stick with a pretty bead handle and ribbon streamer.

A simple version, but not as pretty, can be made by binding the cocktail stick with wide silk ribbon and adding a frill of lace near the handle.

RETICULE
(Fig 101c)

Cut a small rectangle of fabric or soft leather. Turn in the long edges and fold in half. Slightly gather or pleat the top edges and stitch or glue in place. Squeeze a gold or silver filigree jewellery bell-cap or folded buckle over the top of the bag and glue on a bead for the clasp. Attach a short length of matching chain or cord for the handle.

FAN
(Fig 101d)

Pleat or gather about 2in (5cm) of lace and pull up the plain edge tightly. Tuck this between two shell-shaped sequins and stitch together through the lace. Stiffen the fan with colourless nail-varnish or Fray Check. A design can be painted on the lace. Trim with ribbon roses, bow and streamers.

Very pretty fans can also be made with matched feathers, glued into sequins or jewellery 'findings'.

MUFF
(Fig 101e)

A small muff hung around the neck on ribbon looks attractive with a winter outfit. Make the muff from a strip of coat fabric and trim both ends with chenille yarn or un-ravelled bunka 'fur'. A ribbon rose makes an attractive trim. This is a good way to disguise an unfortunate accident with a doll's hand or arm!

SHAWLS

These are effective, but avoid using stiff fabrics. Indoor shawls can be made in fine wool, silk or lace, and large outdoor shawls in brushed cotton tartan or checked woollen fabrics. Finish the edges by pulling away the threads to leave a fringe. Cut a square and fold diagonally, or cut a triangle and hem the diagonal edge or seal with Fray Check, or use a long strip of ribbon. Drape the shawl around the doll's shoulders and tack it in place.

MITTENS
(Fig 101f)

These look very pretty made wrist or elbow length for ladies and girls. Make mittens in delicate lace edging, stitched tightly to the arm, tucking in the raw edges. Take one stitch around the thumb to hold firmly in place.

GLOVES
(Fig 101g)

Gloves made on the hand look clumsy, but a glove shape cut from single-thickness fine leather using really sharp scissors and glued into the hand will look realistic.

BRIDAL VEIL, HEAD-DRESS AND BOUQUET
(Fig 101h)

Use the finest tulle available for the veil, even if it is nylon. This can often be obtained from a florist in 6in (15cm) widths in either white or cream. Cut a piece long enough to fold back to shoulder length. Gather at the fold and stitch to the hair.

For a floral head-dress, tightly gather short lengths of pastel-coloured silk ribbon, interspersed with a little green, or make ribbon roses and stitch in place. Tiny pearls can be threaded on wire and arranged to make a formal head-dress.

A long bouquet is made by mounting ribbon roses and gathered ribbon onto a stiff paper foundation. Cut this to the required shape, cover with ribbon and trim the edge with lace. Make the flowers and glue in place, adding little streamers of 2mm ribbon. Make the handle by tap-ing a short length of pipecleaner or wire to the back of the foundation.

For a posy, choose lace with a definite scalloped edge. Make ribbon roses and glue onto wires. Cut leaves in double-bonded green ribbon and glue to the wires. Twist the wires together, wrap with gathered lace and tie with a ribbon bow.

JEWELLERY
(Fig 102)

The tiniest pearls can only be threaded on wire or waxed silk thread. Hooks are unsatisfactory, so knot or twist the

fig 102
Making jewellery

The Picnic

After an afternoon spent wandering around the castle, they find a quiet corner in the grounds for a picnic tea. She wears an Edwardian Suit and her best hat, he wears clothes made from the Lounge Suit pattern

wire at the back of the neck or around the wrist, and cover with a flat gold bead. To make a necklace lie flat, it may be necessary to use a dab of glue. Wired pearls can be twisted to form a tiny loop and a gemstone glued into this 'setting'.

Ear-rings can be made in the same way, leaving wire ends to be glued under the hair. Very simple ear-rings can be made from single pearlised artificial flower stamens.

Another method of mounting gemstones which will make quite elaborate necklaces is to make a chain by twisting two silver or gold wires together. Twist the wires around a needle of suitable size to make a tiny loop into which the stone can be glued. Twist the wires together again, mount another stone, and repeat as required.

A tiara can be made using either method. Make a wire head-band, curved to fit the head, and use two more

wires twisted to hold the stones. The twisted wires can be arranged in loops or in separate stems from the head-band. (Shown in colour on pp78/79.)

Very effective brooches can be made with threaded beads stitched onto a lapel or the neckline of a dress.

BASKETS
(Fig 103)

All shapes and sizes of basket make good accessories, from tiny flower baskets for children or ladies (filled with ribbon roses on individual stems), to work- or shopping-baskets, trugs for garden produce, laundry baskets with folded washing, or log baskets for the handyman. These can be bought, but they are not difficult to make. One method is to mould dampened embroidery canvas over suitable shapes such as bottle-tops and tins with rounded edges. When dry, trim the top edge straight and finish by

fig 103
Baskets

gluing on strands of fibre. Make handles from strands twisted and glued together.

Baskets can also be made to any shape with 5mm hat-straw using the method described for straw-hats (see p180). To make a large hamper or a Moses basket for a baby, plan the pieces so that there are the minimum of joins, start at the centre of the base and work into an oval. Then, by increasing the tension, work up the sides, finishing off with a slight hood as you would for a bonnet brim. Line and trim the basket with lace.

TOYS
(Fig 104)

Very effective balloons can be made by gluing pressed cotton balls onto florists' wire and covering them with rubber cut from a real balloon. Blow up the balloon first to soften the rubber, cut a piece, pull it over the ball and fasten with thread. Use different colours and bend the wires so that they look as if they are floating.

Make a bucket and spade from a tube or bottle-top and an icecream spoon extended with a toothpick, all painted to match. Make a shrimping-net from a triangle of net stitched into a cone and sewn around a loop of wire fixed to a toothpick. Make a skipping-rope from fine cord with handles made from short lengths of toothpick pushed into beads. Make a hoop from a length of fine cane, soaked to bend and wired to secure, with a small piece of toothpick for the stick.

fig 104
Toys

Acknowledgements

MY SINCERE GRATITUDE TO everyone who has helped to make this book possible – the Sunday Dolls team of needlewomen, especially Janet Clarke, Cynthia Chandler and Elizabeth Hayes for all the help and advice so generously given; Beryl Fox-Sommers for the illustrations; my daughter-in-law, Kate Atkinson, for drawing the patterns; Joy Parker for her advice on mould-making; the kind customers who generously lent their dolls to be photographed; the Secret Garden for providing the garden and particularly Venus A. Dodge whose support with planning and writing was invaluable. My heartfelt thanks to my husband, Bernard, for his endless help and encouragement.

Stockists

All the stockists provide a mail order service. To enquire the price of their catalogue please telephone, or write, enclosing a stamped, self-addressed envelope (International Repy Coupon from overseas). Before visiting, check opening hours as some do not have showrooms.

DRESSED DOLLS-HOUSE DOLLS AND DOLL KITS
Sunday Dolls, 7 Park Drive, East Sheen, London SW14 8RB (No showroom; fairs and mail order only)
Doll kits obtainable in USA and Canada from J. Parker, Box 34, Midland, Ontario L4R 4K6, Canada

HABERDASHERY
Ribbon, braid, lace, fabric, iron-on interlining, hat-straw, hair, beads, buckles, eyelets, spectacles, pearls and gemstones, rosemaker, bowmaker, pleater, Fray Check, Aleene's glue, syringes and doll stands from The Dollshouse Draper, PO Box 128, Lightcliffe, Halifax, West Yorkshire HX3 8RN (Tel: 0422-201275).
(Fairs and mail order only.)

MOULD-MAKING SUPPLIES
Alec Tiranti, 70 High Street, Theale, Reading RG7 5DG (Tel: 0734-302775)

DOLLS' HOUSE
Kevin Mulvany, 2 South Lane, Kingston-upon-Thames, Surrey KT1 2NJ
(Tel: 081-549-2097).

GLOVING LEATHER
Pittards, Sherborne Road, Yeovil, Somerset (Tel: 0935-74321)

EGG-CRAFTING SUPPLIES
Carade, 8 Lawson Close, Woolston, Warrington, Cheshire WA1 4EG
(Tel: 0925-819339)

DOLL MOULDS
Recollect, The Old School, London Road, Sayers Common, West Sussex BN6 9HX
(Tel: 0273-833314).

Bibliography

DOLLS' DRESSMAKING

Dodge, Venus and Martin, *The Dolls' House DIY Book* (David & Charles, 1982)

Dodge, Venus A., *The Dolls' Dressmaker* (David & Charles, 1987)

–.–*Making Miniatures in* $^1/_{12}$ *Scale* (David & Charles, 1989)

FASHION

Blum, Stella, *Fashions and Costumes from Godey's Lady's Book* (Dover Publications, 1985) · *Victorian Fashions & Costume from Harper's Bazaar 1867–1898* (Dover Publications, 1974)

Bradfield, Nancy, *900 Years of English Costume* (Peerage Books, 1938)

Hamilton Hill, Margot and Bucknell, Peter A., *The Evolution of Fashion, Pattern and Cut from 1066 to 1930* (Batsford, 1967)

Laver, James, *Costume Through the Ages* (Thames & Hudson, 1964)

Peacock, John, *Costume 1066–1966* (Thames & Hudson, 1986)

Ruby, Jennifer, *Costume in Context: 1 Medieval Times; 2 The Tudors; 3 The Stuarts; 4 The Eighteenth Century; 5 The Regency; 6 The Victorians; 7 The Edwardians and the First World War* (Batsford, 1988–90)

Schick, I. T., *Battledress – The Uniforms of the World's Great Armies, 1700 to The Present* (Weidenfeld & Nicolson, 1978)

Ulseth, Hazel and Shannon, Helen, *Victorian Fashions 1880–1890* (Hobby House Press, 1988)

COLLECTED PHOTOGRAPHS

Bentley, Nicolas, *Edwardian Album* (Weidenfeld & Nicolson, 1974)

Gernsheim, Alison, *Victorian and Edwardian Fashion* (Dover, 1963)

Ginsburg, Madeleine, *Victorian Dress in Photographs* (Batsford, 1982)

Huggett, Frank E. *Life Below Stairs* (John Murray, 1977)

Mager, Alison, *Children of the Past in Photographic Portraits* (Dover Publications, 1978)

Sansom, William, *Victorian Life in Photographs* (Thames & Hudson, 1974)

Sykes, Christopher Simon, *Country House Camera* (Weidenfeld & Nicolson, 1980)

DOLLS' HOUSES

Eaton, Faith, *The Miniature House* (Weidenfeld & Nicolson, 1990)

Greene, Vivien, *English Dolls' Houses* (Batsford, 1955) · *Family Dolls' Houses* (Bell, 1973)

Hamilton, Caroline, *Decorative Dolls' Houses* (Ebury Press, 1990)

Jacobs, Flora Gill, *A History of Dolls' Houses* (Scribners, 1953) · *Dolls' Houses in America* (Scribners, 1974)

King, Constance Eileen, *The Collector's History of Dolls' Houses* (Hale, 1983)

Stewart-Wilson, Mary, *Queen Mary's Dolls' House* (Bodley Head, 1988)

MAGAZINES

Please enclose a stamped self-addressed envelope with all enquiries.

Dolls' House World (bi-monthly), Shelley House, 104 High Street, Steyning, West Sussex BN4 3RD.

Dolls' Magazine, Shelley House, 104 High Street, Steyning, West Sussex BN4 3RD.

The Home Miniaturist (bi-monthly), Shelley House, 104 High Street, Steyning, West Sussex BN4 3RD.

Dolls in Miniature, The Magazine (quarterly), 3177 E. Bel Air Ct, Camarillo, CA 93010, USA.

International Dolls' House News (quarterly), PO Box 154, Cobham, Surrey KT11 2YE.

Miniature Collector (quarterly), Scott Publication, 30595 Eight Mile, Livonia, MI 48152-9868, USA

Nutshell News (monthly), PO Box 1612, Waukesha, W1 53187-9950, USA.

The British Dollshouse Hobby Directory lists makers, retailers, shops and museums (annually). (£3 + strong self-addressed A5 envelope stamped for 250g).

LDF Publications, 25 Priory Road, Kew, Richmond, Surrey TW9 3DQ.

Index